be returned on or

ADOBE CS PRODUCTION PREMIUM FOR FINAL CUT STUDIO EDITORS

ADOBE CS PRODUCTION PREMIUM FOR FINAL CUT STUDIO EDITORS

LARRY JORDAN

AMSTERDAM • BOSTON • HEIDELBERG • LONDON • NEW YORK • OXFORD
PARIS • SAN DIEGO • SAN FRANCISCO • SINGAPORE • SYDNEY • TOKYO

Focal Press is an imprint of Elsevier

Focal Press is an imprint of Elsevier
30 Corporate Drive, Suite 400, Burlington, MA 01803, USA
Linacre House, Jordan Hill, Oxford OX2 8DP, UK

Library of Congress Cataloging-in-Publication Data
Jordan, Larry, 1950-
  Adobe CS production premium for Final cut studio editors / Larry Jordan.
    p. cm.
  Includes index.
  ISBN 978-0-240-81223-6
  1. Motion pictures--Editing. 2. Final cut (Electronic resource) 3. Digital video--Editing. 4. Adobe Photoshop. 5. Macintosh (Computer)--Programming. I. Title.
  TR899.J6697 2010
  778.5'35--dc22

                                                                                              2009034509

British Library Cataloguing-in-Publication Data
A catalogue record for this book is available from the British Library.

ISBN: 978-0-240-81223-6

For information on all Focal Press publications
visit our website at *www.elsevierdirect.com*

Typeset by: diacriTech, Chennai, India

09 10 11 12 13 5 4 3 2 1

Printed in the United States of America

Working together to grow
libraries in developing countries

www.elsevier.com | www.bookaid.org | www.sabre.org

ELSEVIER   **BOOK AID**
International   Sabre Foundation

Dedication

To Steve Martin of Ripple Training, who changed a life with a simple question

CONTENTS

GETTING STARTED

Why should a Final Cut editor even bother with this book? I mean, does the world need another book on Adobe Photoshop or Apple Final Cut Studio?

In this case, yes.

Here's why. This book doesn't just cover Adobe software or Apple software. It explains specific techniques for using Adobe Production Premium that will benefit an editor who uses Final Cut Pro. For example, tens of thousands of pages have been devoted to explain Photoshop to the Photoshop users. But very few pages, if any, explain how to use Photoshop for video editing to the Final Cut users.

As editors, we have three basic goals:

1. To get our projects done on deadline and on budget
2. To get our projects with the quality that meets the client's specifications
3. To keep the job interesting for ourselves

If we are working smart, we will use the software that helps us meet those goals. For me, my editing application of choice is Apple's Final Cut Studio. However, everyday, I find myself using a wide variety of software to accomplish the tasks that can't be met using Final Cut alone.

That is the reason this book exists. Increasingly, one application, no matter how powerful, cannot meet all the needs of professional-grade video editing. It takes a team.

This book looks at how to combine the power of the software in Adobe Production Premium with Apple Final Cut Studio to accomplish tasks that are impossible with Final Cut Studio alone.

This book will show you how to use these applications in the real world of deadline-driven video editing to get your work done faster and solve problems better while maintaining necessary quality so that you have the free time you quite rightly deserve for things like eating, sleeping, and rediscovering the faces of your family.

If making a living with video editing needs to coexist with having a life outside the edit suite, then this book is for you.

What Do I Mean by "Video"

My career is in video. In my classes, I like to say that "I've made only one film in my life, and my own mother did not like it." However, this is not completely true. Although I *have* made only one film, mom liked it – and I'm sure she was *completely* objective in forming her opinion.

I use the term *video* in this book to include editing using video and film source files. However, you should know that my background is in video production; principally, live events, documentaries, and other nonscripted productions.

The Goals of This Book

The purpose of this book is not to cover every possible feature in each of these applications. I've already written thousands of pages just about Final Cut Pro, and there is still more to write about.

Instead, I want to focus on answering the following question: what does a Final Cut Studio editor need to know about Adobe Production Premium that can make editing in Final Cut Studio better?

This question opens up huge opportunities that I've not seen covered by any other book or on-line training.

But, the process of using these two suites together is not always straightforward. There are lots and lots of hidden tricks, a few traps, and plenty of techniques that we can talk about.

When I was planning this book, I set the following goals:

- Don't just focus on effects; describe clearly how to move files between applications and how to get something started and finished. There are lots of creative books on the market, but very few talk about how software interconnects.
- Illustrate the things you can do with Adobe Production Premium that you can't do with Final Cut Studio.
- Don't attempt to explain every feature of Photoshop, After Effects, Illustrator, or so on. That way lies madness. It is impossible to do in a single book. Instead, highlight the key features that you can put to use today.
- Where possible, show how to get something done faster.

Just What Software Are We Talking About?

Both Final Cut Studio and Adobe Production Premium CS4 are software suites, meaning that they include multiple pieces of software.

For example, here is the list of the software in Final Cut Studio (2009):

- Final Cut Pro 7
- Motion 4.2
- Soundtrack Pro 3
- Compressor 3.5
- DVD Studio Pro 4.2
- Color 1.5
- Cinema Tools 4.5

Here is the list of software in Adobe CS4 Production Premium:

- After Effects CS4
- Bridge CS4
- Device Central CS4
- Encore CS4
- Flash CS4 Professional
- Illustrator CS4
- Media Encoder CS4
- OnLocation CS4
- Photoshop CS4 Extended
- Premiere Pro CS4.1
- Soundbooth CS4

This book touches on most of these Adobe packages but will emphasize some more than others.

What Can We Do in Adobe That We Can't Do in Final Cut?

This is really a good question. So, here's a summary:
Bridge

- Faster image previewing, file handling, and drag-and-drop support between applications
- Improved metadata tracking on all files

On-location

- Preproduction planning
- Monitoring video on set

Soundbooth

- Ability to create text transcripts from media files
- Ability to export text transcripts
- Ability to search media files based on text transcripts

Photoshop

- Video retouching
- Animation creation and simple rotoscoping
- Stills preparation

Encore

- Ability to create Blu-ray Discs with menus similar to standard DVDs
- Ability to export a DVD layout for Web use, that is, to create a DVD interface you can post to the Web

Adobe Media Encoder

- Create Flash movies

In addition, Final Cut users have reported other benefits:

- Tight integration with other Production Premium components: easy access by dynamic link to After Effects and Encore (via Final Cut Pro importer)
- Tight integration of After Effects (a standard in the industry) with other components of the suite
- Improved PSD import with After Effects, Premiere, and Encore
- Clip notes in Premiere Pro and After Effects, which enable you to get client feedback easily

Although this book expects that you'll be principally editing in Final Cut Pro, Adobe Premiere Pro also has advantages compared to Final Cut. These include the following:

- Better titling (that is, adding text) in Premiere than Avid Media Composer or Final Cut Pro
- Native editing of tapeless formats (such as XDCAM EX) without requiring conversion to a QuickTime movie
- Faster rough cut of the dialogue using Speech Search – great for documentary or talking-head footage
- More efficient mixing-and-matching of different footage on the timeline
- More efficient integration of Premiere Pro for effects-heavy projects centered around After Effects than between After Effects and Final Cut Pro
- Smooth roundtrip editing between Premiere, Soundbooth, and Photoshop

A Quick Word about Me

For those of you who haven't read my newsletters, listened to my podcasts, or read my other books, let me digress for a moment to give you a quick snapshot of my background.

I got my start in production when video cameras weighed more than 700 pounds and consisted of a lens turret with no zoom lenses, creating black-and-white images using an RCA TK-14 rolling on a steel pedestal over reinforced concrete studio floors. I was studying Radio/TV/Film at the University of Wisconsin in Madison.

Since then, I've produced and directed programs for broadcast from local stations to ABC and PBS. My specialty was directing live, multicamera special events. Along the way, I became a member of the Directors Guild of America, the Producers Guild of America, won a number of awards, and was nominated for an Emmy award as a director.

My TV career lasted for about 20 years. Then, excited about the emerging personal computer industry, I left television and moved into computers, software, and marketing. One of the highlights of this 15-year part of my life was working in the desktop publishing industry as we developed the technology to display first, black-and-white images on computer screens, then color stills, then, video.

Over the last 10 years, I've been able to integrate my background in broadcast television with my knowledge of computers and software in creating a business (Larry Jordan & Associates, Inc.), which trains people around the world on how to use and improve their video production and postproduction skills. As an Apple-certified trainer, I've written four books on Final Cut Studio (this one is the fifth), and I have two different Web sites: one geared to Final Cut Studio (http://www.larryjordan.biz) and the other to digital video (http://www.digitalproductionbuzz. com). I also regularly produce podcasts, newsletters, on-line training, consulting and seminars all designed to answer questions, showcase new technology, and improve the skills of people who want to communicate visually, which gets to me, to why I'm writing this book. About 6 months ago, Michelle Gallina, the senior product marketing manager for Adobe Systems asked me why I wasn't training people on how to use Adobe Production Premium software. I told her that I was quite happy with Final Cut Studio and had no reason to switch to Adobe Premiere.

After politely waiting a minute to see if I was done, Michelle quietly asked if I had heard of other Adobe software, such as Photoshop, Flash, or After Effects.

I admitted that I had indeed heard of them. At which point, Michelle asked if, perhaps, Final Cut editors might not find that software useful as well.

Duh.

So, with her encouragement, I created a series of seminars on how Final Cut editors can use Adobe software and presented them in 15 cities across North America in the Fall of 2008. In the middle of which, Adobe released the CS4 suite.

This book was born from those seminars and the training I've done since. While it showcases the latest versions of Adobe Production Premium and Apple Final Cut Studio, many of these techniques will work with earlier versions of both.

How This Book Is Organized

There are many ways a book like this could be organized. But, what seems to make the most sense to me is to organize the book around the workflow of production.

In other words, this book follows the flow of planning and pre-production, production, and postproduction.

However, it's probably too much to hope for that you'll read this book for its plot. So, feel free to dip in wherever you want.

Where These Images Came From

One of the hardest challenges in creating a book is finding the right media to use to illustrate the concepts I am trying to teach. This makes me especially grateful to the following people for allowing me to use their images:

Resmine Atis, my lovely actress niece (http://www.imdb.com/name/nm1742686/) for her stunning head shots and modeling of a Civil War–era dress. Whoever thought you'd be acting in a book?

Actors Lisa Younger and Andrew David James for their work on a green screen project shot specifically for this book.

I'm also grateful to Pond5.com, an open marketplace for stock video footage, who provided much of the footage used for this book. They have more than 150 000 clips, very reasonably priced and more arriving every week. Check them out at http://www.pond5.com. Thanks also to the Pond5 artists whose clips were used:

alunablue – Earth in space, peaks 10
artmanwitte – Twin waterfall, icebergs
blueice – Lion rolling over, black bear
cardoso – Polar bear at Toronto zoo
chmiel – Sexy particle girl dancing
crackerclips – Grand Canyon sunset
digitalchaos – Snow blowing thru park
dubassy – Lou dance final10
egleye – Grizzly sow
gmanvideo – Sunset waves, stage curtains, glass woman
julos – Dancing heart
lovemushroom – VJ Loop 025
ownway – Concert lights
paha_l – Dancing girl and fan, girl dance on bridge
seanp – Youth culture
skylight – Rocky mountain big horn sheep
spotmatik – Environmental and green
stockshooter – Tigers playing
vjv2 – Popping breaker
wmsimmons – Icebergs

Dr. Vint Cerf and Alcatel-Lucent for their gracious permission to use video from a speech Dr. Cerf gave in September 2004.

Standard Films and Mike Hatchett for the snowboarding footage (www.standardfilms.com).

Darryl Jordan for his photo of Dean Jordan.

Thanks to Brian Greene and Greene HD Productions (www.greenehdtv.com) for permission to use a still from his Moscow on Ice program.

Katie Fredeen (www.pinktiedesign.com) for her Adobe Illustrator Space Image.

Thank Yous to Important People

A book is not created in a vacuum, and there are a number of people I want to thank.

First is Steve Martin from Ripple Training. Many years ago, when I was unemployed yet again, Steve suggested I become a certified Apple trainer – it was an insightful suggestion, and it changed my life. More recently, Steve gave a lecture on how Final Cut editors could use Adobe software. That speech served as the inspiration for my own research into the topic.

Second is Michelle Gallina, a very, very patient person. As senior product marketing manager for Adobe System's Production Premium, she was an invaluable resource in getting me the help I needed and even reviewing many of these chapters. Any mistakes these contain are my fault, the fact that there aren't far more is due to her hard work. Thank you, Michelle!

Thanks also to Dave Helmly at Adobe, for many e-mails clarifying technical issues that I didn't properly understand.

Dennis McGonagle, my editor at Focal Press, for inventing this book and the patience to get me to write it.

Tom Wolsky, for his sharp eye as a technical editor. I've always felt that my monthly Final Cut Studio newsletter was never really complete until I received his corrections on what I messed up. This book is vastly improved by his discerning comments.

Bruce Nazarian for his review and suggestions of the chapter on Blu-ray Discs and his patience in explaining the complexities of this new format.

Jody Eldred, for sharing elements of his XDCAM HD video of LAPD helicopters for use in this book.

Hana Peters, for her discovery that a degree in Psychology can be a perfect springboard to help research a book on video editing.

Aleesa Adams, who joined my company to do some video editing, never realizing that the word "editing" has many different definitions, did an outstanding job reviewing this manuscript from an editor's point of view.

Debbie Price, probably the finest executive assistant who ever lived and the person who makes it possible for me to run a company.

Mike Chapman, Jeff Evenson, Salvador Garza, Ryan Hasan, Jamie Hurt, George Mauro, Dan Shellenbarger, Mark Spencer, and Simon Walker for contributing real-world stories of their experiences in integrating Adobe and Final Cut software.

Time to Get Started

So, you've got all the background. Now, it's time to get to work. And we'll start by looking at a way to find exactly what we seek – using Adobe Bridge.

2

ADOBE BRIDGE: OUR MEDIA HUB

As projects get bigger and more complex, easily finding, previewing, annotating, and organizing media becomes ever more important. That's the best reason I can think of to start this book with Adobe Bridge – it helps us to get better organized.

Final Cut users were introduced to the idea of metadata working with tapeless P2 (DVCPROHD) media, then, more recently, with Final Cut Server. However, metadata runs throughout all the Adobe applications, and this can be a big help in tracking and locating your files. Also, Adobe has significantly standardized the interface in all its applications – so, by spending time learning the interface in Bridge, you're well on your way to success with the others.

Bridge is an application that allows us to find, preview, manage, annotate, and import our media files and still images. It also allows us to add descriptive information, called metadata, so we can find that proverbial needle-in-a-haystack file when we need it.

In this chapter, we will look at Bridge from six points of view:

- The Bridge interface
- Navigation inside Bridge
- Previewing and file management
- Finding stuff
- Working with metadata
- Integration with Production Premium and Final Cut Studio

Why I Like Adobe Bridge

Final Cut Pro has its Browser, the Finder has Spotlight, and there's even Final Cut Server. Why should we even consider using Bridge?

The answer, for me, is that Adobe Bridge is easier to use, runs independently, and is designed to make even a single editor more productive. While Final Cut Server does more, Server is designed for work in a team environment, and it is both costly and time-consuming to install.

Definition: Metadata

Metadata is "data about your data," that is, information about your files. Common metadata includes file name, creation date, format, file size, and so on.

Tip: Get Bridge to Start Itself!

You can get Bridge to start automatically during start-up or log-in. While Adobe provides this as a choice during installation, most of us probably skipped over that step. So, here's how to configure it now – go to **Adobe Bridge > Preferences > Advanced** tab and check "Start Bridge at Login."

Now, Bridge starts whenever you start your computer. If you need to hide Bridge, press **Command + H**. To display it again, click its icon in the Dock.

Tip: Customizing List View

You can control what information is displayed in List view by Control-clicking any column header and selecting from the list in the pop-up menu.

Unlike the Final Cut Browser, which is optimized for viewing files as lists of names, Bridge is designed for working visually. Bridge is a highly customizable program that provides a variety of ways to display and preview files. It also allows adding extensive metadata that travels with the file, as opposed to being stored solely in a Final Cut Pro project file. As an added bonus, Bridge allows drag-and-drop file importing into both Adobe and Apple applications.

While Final Cut allows us to view files in the Browser using what Apple calls a "light-table" approach, this feature is woefully underpowered compared to Adobe Bridge.

Learning the Bridge Interface

Visually, all the Adobe products have a similar interface approach. So, we will spend a bit more time learning the interface to Bridge because that simplifies learning the interface of other applications.

The Bridge interface is composed of workspaces, panels, and tabs. Workspaces contain panels, panels contain tabs, and tabs contain information.

A **workspace** is what Final Cut would call a window layout – it defines the overall look of all screen elements. Those elements include three panels, which contain collections of tabs.

There are three columns, or **panels**, in a workspace. These columns are on the left, center, and right of the workspace. The center panel is where the content is displayed, generally as thumbnails, but not always. The left panel, by default, displays navigation and search filters. The right panel displays the preview windows, keywords, and metadata.

Inside each panel is a collection of tabs. The panel in the top-left corner contains two **tabs**: Favorites and Folders.

Just as in Final Cut, you can resize or reposition just about everything. You can drag tabs from one panel to another. Increase or decrease the size of each panel. Even create entirely new workspaces and save them as a customized workspace to reuse later (see Fig. 2.1).

Workspace

While the default workspace is named Essentials, you can easily select the workspace that corresponds to the work you want to do. There are eight prebuilt workspaces that ship with Bridge. You can switch between workspaces in one of two places: the Workspace menu at the top of the screen or the Workspace pop-up menu in the main Bridge window (see Fig. 2.2).

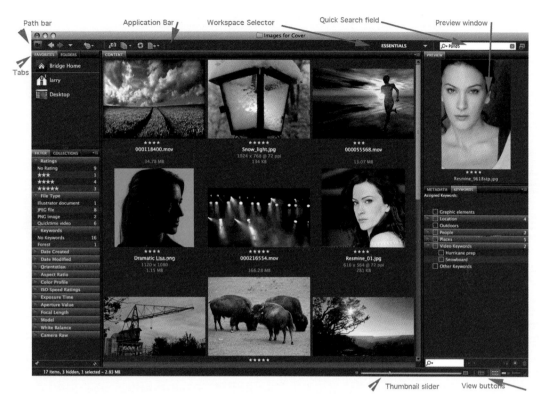

Path bar   Application Bar   Workspace Selector   Quick Search field   Preview window

Tabs

Thumbnail slider   View buttons

Figure 2.1 The Adobe Bridge interface. This is the default workspace, called **Essentials**.

Figure 2.2 Select from one of eight prebuilt workspaces from the Workspace pop-up menu. You can also create and save custom workspaces.

Tip: A Fast Way to Full Screen

To display the Content panel in full screen, press the Tab key (see Fig. 2.7). To get back to where you were, press the Tab key again. The Tab key hides, or shows, all panels except the Content panel. (This trick is similar to the way we hide, or display, the tool palette in Photoshop.)

For instance, Figs. 2.3–2.5 illustrate different workspaces. Each of these variations are just different ways of looking at the same data. The actual files and the associated data have not changed.

One of the nice things about Bridge is that there are many different ways to configure how it looks. For instance, in the lower right corner of the main Bridge window are the View Mode icons. These configure how the main Content panel looks. Figure 2.6

Figure 2.3 Filmstrip workspace. Note how all the large thumbnails are now reduced in size and lined up at the bottom, allowing for a much larger preview window.

Figure 2.4 Metadata workspace. Note how the thumbnails are very small, allowing more access to entering and changing the metadata.

illustrates the three choices – display as large thumbnails, small thumbnails with file information, or just metadata.

Customizing Your Workspace

Creating custom workspaces is a great way to save time, because you can select the workspace that most closely resembles the work you are doing: reviewing clips, adding metadata, organizing files, or whatever.

Figure 2.5 Keyword workspace. Note that the image size is reduced to allow more room for keywords.

(a)   (b)   (c)

Figure 2.6 Three view modes on how the Content panel is displayed: (a) Thumbnails, (b) Details, and (c) List.

Figure 2.7 Press the Tab key to make all side panels disappear. Press the Tab key again to bring them back.

There are three panels, or columns, in Bridge: left, center, and right. To resize a panel, grab the handle that separates one panel from the next and drag it.

To resize a panel, grab the edge of it and drag. Looking for a good place to grab? Try the two parallel lines at the edge (see Figure 2.8).

Control-Click or Right-Click – oh, How to Choose?

At the beginning of time, Macintosh computers shipped with single-button mice. So, for years and years, we needed to Control-click, meaning to press the Control key while clicking the mouse, to access certain hidden menus. Recently, Apple, and many third-party companies, began shipping two-button mice. Control-clicking is the same as right-clicking a mouse button. However, old habits die hard. I use both terms in this book, and they both do the same thing – access hidden contextual menus in an application.

Figure 2.8 To resize a panel grab the edge between two panes and drag left or right.

You can move entire panels, or groups of panels, and not just tabs, to customize your own workspace. To reposition a panel, drag the panel "gripper" to a new location.

To reposition a tab, grab the tab itself and drag it where you want it to go.

To save a customized workspace, make your changes, select **Workspace > New Workspace**, give it a name, then click **Save**.

Using Tabs

There are 10 tabs inside Bridge. Specifically,

- **Collections**. These group files by common parameters, such as file type.
- **Content**. This is where thumbnails are displayed.
- **Favorites**. This is where you put servers, drives, folders, or files you want to return to often.
- **Filters**. These are search criteria used to narrow an existing search.
- **Folders**. These are the folders stored on your hard disk(s).
- **Keywords**. These are the words or phrases used to categorize your files, like "Exterior" or "Interior."
- **Metadata**. This is detailed information about each file, such as "Date shot," "Photographer name," or "Silent."
- **Output**. This displays files you want to output to a particular format, for example, still images you want to output as JPEG.
- **Output Preview**. This is a preview of what your soon-to-be-output files will look like after outputting.
- **Preview**. This is where you see a larger version of the selected file.

Tabs are stored in panels to move a tab, grab it and drag it where you want it to go. You can shuffle the tabs until your heart's content. You can also compress or expand them.

Three Ways to Run Bridge

Like most applications, Bridge is designed to run in Full-screen mode. The problem with this is that many times the full-screen window blocks what we want to see below it.

To solve this problem, Bridge has three different running modes:

- **Full Screen**. All panels are visible, and Bridge can be hidden by other applications.
- **Compact**. All panels are hidden, and the Content window is smaller. Bridge floats on top of all other applications.
- **Ultra-compact**. Both panels and Content window are hidden. This window, too, floats on top of all other applications.

To switch between these modes, click the **Switch to Compact Mode** (Fig. 2.10) or **Switch to Ultra-compact Mode** buttons in the top-right corner of the main Bridge window. This button changes role, depending upon the current display mode.

To switch back to Full-screen mode, click the **Switch to Full Mode** button, which is also in the top-right corner.

Navigating in Bridge

Navigation is the process of pointing Bridge to different sections of your hard disk, so you can see the information that is contained there. At its simplest, navigation means clicking the hard disk, folder, or file to view its contents.

We can make this navigation more sophisticated, and vastly more powerful, by using Quick Searches, Keywords, and Metadata to look for all files that meet a certain criteria regardless of where they are stored on your computer or hard disks.

For now, though, let's keep things simple.

Near the upper left corner of Bridge is a tab labeled "Folders" (Fig. 2.11). This is a list of all the hard drives and servers attached to your system and the folders they contain. As an experiment, just start clicking them and watch what happens in the Content tab.

Tip: A Fast Way to Compress, or Expand, a Tab

 If speed is your goal, double-click a tab to collapse it (see Fig. 2.9). To bring it back, double-click it again.

Figure 2.9 A compressed tab. To reveal it, double-click the tab name.

Tip: Fast-Mode Switching Shortcut

 Here's a keyboard shortcut you won't find in the Bridge manual: to switch between Compact and Full mode, press **Command + Return**.

Figure 2.10 To switch to Compact mode, click the "Switch to Compact Mode" button in the top-right corner of the main Bridge window.

Figure 2.11 The Folders tab. This is a list of all the hard drives and folders on your computer.

Each folder opens into the Content tab, displaying its contents. If it is a file that Bridge can display, a thumbnail appears. Otherwise, only a generic file or folder icon appears.

Not only can you navigate by clicking folder names in the Folders tab, you can also navigate by directly clicking folders in the Content window. This is directly analogous to opening folders in the Finder (see Fig. 2.12).

(As an aside, just like in the Finder, if you double-click a file in Bridge, it opens the file. But, I'm saving that trick for the next section on previewing.)

As you open successive folders inside the Content window, the path to those files is displayed in the main Bridge window. What's really cool is that each element in that file path is clickable. For instance, in Fig. 2.12, to go back two folders, click the word "Larry," and Bridge instantly shifts back. I use this feature a lot!

Creating a Favorite

Let's say you have a folder, filled with the finest files. (In fact, they are so desirable that you want to come back to this folder time and time again.) However, they are buried 55 folders deep.

Now, you could wear out your mouse-button clicking in the Folder tab to get here each time. But, there's a better way – create a Favorite! (See how cleverly I worked the letter "F" into that last paragraph to help you remember *Favorites*? I am renowned for my subtlety.)

Tip: Thumbnails Take Time to Build

If you have an especially complicated image, or if you are displaying a large number of thumbnails for the first time, it can take a while to create thumbnails. If so, this screen may take a while to draw. The speed of creating thumbnails is directly dependent upon the speed of your processor.

Figure 2.12 The file path. This path, located at the top of the Bridge window, shows the route to the images displayed in the Content tab. Each element of this path is also clickable.

To create a Favorite folder, simply select the folder you want to make a Favorite and choose **File > Add To Favorites**, or right-click the file and select **Add to Favorites**.

There's no limit to the number of Favorites you can create. On the other hand, if everything is a favorite, then you really haven't made your life any easier, have you?

Tip: Faster Favorites for the Impatient

 Here's a faster way to create a Favorite folder – simply drag it into the Favorites tab (see Fig. 2.13). Best of all, you can create Favorites by dragging from the Folders tab, the Contents panel, or even the Finder!

Figure 2.13 Drag a folder from the Finder directly into the Favorites tab to set a favorite location.

Previewing Files and File Management

Now that we have a basic understanding of how Bridge works, its time to put it to some practical use: previewing files.

Adobe Bridge will preview any file that can be created, or displayed, in an Adobe application. This includes the following:

- Video files
- Audio files
- Bitmap image files
- Vector image files
- PDF files

The easiest way to preview a file is to click it, which selects it. A preview of the image appears in the Preview window. Grab an edge of the Preview window to resize it. If you select multiple images, then all the selected images will appear in the Preview window.

Tip

 You can change the size of the thumbnails by dragging this slider at the bottom right edge of the Bridge window. Click the small box to the left of the slider or the larger box to the right of the slider to change the thumbnails in increments (see Fig. 2.14).

Figure 2.14 Change the size of your thumbnails in the Content window by dragging this slider or clicking one of the boxes on either side of the slider.

Tip: What's Missing

Image size is displayed for still images, but not for video. Also, the Metadata tab does not display the compression codec for video. Both of these would be really helpful and, hopefully, will be added in future versions.

Since Final Cut prefers images that are smaller than 4000 pixels on a side, I long ago got into the habit of checking the dimensions of an image before I import it. Bridge makes this even easier by displaying key information under the thumbnail.

By default, it just shows the file name. But, if you go to **Adobe Bridge CS4 > Preferences > Thumbnails** tab, see Fig. 2.15a, you can select other information to display under the thumbnail. As Fig. 2.15b illustrates, I added image dimensions and file size to the display. You can also see this information in the Metadata tab under the Preview window.

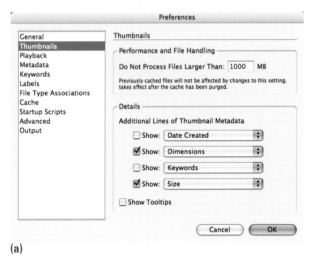

(a)

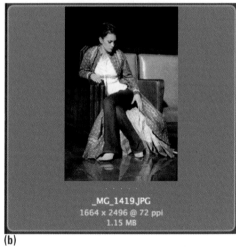

(b)

Figure 2.15 (a) You can change the text displayed below a thumbnail from the Adobe Bridge CS4 > Preferences panel. (b) This shows the results of changing the thumbnail preference setting.

Tip

To lock your thumbnails so that they don't change position as you resize the window, click the Lock Thumbnail Grid button next to the Thumbnail slider (it looks like a Tic-Tac-Toe board) as shown in Fig. 2.16.

Figure 2.16 Click the Lock Thumbnail Grid button to lock your thumbnails so that they don't keep moving into different row and column layouts as you resize the Bridge window.

The Spacebar performs a number of functions. If you are previewing a still image, pressing the Spacebar displays it as large as your monitor will support. If you are previewing a video clip, the Spacebar plays, or stops, the clip. Previewing an audio clip automatically plays it. Pressing the Spacebar stops playback.

Figure 2.17 You can turn off automatic audio playback by unchecking "Play audio files…" in Bridge > Preferences > Thumbnails.

Tip: Turn Off Automatic Audio Previewing

By default, Bridge automatically plays any previewed audio file. You can turn this feature off in **Adobe Bridge > Preferences > Thumbnails** (see Fig. 2.17).

To zoom in, or out, of a preview, press the + (plus), or – (minus), keys. You can zoom in up to 800%!

To change the order of your thumbnails, select and drag the thumbnails you want to move to their new location. The yellow bar that appears shows you the new location for your thumbnails (see Fig. 2.18).

Tip

Double-click any still image, and it will open in Photoshop for editing. Save the edited file, and the thumbnail will automatically update in Bridge.

Figure 2.18 To move a thumbnail, or group of thumbnails, select and drag it to its new location. The yellow bar shows where it will be placed.

Using Review Mode for Thumbnails

If you are looking at still images, you can switch to Review mode, which presents still images in full screen, refines what you've selected, or does basic editing. While Review mode allows you to preview video clips, it is much more helpful in looking at stills. Here's how it works.

Figure 2.19 To quickly review a group of images, select the images and press **Command + B.**

Select one or more thumbnails, then choose **View > Review mode** (or type **Command + B**). To exit Review mode, either press the **Esc** key or click the **X** button in the lower right corner.

Depending upon the number of still images selected, they are shown in a rotating display as shown in Fig. 2.19. To move between the images, click an image, press the **Tab** key, or click the left or right arrows in the lower left corner of the window. To remove an image from your selection, click the down-pointing arrow in the lower left corner (see Fig. 2.20).

The "Loupe" is a magnifying glass you can use to see details in your images. To display the Loupe, either click in the foreground image or click the Loupe icon in the Window controls in the lower right. To create a Collection, which I will talk about a little later, click the Collection icon. And to close this window, click the **X** button (Fig. 2.21) or press **Escape** key.

Figure 2.20 Click the left arrow to move left through your images, the right arrow to move to the right, and the down arrow to remove an image from your selection.

Previewing Tips for the Preview Pane

There are many things we can do in the Preview window. Let's start by looking at still images, then move into media clips.

I've already mentioned that we can change the size of the Preview window by dragging the vertical bar separating the

Preview window from the Content window. However, the Preview window allows us to do much more.

First, click anywhere inside your image, and the Loupe pops up. This shows a detailed view of the point at which you clicked. Notice there's a small "pointy-part" in one of the corners (Fig. 2.22 shows the arrow in the top-left corner.) This indicates the portion of the image that is magnified.

Figure 2.21 Click the Loupe icon (above left) to display a detail from the foreground image, the Collection icon (center) to create a Collection, and the X button (right) to close the Review mode window.

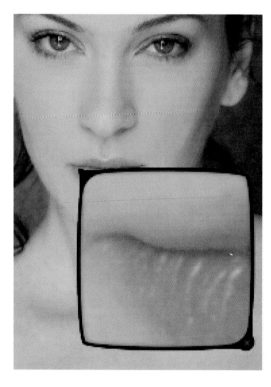

Figure 2.22 Click anywhere inside your image in the Preview window to see a magnified detail of your image.

Tip

In Review mode, if you need to rotate an image 90°, select it using the Tab key or by clicking it, then press the **[** or **]** (square brackets) key.

Extra-Secret Tip

Press the **H** key for a list of all keyboard shortcuts available in Review mode.

Drag the Loupe around inside your image to see other details. By default, it shows the image detail at 100%. Either click the mouse again or click the small close box in the lower right corner to make the Loupe disappear. You can only use one Loupe per image.

Previewing Media Files

Everything we've already learned about images, thumbnails, and previews works exactly the same with what Adobe calls "Dynamic Media," media that changes over time. I just call them clips.

Bridge can preview just about any video, audio, or 3D clip that can be played in QuickTime.

Tip

To zoom in, or out, with the Loupe, you can use your mouse scroll wheel or the plus and minus buttons on the main keyboard. The zoom range is from 100 to 800%.

However, there is one gotcha that you need to watch for. Because Adobe Bridge is cross-platform, that is, it runs on both Macintosh and Windows computers, it expects all media file names to have an extension. For instance, to preview a QuickTime movie, the file name needs to end with ".mov" (see Fig. 2.23). If a media clip doesn't have a file name extension, Bridge displays it as a still image if it's a video clip, or with a generic icon if it's an audio clip.

Figure 2.23 A selected video clip shows up in the Preview window. Press the Spacebar, or click the small Play arrow to left of the slider, to play the clip.

To preview a video clip, or a group of clips, select what you want to preview to display it in the Preview window. Click the Play arrow in the Preview window, or press the Spacebar, to play a clip. To stop playback, press the Spacebar again.

However, unlike a still image, double-clicking a video clip will open it into the application that created the clip; it will be Final Cut Pro for clips that are captured or created in Final Cut. However, most of the time, I would prefer that all my video clips open in QuickTime player. It's faster and simpler to work with for previewing video.

There are three ways to get around this problem. First, to open an individual clip, right-click the clip and select **Open With > QuickTime Player** from the pop-up menu (see Fig. 2.25).

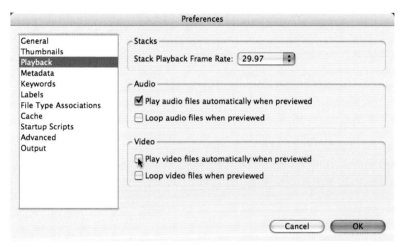

Figure 2.24 Adjust Playback preferences to play audio or video clips automatically when selected. In general, I uncheck all four checkboxes.

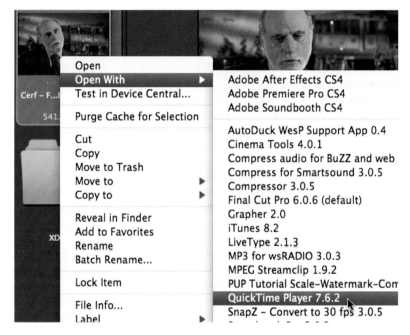

Figure 2.25 Control-click a thumbnail to select the application you want to use to open a clip.

To set a clip, or group of clips, so that they permanently open in QuickTime (this does not affect their ability to be edited inside Final Cut), we need to make a trip to the Finder and make some changes. Figure 2.26 shows how.

- Select all the clips that you want to change so that they open in QuickTime Player (remember, this will not affect Final Cut's ability to edit them).
- If you have only one clip, select **File > Get Info** (or type **Command + I**).

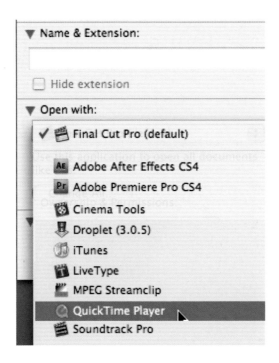

Figure 2.26 Select a clip in the Finder and choose **File > Get Info**. Changing the Open With menu to "QuickTime Player," allows you to double-click a media file in Bridge to open it in QuickTime Player.

Tip: Change All Changes All Files

If you click the Change All checkbox, all .mov files will open in QuickTime. This is a fast way to set all your movies to open the same way.

Note

Bridge doesn't preview Final Cut Pro, Soundtrack Pro, Motion, or LiveType project files. However, it will preview the media files that are the components of those projects.

- (If you have more than one clip, hold the Option key down and select **File > Show Inspector** or type **Option + Command + I**).
- Change the **Open with** pop-up menu to **QuickTime Player**.
- Close the dialog box.

Now, when you double-click a video clip, it automatically opens in QuickTime Player.

The third option is to change which application Bridge uses to open a file. To do this choose Adobe Bridge > Preferences, and select File Type Associations. While these settings only affect Bridge, many times they can save you a trip to the Finder.

File Management

There are a number of file management tasks that can be done inside Bridge. Sometimes, it may be easier to do these in the Finder. Other times, it may be easier in Bridge. The nice thing is, once you know both, you get to pick your favorite.

Creating Stacks

Stacks are collections of files that are grouped under a single thumbnail. For instance, you could group all the still images of a single subject into a stack.

To create a stack, select the images you want to group and select **Stacks > Group as Stack** (or type **Command + G**).

To view the images in a stack, click the small number in the upper left corner to preview the elements of the stack. To collect the images back into a single stack, click the number again (see Fig. 2.27).

Tip

Bridge stacks are not the same as Photoshop stacks. In Bridge, a stack is simply a way to organize a group of images, whereas in Photoshop, a stack converts multiple images into separate Photoshop layers in a single Photoshop document.

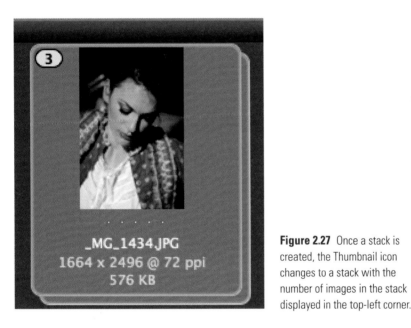

Figure 2.27 Once a stack is created, the Thumbnail icon changes to a stack with the number of images in the stack displayed in the top-left corner.

To unstack the images, select **View > Ungroup from Stack** (or type **Shift + Command + G**).

Everything you can do to one image you can do to a stack. While stacks are handy for still images, I don't find them particularly useful for Dynamic Media. A better choice for me is to create a Collection.

Creating a Collection

A Collection is a handy way to group media in one place, even if they are stored in different locations, or even in different hard disks.

There are two types of Collections: a regular Collection, the contents of which don't change, and a Smart Collection, whose contents change dynamically based upon the results of search criteria that you specify.

To create a Collection, select the thumbnails you want to group together, click the **New Collection** button at the bottom of the Collections panel (Fig. 2.28), and give the Collection a name.

The new collection shows up in the Collections panel. To add files to the Collection, drag the thumbnails onto the name of the

Figure 2.28 To create a Collection, select the images you want to include and click the New Collections button at the bottom of the Collections panel.

Collection. To remove files, Control-click and select **Delete** from the menu as shown in Fig. 2.29.

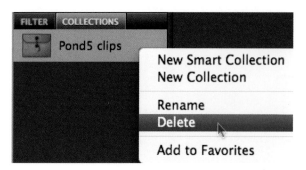

Figure 2.29 To remove files from a Collection, Control-click the Collection name and select "Delete."

- You can rename Collections – double-click the name.
- You can delete Collections – highlight the name and click the trash button at the bottom of the Collections pane.
- You can create more collections.

Collections make it easy to group all related files, so they are easy to review, regardless of where they are stored.

But, the really neat part of Collections is a Smart Collection, which is dynamic. We'll talk about that in the Finding Stuff section.

Other File Management

In addition to grouping files, Bridge allows us to manage our files. Specifically, we can do the following:

- Open a file in another application
- Cut, copy, and paste files
- Move files to the Trash
- Move files to recently opened folders, or any folder we choose
- Copy files to recently opened folders, or any folder we choose
- Reveal files in the Finder
- For files in Collections, reveal the source file in Bridge
- Add files, or folders, to the Favorites panel
- Rename files
- Batch rename files
- Label files
- Sort files

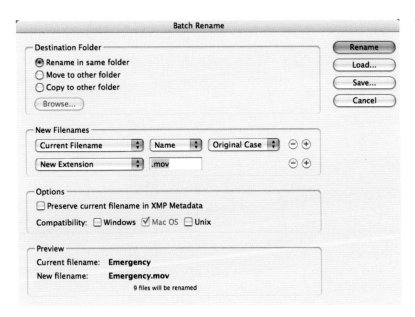

Two Important Notes

Batch Rename is not undoable. If you make a mistake, you'll need to correct it using Batch Rename again.

Also, when you change a file name, you break the link that Final Cut Pro has with the file. This means that Final Cut will show the file as off-line. Fixing this requires using Reconnect Media inside Final Cut to reestablish the links with the files.

Figure 2.30 Use these settings to add extensions to a group of selected QuickTime movies.

While most of these functions are self-evident, the Batch Rename feature is especially helpful to Final Cut users. Earlier, I mentioned that in order for Bridge to play a media file, that file needs to have an extension. The problem is that often, Final Cut does not add extensions during normal capture operations.

This means that editors would need to manually rename every file. While possible, this ain't fun.

That's where Batch Rename makes our life really easy. Here's how:

- Select the files you want to rename in the Content window.
- Select **Tools > Batch Rename** (or type **Shift + Command + R**).
- Change the settings to match those in Fig. 2.30.
- Click **Rename**.

Almost instantly, all your clips have extensions added and are ready to preview.

To see all the options you have in file management, **Control-click** any thumbnail, and the menu shown in Fig. 2.31 is revealed.

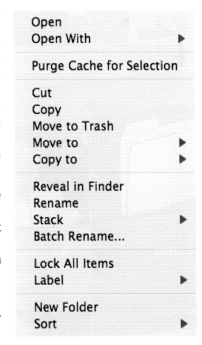

Figure 2.31 For a list of all file management options, Control-click a thumbnail.

Adobe and Apple Differ on Metadata

Adobe has implemented extensive metadata support that is shared and readable across all their applications, using an XMP architecture.

Sadly, Final Cut Pro does not read XMP metadata natively. So, there is no way to get this data, easily, into Final Cut Pro. Final Cut Server does read metadata, provided it is contained in still image data. At this point, Final Cut Server does not read XMP data from sidecar or media files.

Adding Metadata

Metadata – which is the information that describes your files – is where Bridge really shines. The whole reason for spending time adding metadata – and it does take time – to our files is to allow us to find the files we need when we need them with a minimum of wasted time and steps.

As we fill up more and more hard disks with media, being able to find exactly the clips we need becomes increasingly challenging, especially if you have multiple clips all named "Scene 23 WS Tk 2." It made sense at the time, but a year later, as you are looking for that clip, it's going to be hard to locate.

That's where metadata comes in. We can add data to our images and media in several ways:

- Ratings
- Labels
- Keywords
- Metadata

We use all this metadata to help us describe our clips in a way that makes it easy to find later.

Using Ratings

Ratings are cool.

Underneath every thumbnail is a series of five dots. Click on a star or drag your mouse across those dots, and they turn into star ratings, just like in iPhoto. These stars can mean anything you want – the cool part is that you can search for files based on their star ratings (see Fig. 2.32).

To change the rating, simply click or drag across them again. In fact, as you change a rating, you'll see an otherwise invisible button on the left, which allows you to remove any rating from a clip. Ratings are displayed in both the Content and Preview windows.

Tip

You can also apply star ratings from the Label menu, but this is nowhere near as cool as dragging with the mouse.

Sidebar: An Opposing Point of View

I asked Tom Wolsky to tech edit this book because I value his opinions. Tom disagrees with my comments on ratings: "I think ratings are great for stills, not so much for video. Projects change. The flow of a movie, fiction, or nonfiction, can change in the process, especially a program with a lot of material or one that goes on for a long time. A one or no star clip, which might be ignored, might in reality be just the right piece for the project as it develops. The idea that you are excluding material early in the process just seems wrong to me."

Figure 2.32 Add your own star ratings at the bottom of every thumbnail. Ratings can be modified at any time.

Using Labels

Like ratings, labels are easy to apply and can also be searched on. However, there are only five labels available, so the first thing you will probably want to do is to change them from their defaults.

To do so, go to **Adobe Bridge CS4 > Preferences > Labels**. Here, you can change the text associated with each label and decide if you want to use the Command key, along with the number, to apply a label to a selected clip (Fig. 2.33).

However, just like the labels in Final Cut, we are stuck with the colors.

Once you've configured your labels, simply select the thumbnails you want to apply the labels to and choose the appropriate label from the Label menu.

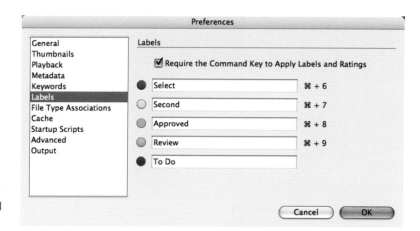

Figure 2.33 Use this preference panel to configure your own label text.

Tip

 The best keywords are those that span clients or projects. For instance, something specific to a small number of clips, such as the project name or the client, would be best stored as metadata. File types don't need keywords, since they are tracked automatically in metadata. Useful keywords might be "sea shore," "kitchen," "dawn," and "no people."

Using keywords this way allows Bridge to "find all .mov clips that I shot at dawn at the seashore that don't show any people in them, regardless of which project it was for."

Using Keywords

Keywords are words or phrases that describe categories that we want to apply to our clips.

Keywords are stored in the Keywords panel. While there's no practical limit to the number of keywords you can create, keywords work best when there are not a lot of them. This is not to say you should only use a dozen, but if you need more than 50–60 keywords, you might want to rethink your organization.

This is an important point. Keywords work best when you don't create too many of them. Spend some time thinking about how you want to track and retrieve files – for instance, location, year, time of day, subject matter – before you start creating keywords.

To apply a keyword to a clip, select the clip, then from the Keywords tab, click the checkbox for all the keywords you want to apply to a clip. You can check as many keywords as you like (Fig. 2.34).

Figure 2.34 Apply a keyword to a selected file by checking the checkbox.

To create new keywords, select a keyword at the same level as you want the new keyword to appear and click the **New Keyword** button (Fig. 2.35a). To create a subkeyword, that is, a subdivision of an existing keyword, click **New Sub Keyword** (Fig. 2.35b). To delete a keyword, select the keyword and click **Delete Keyword** (Fig. 2.35c).

(a)

(b)

(c)

Figure 2.35 These buttons are all located in the lower right corner of the Keyword panel. (a) New keyword. (b) Sub Keyword. (c) Delete Keyword.

Adding Metadata

When it's time to get specific, it's time to use metadata.

There are 15 specific metadata categories inside Bridge; however, not all are visible on every file. While we are not able to create new metadata fields, there are plenty of options to choose from. These six categories are used most frequently by video editors:

- File properties
- IPTC Core
- Audio
- Video
- DICOM
- Mobile SWF

File Properties. This is similar to the metadata kept inside the Final Cut Browser – file name, type, size, resolution, and so on. This data is automatically tracked by Bridge for us. However, and this is important, Bridge does not read Final Cut Pro Browser fields, which means you need to manually reenter any data that is not tracked automatically.

IPTC Core. This is the metadata that you would track inside Photoshop. There are 31 fields of information ranging from the name of the creator to the status of copyright. You don't need to use all these files, but it's nice to know you've got them available.

Audio. This is more iTunes-oriented than I'd like, but keep in mind that each audio clip also has the full range of IPTC metadata to supplement anything missing in this category.

Video. This is almost identical to the data we enter in Final Cut's Log and Capture/Log and Transfer window. However, Bridge does not read the Reel ID field stored in the QuickTime movie.

DICOM. This is short for Digital Imaging and Communications in Medicine and is used for tracking x-rays and other medical imagery.

Mobile SWF. This lists data on SWF files for cell phones.

You can select what metadata should be displayed – from hundreds of possible fields – by choosing **Adobe Bridge CS4 > Preferences > Metadata** (see Fig. 2.36).

To apply metadata to the thumbnails you selected:

- Double-click the metadata header, such as IPTC Core, to display the fields inside.
- Click to the left of the Pencil icon on the right side of the panel. Those fields that change to a lighter shade of gray allow data entry, such as the name of the photographer. Those that don't calculate their field contents automatically, for example, with the name of the file (see Fig. 2.37).
- If you are satisfied with your entry, click the checkmark in the lower right corner of the pane. If you want to throw away all your new entries, click the **Cancel** button, next to the checkmark (Fig. 2.38).

Metadata can be changed at any time by simply clicking in the field you want to change and making your corrections. To delete metadata, select the entire contents of the field and press the **Delete** key.

Tip

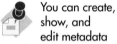

You can create, show, and edit metadata templates using the Tools menu. You can also use these templates to import metadata into multiple files at once. The Bridge User Manual describes how.

Figure 2.36 With hundreds of metadata fields to choose from, this preference allows you to control which fields Bridge will display. Note the checkbox allowing you to hide empty fields.

Where Metadata Is Stored

Most of the time, metadata is stored in the file itself. This is true for most documents. This means that metadata will always travel with the source file and not get lost.

However, QuickTime files are an exception. The QuickTime spec does not contain all the metadata fields that Bridge supports. In which case, Bridge creates what's called a "sidecar" file. This is a file with the same file name as the QuickTime movie, but with an .XMP extension, which is stored in the same location as that of the QuickTime movie.

While Bridge handles sidecar files transparently for most operations, you need to be careful when copying files because you need to copy both the QuickTime movie and the related sidecar file as well.

Finding Stuff

Since the reason for adding metadata is to allow us to find the files we need, in this section we take a look at how Bridge allows us to find stuff.

We will look first at simple ways to find the files, filter them using specific criteria, create a Smart Collection, and then wrap up by sophisticated searches using keywords and metadata.

The best part of this whole process is that it isn't hard.

Tip

The QuickFind box uses the Spotlight indexing built-into OS X for really fast searches.

Simple Finds

Some examples of simple finds include finding by file name, file extension, star ratings, or labels.

Here's an example of finding by file name. Say we want to find all files that have "Snowboard" in the file namc.

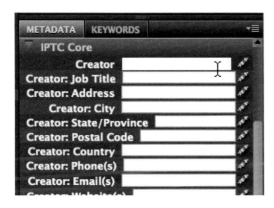

Figure 2.37 Metadata can be entered into any field that is light gray in color.

Figure 2.38 To accept your metadata, click the checkmark; to discard all entries, click the Cancel button.

Figure 2.39 Type the word or phrase you are looking for in the QuickFind text box and then press Enter.

- Click the Folders tab and select your computer, or a hard disk, that you want to use as the source of your search.
- Double-click the hard disk you want to search to load it into the Content window.
- In the QuickFind box in the top-right corner of the Bridge window, type the word "Snowboard" and press **Enter** (see Fig. 2.39).

Cool. Several files were almost instantly displayed in the Content tab.

More Complex Finds

Let's try something a bit more complex. Let's look for all .mov files on our hard disk.

- Choose **Edit > Find** (or type **Command + F**).
- In the Find dialog box, set the **Look In** pop-up menu to the hard disk you want to search. In this case, we are looking on our boot disk.
- In the Criteria section, set the first line of the search criteria to **Filename**, **Ends with**, **.mov**. This will display all files on the specified hard disk with an extension of .mov.
- Click the **Find** button.

Dozens of files are displayed in the Content window really, really fast. Hmmm… Hundreds of files. Worse. Thousands of files. There are, wow, way too many! Help (see Fig. 2.40).

Working with Filters

Whoa! Houston, we have a problem. We need to limit the number of files found by this particular Find.

Ta-DAH! Filters to the rescue!

In the left panel is the Filter tab (Fig. 2.41). This tab filters, or limits, the results of a search. What's cool about this is it shows all the different categories associated with the files currently displayed in the Content window. While it would be nice to include a few more technical categories – like codecs, frame rates, and image sizes – this is still a great way to narrow the field.

So, in this case, we found 55 files: 52 have no star rating, 2 have a three-star rating, and 1 has a four-start rating.

Figure 2.40 Our simple file extension search found way too many files. In this case, 85!

Figure 2.41 The Filters tab is dynamic. It instantly displays statistics about the files currently displayed in the Content window.

Tip

To apply a filter, click the name of the filter, for example, the three stars. To remove a filter, click the name again.

Click the three-star line and instantly, from those 55 files, the two that you've assigned three stars to are displayed.

Let's do a multilevel search. When we click the QuickTime video filter, our 55 files are narrowed to 45. Then, when we click Snowboard, from all those files, we found exactly two that meeting all our criteria: a QuickTime movie about snowboarding.

Just remember, filters narrow an existing search.

Creating a Smart Collection

Let's say that we want to keep a dynamic collection of Snowboard QuickTime movies, so that we can instantly see all the files that are available. Piece of cake – it's called a Smart Collection. Here's how to create one.

- Click the Collections tab in the left panel.
- Click the Smart Collection button at the bottom.
- In the Smart Collection dialog (which looks suspiciously like the Find dialog we just worked with), set **Look in** to the hard disk you want to search.
- Set the criteria to the types of files you are looking for. This can rarely be done using a single line. That's OK, we have lots of lines to work with. Set the first line to **Filename**, **Ends with**, and **.mov**.
- Click the **Plus** button on the right side of the first line to add another search criteria.
- Set the second line to **Keywords**, **contains**, **Snowboard**.
- Change the Results Match pop-up to **If all criteria are met**. This means that a file must match both criteria to be displayed. The default is that a file needs to match any one criteria.
- Click **Save**.
- In the Collections tab, rename the Smart Collection to, in our case, **Snowboard videos**.

And that's it.

Now, whenever you click that Smart Collection, it will use those criteria to re-search your hard disk and find all the files that match the criteria. So, you can keep adding new files without worrying about whether Bridge will find them.

Finding Using Metadata

So far, our searches have been simple. But, as you start to get more and more files, you'll want to make your searches more specific, so you don't waste time searching through hundreds of files you don't need. That's where metadata comes in.

And, best of all, you already know how to use it.

- Select the hard disk(s) you want to search.
- Choose **Edit > Find**.
- In Criteria, select the Metadata you want to search for. If you need to restrict your search, add as many additional search criteria lines as you need. Or, select **All Metadata** to search all metadata fields.
- After that, the Find operation is exactly the same as those you've already done.

This powerful search ability makes finding and managing files, especially files used across multiple projects, much faster and easier than working with them in Final Cut Pro, or even the Finder.

Integrating Bridge with Final Cut Studio

Learning Bridge is useful in itself, but what makes it worth learning for Final Cut Pro editors is that it integrates smoothly with the applications in Final Cut Studio.

For instance, Fig. 2.42 illustrates two files that we want to add to Final Cut Pro. Simply drag the files from Bridge into the Final Cut Pro Browser. This is much faster than importing with the added benefit that Bridge is able to track and maintain the metadata from the clips while Final Cut is busy editing them.

This drag-and-drop process works the same when dragging a clip into the Timeline for Soundtrack Pro (see Fig. 2.43), the Layers or Canvas windows of Motion, or the Assets tab of DVD Studio Pro.

Because Bridge normally takes up the full screen, be sure to switch to Compact mode **(Command + Return)** to make it small enough that you can move files from Bridge into Final Cut.

In other words, if you can find it in Bridge, you can bring it into Final Cut Studio.

TIP

It is always better to drag a file into Final Cut Pro's Browser, than directly to a sequence in the Timeline. If you ever accidentally delete the sequence, you've lost the link to that clip. However, dragging clips into the Browser preserves the link, regardless of what happens to an individual sequence.

Figure 2.42 To import files into Final Cut Pro, just select them in Bridge and drag them into Final Cut's Browser.

Figure 2.43 To import files directly to Soundtrack Pro's Timeline, select the files in Bridge and drag them over.

Bridge Keyboard Shortcuts

Here's a collection of useful keyboard shortcuts for Adobe Bridge CS4.

Shortcut	What it does
Command + F	Finds
F5	Refreshes Contents panel
Command + Return	Switches between Full-screen and Compact mode
Command + \	Switches between workspace views
Control + F1	Resets default workspace
Tab	Shows/hides panels
Spacebar	Previews a media clip or displays a still image full screen
Command + B	Switches to Review mode
Option + Shift + Command + I	Shows file info
Command + + (plus)	Increases thumbnail size
Command + ((minus)	Decreases thumbnail size
Command + [1–5]	Shows items with star rating of 1–5, or higher, in Filters panel
Command + Option + A	Clears all filters
+	Zooms in with Loupe
−	Zooms out with Loupe
Command + ,	Decreases star rating
Command + .	Increases star rating

At the end of most chapters, I'll present stories written by editors working on real-world projects illustrating how they integrate Adobe Production Premium software into a Final Cut Studio workflow.

My Story

Salvador Garza Roehll
Pixelop Studio
www.pixelopstudio.com

At Pixelop Studio, we're a boutique-style production house and home to only four creative professionals. We like to think of ourselves as a high-performing multidisciplinary team, always looking for a more efficient and better way of doing things.

For the past 5 or 6 years, a large percentage of our work has been producing corporate, annual report and product videos for GCC (www.gcc.com), a multinational business group that produces cement, ready-mix concrete, aggregates, and innovative solutions for the construction industry. Each year GCC delivers its annual report to its stockholders by the end of April. So, every year, we make a 2-month trip and visit each and every one of its locations. With the annual report video being our primary objective during the tour, we also shoot additional footage with the idea of building a stock footage library for future projects. We started out shooting with a Panasonic DVX-100 and have moved up to a HPX-170, a P2 tapeless workflow.

Managing almost 6 years worth of stock footage has become a challenge. We've got everything online on an Xserve hosting nearly 6 TB of footage and project files to a four-seat NAS system (a SAN exceeds our requirements and budget). Adobe Bridge has become an essential part of our workflow. After 2 years of working with a P2 tapeless workflow, the renaming feature in Bridge has been a real life-saver. We usually log and transfer all the footage on our P2 cards, use Adobe Bridge to quickly navigate, and playback the footage. We delete any unwanted shots, then batch rename the files according to the content and our file naming conventions. We can't imagine having to go through 2 years of 0001XU.mov files or manually renaming them in Final Cut Pro!

We've been working with Final Cut Pro from 2003 and just love the program. I prefer working with FCP's Browser in list view, and although the interface is highly customizable, unfortunately, the thumbnail size can't be customized in this view mode. After long hours, it's hard to see the images at 2.5 ft. from a 30-inch Cinema Display. Even in large icon view, Adobe Bridge's automatic playback feature wins me over. Being able to drag clips from Bridge directly into any of Final Cut Pro's windows (Viewer, Canvas,

Timeline, and Browser) is very efficient. I use Bridge to quickly preview thousands of clips and select the footage I plan to work with, drag into Final Cut Pro's Browser, and continue from there. Exporting the thumbnail cache to the folders on the server means that valuable time is saved when other seats use Bridge to browse the library. Recently, we've even been using Bridge to navigate, locate, and playback music files in our royalty-free music library.

Using both Adobe Bridge and Apple's Final Cut Pro has significantly increased our productivity, enabling us to focus exclusively on the creative direction of our projects.

3

ADOBE ONLOCATION: PREPRODUCTION PLANNING AND ON-SET MONITORING

Adobe OnLocation is new to the Mac with CS4; prior to that it was Windows-only. In the CS4 version, OnLocation has an all-new interface, cross-platform support, and better metadata integration. In this chapter, we'll take a look at how to use OnLocation as an aid in production.

Prior to the shoot, OnLocation helps us get organized by creating and organizing shot lists and entering metadata. During production, it allows us to capture our shots directly to the computer, monitor their quality, and review them on set or after. Following production, we can use it to add or modify metadata.

In preparation for writing this chapter, I rented a small stage, hired actors, and brought in a couple of cameras to show how OnLocation works. While there, I also shot some green screen footage to use later in this book as illustrations.

So, to get ready for this shoot, I'll use OnLocation to help me plan, then take it to the stage for the shoot and use it to capture my shots.

With that as background, let's take a closer look at how OnLocation can help me in preparing and shooting this material.

Learning the Interface

One of the advantages in spending time learning the interface to Adobe Bridge is that now we already know how to use OnLocation – the interfaces are similar: workspaces contain panels that contain tabs (see Fig. 3.1).

There are four workspaces inside OnLocation:

- Preproduction
- Calibration

Figure 3.1 This is the Production workspace for OnLocation.

Figure 3.2 To relocate a panel, drag the small gripper icon next to the name of a panel to a new location.

- Production
- Full-screen

Preproduction. This workspace allows you to create a list of shots you want to get during production by displaying the Shot List and Metadata panels.

Calibration. This displays a live video feed directly from your camera, plus audio-level meters, waveform, vectorscope, and histogram video scopes.

Production. This reorganizes panels to make it easy to record, review, and analyze clips.

Full-screen. Almost any panel can be made full-screen; this option allows you to display a panel, such as the video monitor (called the Field Monitor) or any individual video scope, full screen with tabs to select other panels.

Here's another neat trick. You can move tabs to customize your own workspace. To reposition a tab, drag the "gripper" just to the left of the tab name to a new location (see Fig. 3.2). Notice when you click a gripper, the tab displays an orange boundary, indicating what you are about to move.

To resize a panel, drag the dividing line between panels. If you can't find a panel or workspace, display it using the Window menu at the top of your screen.

Just like Final Cut Pro, OnLocation will remember the last window layout you were using when you quit the application and reopen the same layout the next time you launch the application. If you want to save a particular workspace to use again in the future, choose **Window > Workspace > New Workspace**. Enter a name for your new layout and click **OK**.

For the rest of this chapter, we'll use the standard workspaces that are built into the application.

On Using Two Monitors

One thing I've noticed is that when using two monitors, if OnLocation is displayed on the second monitor and the menu bar is assigned to that second monitor, OnLocation will often open such that the top part of the window will be underneath the menu bar. If this happens to you, open **System Preferences > Display** and move the menu bar to the other monitor. In the Finder, reposition OnLocation away from the top of your screen. Then, move the menu bar back to the second monitor.

Using OnLocation in Preproduction

Preproduction is all about planning. The more time you spend planning the different elements of your production – from budgets to script to staffing to tech – the smoother your production days will run, and the more likely you are to get the shots you really need.

OnLocation can help in that it allows us to plan our shots and begin the process of entering metadata in the less-stressful environment before shooting starts rather than the high-stress world of shooting on-set.

In this section, I want to show you how to create a new project, create a shot list, and begin the process of entering metadata.

Working with Projects

To create a new project, either select **New Project** from the Start screen that opens when you launch the application (Fig. 3.3), select **File > New Project**, or type **Command-N**. Give your new project a name and save it to your second drive.

To open an existing project, either select **Open Project** from the Start screen, use **File > Open Project**, or type **Command-O**.

You can easily move projects between hard drives, or even computer systems, by dragging the entire project folder, which contains both your project file and the Clips folder, to the new location. You need to move the entire folder; if you just move the project file itself or if you rename anything, either the project file won't open or all the media clips will be marked as off-line.

To delete a project, or the media files associated with a project, simply drag the project file, the Clips folder, or the entire project folder from the Finder to the Trash.

Understanding Recording Modes

One of the key benefits to using OnLocation is its ability to help you plan your shots before you get on set. The better your planning, the more efficient you can be when under pressure on set.

Figure 3.3 To create a new project, click the New Project button on the Start screen.

Definition: Off-line

 An off-line media clip is a clip that is not available to a project. This could be due to the file being erased, moved, renamed, or not yet captured. The project file knows it should be there, but just can't find it.

Really, Really Important!

Unlike Final Cut Pro, OnLocation does not use scratch disks. This means that your media will be saved to the same place you save your project file, in a folder named **Clips**. In my opinion, it is really important that you save both your OnLocation project and media files to a hard disk other than your boot drive to reduce the risk of dropping frames during data capture.

In reviewing this point, however, Adobe disagrees. In their comments, they wrote: In nearly five years of testing DV Rack [the precursor to OnLocation] and OnLocation, more often than not recording to the boot drive, I have seen frames dropped only a few times, and we've never attributed it to the project being on the boot drive.

"For my money, the top reasons to record to a secondary drive, ideally an external [drive], are [better] disk space, defragmentation, and convenience for transferring to the media server."

While I find these comments reassuring, I will restate that recording media to a second drive is an excellent practice. In addition, avoid using USB hard drives (even USB2) for media recording on a Macintosh. While providing acceptable performance on a PC, they rarely work fast enough on a Macintosh. Though both DV and HDV have very small data rates, when compared to other HD formats, connecting drives using USB on the Macintosh is generally a poor choice.

When it comes to file handling, my recommendation is to create a project folder on your media hard drive, then store your OnLocation project file inside that project folder. As you will see, during production, OnLocation creates other folders stored in that project folder automatically.

OnLocation Does Not Support All Cameras

OnLocation supports NTSC and PAL DV cameras, as well as some HDV and DVCPRO cameras. The key requirement is that the camera must attach to the computer using FireWire. OnLocation does not support cameras that record to DVDs, Blu-ray Discs, hard disks, or any type of flash memory cards.

To help in this regard, OnLocation has two recording modes:

Shot-Recording mode. If you only plan one take (or version) for each shot or when you don't have time to plan, this mode creates a new shot every time you select it.

Take-Recording Mode. If you expect multiple takes (or versions) of each shot, for example, when you have time to plan a detailed shot list prior to starting production, this mode allows multiple takes for the shot. This simplifies tracking all these takes later.

Both these modes allow you to capture your video directly to your hard disk, monitor your images, and add metadata. To plan the upcoming shoot and to create multiple takes for each shot, we will take a closer look at creating a Take List.

Creating a Take List

As I mentioned at the beginning of this chapter, my plan is to shoot a variety of green screen shots, which I can use as examples later in this book. Here's an outline of how to create this shot list using OnLocation. I'll provide the details next.

- Select the **Preproduction** workspace (see Fig. 3.4).
- Switch to **Take-Recording Mode**.
- Create a placeholder for each shot.
- Add sufficient metadata, so you can sort your shots by format (for example, HD vs. SD).

Figure 3.4 This is the Preproduction workspace. It consists of two tabs: Shot List and Metadata.

- Set a priority for each shot so that if time runs short, you can quickly find your most important shots. Priorities are not the same as ratings.
- Sort your shots in the order you want to shoot them.

To get started, the first thing I do is set my workspace to **Preproduction**. This reduces the number of open panes to two: Shot List and Metadata. This allows me to concentrate on creating the shots I need, without getting distracted by parts of the interface that are unnecessary until I get to production.

Before creating individual shots, we need to set the recording mode. In this case, as I expect to create more than one take of each shot, I'll use **Take-Recording Mode**. To set this, right-click either the Shot List tab or the fly-out menu in the top-right corner of the Shot List tab (Fig. 3.5).

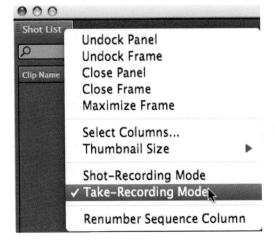

Figure 3.5 Switch modes by right-clicking the Shot List tab.

Next, I add a shot placeholder by clicking the **Add Shot** placeholder button in the lower left corner of the Shot List panel (Fig. 3.6). This creates a new shot at the top of the shot list. (Notice that it numbers Sequences as 10, 20, 30, ... This allows you to easily add new shots without renumbering everything.)

Before entering the shot description (which is another way of saying "entering metadata"), I want to change the columns that are displayed in the Shot List. This way, I can configure the Shot List to track the specific information that I need for my shoot.

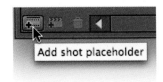

Figure 3.6 To create a new shot in your project, click the Add Shot placeholder button in the lower left corner of the workspace.

When Should You Add a Take?

You add a take when you are in production and you realize that you need to record another take of a shot you've already recorded. When you are creating your shot list in preproduction, you only need to add shots. (By the way, when you create a new take [Fig. 3.7] to an existing shot, OnLocation copies the Sequence, Good, and Rating metadata.)

Figure 3.7 To create a new take to an existing shot during production, click the Add take placeholder button.

Changing Column Order

While you can't change the order of columns by dragging in the Change Selection dialog, you can change column order by dragging the column headers left or right in the Shot List tab until they are in the order you want. This is similar to the way we reorganize Browser columns inside Final Cut Pro.

Either control-click the Shot List tab or go to the fly-out menu in the top-right corner of the Shot List, and pick **Select Columns...** From the Column Selection dialog, check the columns I want to display and uncheck those I am not interested in (Fig. 3.8). Obviously, your priorities may differ, so select the columns that are most relevant to you in planning your own projects.

Based on what I want to shoot, I selected the following columns:

- Clip Name – to create the file name for the clip
- Sequence – a number that determines shot order and can be used to set priorities for production
- Location – green screen or office
- Description – general description of what I want to shoot
- Scene – description of that particular shot
- Take – calculated automatically by OnLocation
- Camera Label – I'm using this to flag whether this is an HD or SD shot
- Good – a checkbox to indicate whether I like the shot

As you create placeholders, notice that you don't need to save anything. All updates are saved automatically. Think of this as entering data into a database, you don't need to save each record you enter. The database does it for you.

There are times when I want to duplicate a placeholder because almost all the metadata is the same, for instance, two identical clips where one is HD and the other is SD. Duplicating clips is easy, but hidden. **Control-click** anywhere in the placeholder and select **Make Duplicate Placeholder** (Fig. 3.9).

Once I'm done entering my shots, I can sort them by clicking the header of any column. Click again to sort in descending order. However, unlike Final Cut's browser, you can only sort on one column at a time.

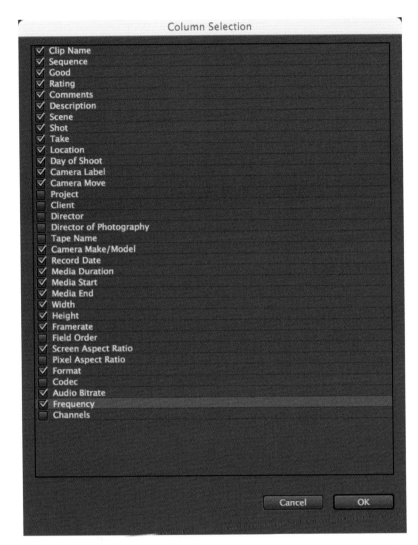

Figure 3.8 The Column Selection dialog allows you to determine which columns you want to display.

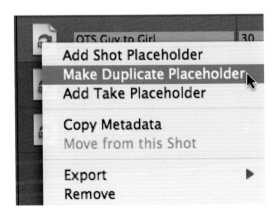

Figure 3.9 Right-click the placeholder name and select Make Duplicate Placeholder to quickly duplicate clip data.

To delete a shot, highlight the shot in the list and press the **Delete** key.

Figure 3.10 illustrates my completed list of shots.

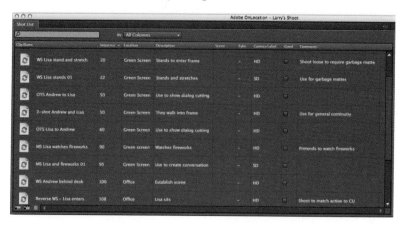

Figure 3.10 Here is a list of all the shots I need to get at my upcoming shoot.

Adding Metadata

To get a jump on tracking my clips, I can start entering metadata into placeholders. As I capture each clip, the metadata is automatically transferred to the clip itself.

Just as in Bridge, metadata has its own panel called, not surprisingly, the Metadata panel. (No, I'm not making this stuff up!) There are 12 categories of metadata, as Fig. 3.11 illustrates. In fact, there are hundreds of fields of potential metadata that can be entered for each clip.

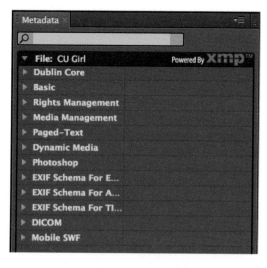

Figure 3.11 OnLocation tracks 12 different categories of metadata information.

You can select the metadata groups you want to display from the Options menu in the top-right corner of the Metadata panel;

Metadata Is Not Meaningless

Metadata is a fancy word for information about each shot. Whether it is as simple as a file name and description, or a complete listing of every actor, spoken word, costume, and camera setting by shot, metadata helps us keep track of our shots. OnLocation, in fact the entire suite of Adobe products, has an extensive list of information (metadata) that is tracked for each shot.

Metadata Reminder

In many cases, metadata is stored directly in the file itself. This is true for EXIF, GPS, and TIFF files. While many QuickTime files, store metadata inside the file, HDV M2T files recorded by OnLocation store metadata in a separate file with an .xml extension, called a "sidecar."

limiting your metadata choices makes it a lot easier to concentrate on entering the data you need.

All the Adobe applications use a format of metadata called XMP (Extensible Metadata Platform). Built on a foundation of XML, metadata makes exchanging information about your clips between applications a lot easier.

Mostly.

Sadly, Final Cut Pro does not read XMP metadata natively, but Final Cut Server does – provided it is contained in still-image data. At this point, Final Cut Server does not read XMP data from either sidecar or media files.

Whether you enter metadata prior to production, during production, or after production, the process is still the same: select the clip you want to work with, click in the metadata field to select it, and type away.

Metadata Is Not Always Stored in the Media File

Graphics images, especially those using fairly recent formats like PNG, are designed to hold metadata in the graphics file itself. That is not necessarily true with video.

Metadata sidecars have the same name as the media file, but use .xmp as the file extension (see Fig. 3.12). For OnLocation and Bridge and other Adobe programs to find files, it is essential to store the XMP file in the same location as the media files.

Making this even more confusing, as of this writing, Final Cut Studio does not read XMP files. This means that you can't access all this metadata when working in Final Cut Pro. The way I work around this is to use Bridge to search for clips, drag the clips into Final Cut Pro (FCP) for editing, and then do any metadata cleanup back in Bridge. This is a bit cumbersome, but much better than not being able to find the clip you are looking for when you really need it.

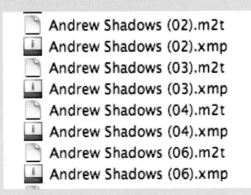

Figure 3.12 While most graphics files hold metadata in the file, some media files, such as HDV, use sidecars. These are separate files filled with metadata with an .xmp file extension.

Lots of Fields to Choose From

 Because I want this book just chock-full of useful information, I counted the number of metadata fields just in the Dynamic Media category alone. There are 104. Sheesh! There are plenty of places to store information about your clips!

Exporting Shot Metadata

 By default, when you export a clip, the metadata travels with it. However, if that causes problems with your version of Final Cut, you can turn off metadata export in the **OnLocation > Preferences > Recording** tab.

Figure 3.13 The Metadata Display window allows you to limit the amount of metadata displayed in the Metadata tab.

Changing metadata is just like changing data in a database. Select the field and start typing.

Deleting data is just as easy: select the data you want to remove and press the **Delete** key.

Looking at the Metadata panel, the three categories that will probably be the most useful to video editors are

- Dublin Core
- Basic
- Dynamic Media

Just as you would in Bridge, twirl down a category to see individual line items. Double-click a line item to enter data. When you are done, tab to another field.

You can select which metadata categories are displayed in the Metadata tab by clicking the Options menu in the fly-out menu in the top-right corner of the Metadata tab and selecting **Metadata Display**. Uncheck the categories, or even the specific metadata, you don't want to track (Fig. 3.13).

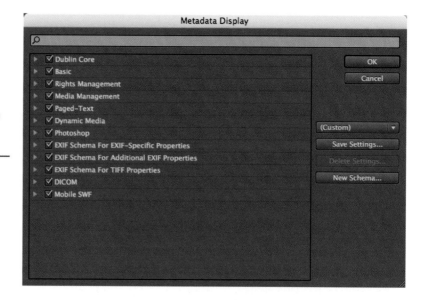

Search: The Reason behind Metadata

I'd be lying if I said entering metadata is fun. Personally, I'd rather watch paint dry. So, there has to be a reason to do this beyond the sheer enjoyment of the process. Actually, metadata makes finding your clips a lot faster and easier.

As we saw in Chapter 2, if you only have 10 clips, finding what you want is easy. If you have 10,000 clips, finding anything is darn near-impossible if you don't have some organized way to track them.

Comments from Adobe

In reviewing this chapter, Adobe wrote: "OnLocation is not specifically designed for managing huge projects, we suggest keeping all the shots for a project in one project file, with all media stored in one folder. This makes it easier to review content, check for continuity, and keep track of what you've done."

That's what metadata does.

Deciding how to organize your files, the metadata to be used, and the specifics of implementation will vary by individual and project. However, the key to good editing is good organization, and OnLocation makes getting organized easy.

You probably won't do a lot of searching inside OnLocation. However, all metadata entered in OnLocation can be searched for in OnLocation, Bridge, or other Adobe applications, which means that you already know how to find and organize your files once they are captured to disk.

Whew!

Now that our preproduction work is done, it's time to head into production.

Using OnLocation in Production

There are four basic production tasks that OnLocation can help with:

- Monitoring video and audio feeds from the camera
- Capturing clips directly to the computer's hard disk
- Reviewing clips for content, quality, or continuity
- Adding metadata, including ratings and comments, to our clips

Calibrate Your Camera

As Adobe's manual states: "If focus is crisp, white balance is correct, and exposure and lighting yield maximum dynamic range, you can achieve high quality video even with a modest camera."

One of the tools provided in the box set for Production Premium, and available for download on Adobe's Web site, is the Focus and Exposure chart. This chart, combined with SureShot, Adobe's camera calibration utility, can make a big difference in the quality of your images.

To learn how to calibrate your system using SureShot, refer to pages 15 and 16 in the OnLocation manual.

From Experience

Let me illustrate this point of having accurate monitors with a personal example. As I mentioned, to help me with writing this chapter, I rented a stage and lights, hired actors, brought in both an SDV and HDV camera, and brought my computer with OnLocation to help create illustrations for this chapter.

Because OnLocation only works with FireWire-connected cameras, we were shooting HDV. We decided to record all our scenes to tape, and then record them using OnLocation. Because the camera operator wanted to be sure he was getting good pictures, he had two monitors on each camera: one was the monitor that came standard with the camera and the other was a larger, outboard monitor.

We adjusted our shots, double-checked our composition and exposure, and started shooting.

Everything went great until we hooked up OnLocation. Then, we discovered by looking at OnLocation's scopes that both camera monitors displayed the picture much brighter than it actually was. Shots that we thought would be about one-stop underexposed were actually three to four stops too dark.

We would never have discovered this on-set if we had not used OnLocation. Monitoring using scopes is *critical* unless you like reshooting your footage over and over.

Calibrating Your Monitor

Calibrating a monitor is critical. What calibration means is that the exposure and colors you see on your screen closely match the actual exposure and colors being captured by the camera.

The basic problem is that computer monitors use entirely different settings for color compared with video cameras. Because of this, we cannot trust our computer to make critical color decisions.

Complicating matters further, the LCD monitors on most low-end cameras are notorious for their inability to accurately display the video being captured. This puts the camera operators in a very difficult position where they cannot trust what they see at the precise moment of production.

However, the scopes in OnLocation have limitations. The waveform monitor defaults to the RGB scale of 0–255 rather than the video scale of 0–235. Also, the manual gives incorrect settings for black level. All black levels in all digital formats – SD and HD – should be set to 0, not the 16 (or 7.5 IRE) recommended by the manual. (I'll show you how to do this on page 56.)

It is beyond the scope of this chapter to show you how to properly calibrate a monitor. However, chapter 4 in the OnLocation user manual does an excellent job showing how to calibrate a monitor, and chapter 5 does an excellent job showing how to use the grids in OnLocation as an aid in framing and image composition.

Note: Make Sure OnLocation Can See Your Camera

Not all FireWire video cameras are supported by OnLocation. If you connect a camera that it doesn't support, you'll see an error message (see Fig. 3.14). This can often be caused by incorrect camera settings. Try changing your frame rate, your image size, or scanning (progressive vs. interlaced) to see whether that allows for a connection.

The number one rule is: "Test your gear before starting production."

Monitoring Your Video

For me, one of the really powerful features of OnLocation is its ability to monitor audio and video in real time on set.

No video Input found. Connect a camera to your computer, or check your current camera's connection and power.

Figure 3.14 This error message is displayed immediately below the video image when OnLocation can't connect to your camera.

Now that the monitor has been properly calibrated, all that's left is to connect the camera to the computer via FireWire then power everything up. Remember, as with all FireWire devices, turn on your camera or deck first, hard disks second, computer third, and then start OnLocation. This order makes sure your software can find all your peripherals.

Time to switch workspaces from Preproduction to Production. The Production workspace adds the following monitors and scopes:

- Video monitor, called the Field Monitor
- Audio monitor
- Waveform video scope
- Vectorscope
- RGB Parade monitor (in OnLocation, this is a mode of the Waveform monitor rather than a separate scope as in Final Cut Pro)
- Histogram
- Scrub bar, with audio waveforms (Adobe prefers not to call it a Timeline)

As you watch your camera in OnLocation, you'll notice a delay, called *latency*, between seeing the movement of your talent on set and seeing the same movement on your computer screen. This latency can vary between a quarter second and a full second and is due to all the video processing that's going on behind the scenes. Don't panic. Your audio and video are being recorded in sync properly. Also, you should always operate your camera looking at the camera monitor, not at the computer monitor.

To the right of the Field Monitor are the audio meters (see Fig. 3.16). Most FireWire cameras, whether DV or HDV, only support two audio channels. (Though both formats can support up to two linear and two multiplexed audio channels.) Audio channels are monitored with the audio meters. Although it would be nice if the actual dB settings were indicated on the meters (Soundtrack Pro had the same problem when it was first released), the key benefit to using the meters are the two small yellow or red lights at the top of the meters.

Adobe flags two types of audio: pops and distortion. An audio pop is a sudden increase in audio level (12 dB or more) compared to existing audio levels, but not enough to distort. Audio pops cause these lights at the top to glow yellow. You can even see yellow flags in the Scrub bar, indicating pops while recording.

Much more important than pops is distortion. If your audio volume is too loud, it will distort, destroying your audio.

Note: Seeing All the Scopes

By default, both the RGB Parade and Histogram scopes are hidden. I will explain where to find them in a few pages.

Note: If You Don't See Your Camera in the Video Monitor

Most of the time, your camera will automatically appear in the video monitor. If it doesn't, you can either turn your camera off, wait 30 seconds, then turn it back on again; or click the View Camera button in the lower left side of the Video monitor window to reestablish the connection (Fig. 3.15). Also, you may need to click this button when you switch between watching recorded clips and live video.

Figure 3.15 The View Camera button tells OnLocation to reconnect to the camera to make sure your connection is good, then display the image.

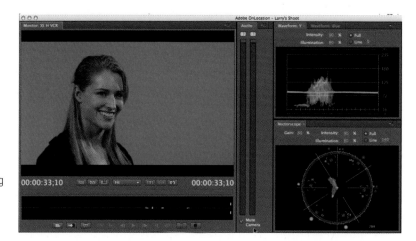

Figure 3.16 Here, we are looking at Lisa, live, directly from the camera. Notice the audio meters and video scopes on the right.

Distortion causes these small lights at the top of the audio meters to glow red. It is critical that you keep your audio levels low enough that these two red lights never glow red. Once audio is recorded with distortion, there is no technology on the planet that can fix it. Your only option is to re-record. This is a big deal, and you need to pay attention. These audio meters will help.

To the right of the audio meters are the video scopes. By default, OnLocation displays the Waveform monitor and Vectorscope. An RGB Parade display and histogram are also available, as I illustrate next.

To get the OnLocation Waveform scope to match the display of Final Cut's scopes, click the small Options icon in the top-right corner of the Scopes panel and select **IRE: Y (0 setup)** (see Fig. 3.17). In this same menu, you can switch the Waveform monitor to an RGB Parade scope by selecting **RGB: Parade**.

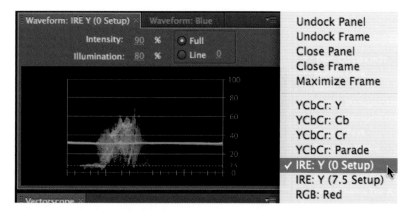

Figure 3.17 Use this menu to switch between scopes. To match the scope markings with Final Cut, select IRE: Y (0 setup).

Entire books discuss how to interpret scopes. So, here are just some highlights to keep you out of trouble. Remember, you are only monitoring your color and exposure here. If you see errors, you need to re-adjust the camera. You don't apply any color-correction settings in OnLocation.

- Black levels for digital video should be at or near 0%.
- White levels for video destined for DVD or broadcast should not exceed 100%; they can go higher for video that will only appear on the Web.
- Caucasian skin should be between 45 and 65% on the waveform monitor.
- Asian and Hispanic skin should be between 35 and 50%.
- Black skin should be between 15 and 35%.
- All skin color, regardless of race, should fall somewhere along the flesh tone line in the Vectorscope, illustrated by the pointing cursor in Fig. 3.18.

Figure 3.18 The Vectorscope measures colors. Skin color, regardless of race, should fall along the flesh tone line, illustrated by the cursor location, assuming no unusual lighting conditions.

While there are exceptions to all these rules, following them will keep you out of trouble most of the time.

Staying Alert

OnLocation will alert you if your audio levels are too loud or if your video levels exceed an amount that you specify. Alerts are displayed in the Scrub Bar just below the Field Monitor.

You set the alert amounts for audio peaks and video levels you want to stay within using **OnLocation > Preferences > Quality Monitoring** (Fig. 3.19). Although you can change them, the default settings are OK.

Tip: Navigating to Alerts

You can jump to the next, or previous, alert in the Waveform area by either clicking the Next/ Previous Alert button or pressing **Command + Left arrow** to jump to the previous alert, or **Command + Right arrow** to go to the next one.

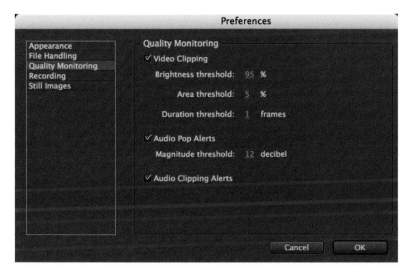

Figure 3.19 You set the levels at which you want audio or video alerts to occur in the Preferences > Quality Monitoring tab.

Then, if video levels exceed these levels, a white bar will be displayed in the waveform area below the Field Monitor at the location of the alert.

Figure 3.20 An audio pop alert is created when there is a sudden jump in audio level, but not enough to cause distortion.

If your audio has a sudden surge in volume, but not enough to distort, a yellow tick mark will be displayed in the waveform area (see Fig. 3.20). If the audio is so loud that it distorts, red tick marks will be displayed in the waveform.

The nice thing about alerts is that they can instantly warn you where problems occur so that you can decide whether you need to reshoot a scene while you are still on set with everything you need in place.

Capturing Video

Once you check your picture and sound to make sure everything is framed properly and looking great, it's time to capture your media. OnLocation makes that one-button easy.

In the Shot List, select the shot you want to capture by clicking it. Then, click the red **Record** button in the lower right of Field Monitor (Fig. 3.21). OnLocation immediately begins recording your scene to disk.

When you are done recording, press the blue **Stop** button (next to the Record button).

If you need to record multiple takes of the same shot, simply start recording again without selecting any other shot in the Shot List. OnLocation will automatically create a new take, with the same shot name in the Shot List and append a take number (see Fig. 3.22).

To record the next shot, select it in the Shot List and press **Record**.

To add a shot that is not in your Shot List, create a new shot placeholder, select it, and click **Record**.

Figure 3.22 Here is an example of a shot with three takes. The take number is at the end of the shot name. Shot names are also used as file names when stored to disk.

Clip Name	Sequence
Andrew Shadows (03).m2t	22
Andrew Shadows (02).m2t	22
Andrew Shadows.m2t	22

Figure 3.21 Recording is easy. Select the clip you want to capture and click the Record button.

Record

Where Does OnLocation Store Your Video Files?

OnLocation stores captured video files in a Clips folder at the same location as you stored the project folder. This is why I recommend creating a project folder to store all these files and folders. Be sure to store all your files to a drive other than your boot drive.

A Note on Timecode

When recording to a QuickTime format, OnLocation handles timecode differently, depending upon what is controlling the recording. When you control recording from a camera, the timecode on tape matches the timecode in the Adobe OnLocation clip. When you control recording from Adobe OnLocation, the timecode depends on whether tape was rolling in the camera. If the tape was rolling or the camera was generating free-run timecode, the clip adopts the timecode from the camera. If not, the timecode starts at 0:00:00. When recording HDV using M2T files, timecode passes from the camera to the computer.

Figure 3.23 To create a freeze frame, what Adobe calls a still image, click the Still Image Grabber button below the Field Monitor.

Where Does OnLocation Store Your Freeze Frames?

OnLocation stores freeze frames (what Adobe calls still images in a Grabbed Stills folder at the same location as you stored the project folder. This is another reason why I recommend creating a project folder to store all these files and folders.

To create a still image click the **Still Image Grabber** button in the toolbar below the Field Monitor (Fig. 3.23).

Figure 3.24 Click the fly-out menu in the top-right corner of the Preview window to access HDV export settings.

Figure 3.25 If you use a fast, Intel-based Mac, change Resolution to Full and Frames displayed to All for highest HDV playback quality.

By Default, HDV Stills Are Not Output at Full Quality

By default, to save CPU cycles, OnLocation defaults MPEG decompression (used for HDV) to half resolution. It captures the image properly but does not display the image at full resolution. It does not store screen grabs at the correct resolution. If you need the highest quality screen grabs, go to the Options pop-up menu in the top-right corner of the Field Monitor (see Fig. 3.23) and change the resolution to **Full**. For smoothest playback, change the Frames displayed to **All**. If your computer has problems with playback of HDV, change these settings back to **Half** and **I+P** (see Figs. 3.24 and 3.25).

Also, still images can be stored as JPEG, PNG-24, or BMP images. The default setting is JPEG, which does not have the quality of PNG. To change the format, go to **OnLocation > Preferences > Still Images** and set the Image Format to PNG-24.

Grabbing Still Images

One of the more helpful functions of OnLocation is that you can quickly grab a freeze frame from a live camera or recorded shot (see Fig. 3.23).

Reviewing Clips

Adding Comments to Shots

Another cool feature of OnLocation is the ability to add comments linked to specific timecode in a shot. These special markers allow you to annotate your clips either during production or later, as you review your work. You can add comments during recording or playback.

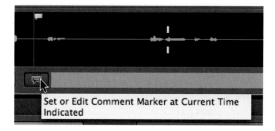

Figure 3.26 To add a comment to a clip, put the playhead where you want the comment marker to appear and press the Set Comment button.

To add a comment to a clip, double-click the clip to load it into the Field Monitor and move the playhead to the position you want to add the comment.

Press the **Set or Edit Comment** button (see Fig. 3.26).

This sets a comment marker in the timeline into which you can enter a comment. When you are done typing, press **Enter** to save your text.

To jump between markers, use the **Go to Previous Marker** or **Go to Next Marker** buttons (see Fig. 3.27a and b); there are no keyboard shortcuts to jump between markers.

Figure 3.27 To jump between markers, use the Go to Previous Marker or Go to Next Marker buttons.

Strengths and Weaknesses of OnLocation

I'm of two minds about OnLocation.

I really like its ability to plan and organize my shots prior to production. The ability to think about and organize what I want before the pressure of production begins is a big plus.

I also like its ability to directly monitor a camera during production. As I mentioned earlier, checking my camera against a scope allowed me to see that both camera monitors were wrong and that I needed to make serious exposure adjustments. This kept me from losing a day's worth of shooting.

Those two features alone make OnLocation worth having in my arsenal.

Its ability to add metadata to individual clips, capture directly to my computer's hard disk, and a highly customizable interface all add up to a very attractive package.

On the downside, however, is that it only supports cameras attached by FireWire. Since all cameras use a FireWire 400 connection, this limits my camera to a 15-foot cable between camera and computer, severely restricting its mobility, unless I invest in FireWire repeaters, which can extend the distance of the camera from the computer to hundreds of feet.

Since OnLocation only supports FireWire-connected cameras, as we move to tapeless acquisition, especially for HD formats, this reliance on FireWire becomes a significant limitation.

Finally, I wish that it had a built-in ability to convert native .m2t HDV files into a much more useful .mov file.

Also, and this isn't Adobe's responsibility, Final Cut needs to access all XMP metadata. Adobe is way ahead of Final Cut in how it manipulates metadata. At this point, Final Cut stores metadata solely in the project file, while Adobe makes it available between applications and platforms. And, the latest release of Final Cut Studio hasn't addressed this problem.

Special Notes on Working with HDV and DVCPROHD

As we move into the world of HD, OnLocation is there to help. But there are special considerations to keep in mind.

First, both HDV and DVCPROHD are video formats that can record to tapeless media, such as hard disks and P2 cards, yet OnLocation can only capture files that come in via FireWire.

When you capture DVCPROHD, you need a hard disk capable of recording 15 MB/s. Most 7200 RPM FireWire 400 hard drives can do this. The USB drives, generally, cannot. Be sure, also, that you always save HD media to a second drive. The boot drive won't be fast enough to reliably capture your media.

Also, OnLocation does not support 24pN or 30pN frame rates from Panasonic P2 cameras, because those frame rates are not transferred from the camera using FireWire. OnLocation only supports FireWire transfer.

Adobe's manual for OnLocation recommends always dedicating a hard drive specifically for media, defragmenting regularly, and starting each project with an empty hard drive. While I agree with dedicating a hard drive for media, defragmenting does less good than it used to, and always emptying your drive before a project is rarely possible when you are editing multiple projects at the same time.

Instead of defragmenting, make a point of regularly running Disk Utility (**Utilities > Disk Utility**) and verifying your hard drives. In addition, once a month, run Alsoft's Disk Warrior X to optimize your hard drive directories, which will go a long way to keeping your system running with peak efficiency.

Second, OnLocation captures media in the native format of the camera. This means that HDV is captured using the MPEG-2 Transport stream format. (It has an extension of .m2t.) This is not a format that Final Cut Pro can read directly, which means that you can't simply import HDV files from OnLocation into Final Cut Pro. You need to convert them first.

There are a number of ways of converting .m2t files into the .mov files that Final Cut needs. Probably the best is MPEG Streamclip from Squared 5 Software (www.squared5.com). This free utility converts a wide variety of video formats.

If small file size is most important, transcode (convert) your files into an HDV format that matches the image size, frame rate, and scanning of the original material.

If compositing quality, faster rendering, and faster output are important to you, transcode them into ProRes 422 (normal quality).

Once the files are converted into QuickTime movies, import them into Final Cut Pro and you are ready to go.

Keyboard Shortcuts

Here are some handy keyboard shortcuts for OnLocation.

Shortcut	What it does
F2	Start recording
Esc	Stop recording
Home	Jump to beginning of clip
End	Jump to end of clip
Command + Left arrow	Jump to previous alert
Command + Right arrow	Jump to next alert
Up arrow	Jump to previous clip
Down arrow	Jump to next clip
Command + 5	Grab still image

4

SPEECH-TO-TEXT TRANSCRIPTS IN CS4

Like Soundtrack Pro in Final Cut Studio, Soundbooth is a powerful audio program. The latest version of Soundbooth allows you to listen to audio, edit audio, repair poor audio, create musical scores, and perform multitrack mixes.

However, where it stands apart from Soundtrack Pro is in its ability to import your video or audio and generate a transcript of a clip's dialog track, search on that text to jump to a specific place in your media, and increase your ability to add more metadata to your clips. This is one of the most fascinating new features in the Adobe CS4 software suite.

Although not 100% accurate, the generated transcripts can significantly help you organize how you plan to edit your material (especially when editing a documentary), speed up finding a specific statement in your clips, or help you review what you've already shot.

For me, as a video editor, the two biggest benefits in upgrading to CS4 are its extensive support for metadata and its ability to create text transcripts from our media files.

There are, of course, several other features in Soundbooth besides the Speech-to-Text Transcribing that make it worth considering for your audio projects. I'll talk more about them toward the end of this chapter.

Selecting an Audio Format

Soundbooth supports a range of QuickTime video formats, as well as a variety of audio formats – AIF, WAV, MP3, AAC, AC3, SDII – which one should you use?

Final Cut Pro only works with uncompressed audio files: AIF, WAV, and SDII. (By the way, AIFF and AIF are the same format using two different filename extensions.)

Windows applications tend to prefer WAV files, while Macintosh apps prefer AIFs. There is no difference in audio quality between WAV and AIF files. The only difference is the information at the beginning of the file, called the file header, which describes the format the audio is stored in. The actual audio information is the same in both.

To keep things simple and reliable, you should work with sample rates of 44.1 or 48 kHz and always use AIF files. These work perfectly for both Final Cut Studio and Soundbooth. The AIF files support both mono and stereo files with no problems.

Creating a Text Transcript

A text transcript is a word-for-word conversion of what a speaker says in an audio or video clip into text that can be entered into a word processor or viewed on screen. Transcripts can be made from audio-only files or video and audio files.

The Old Way

Before we look at how Soundbooth creates transcripts, let's look at how the process normally works. Let's say you need a word-for-word transcript where each paragraph is referenced to the timecode of the clip.

- You create a videotape, DVD, or QuickTime file of your video with burned-in timecode. This generally requires that you add the burned-in timecode in either Final Cut Pro – which requires rendering – or Compressor – which requires extra compression time.

Important Note on File Extensions

Because all the applications in Adobe Production Premium work on both Mac and Windows systems, Adobe expects all files to have a file extension. If a file, such as an AIF recorded using Final Cut Pro's voice-over tool, doesn't have an extension, it won't open in Soundbooth. It should, but it doesn't. So, if a file won't open or preview, be sure it has the appropriate file extension.

Sample Rate and Audio Fidelity

The sample rate determines the audio fidelity of a media clip. Sample rates are defined by the number of readings, or samples, of audio that are captured each second by the computer. The higher the sample rate, up to the limit of human hearing, the closer the digital file comes to exactly reproducing the original sound of the file.

For instance, this table, from the Adobe Soundbooth manual, lists sample rates and their approximate analog equivalents.

Samples per second	Also called	Quality level
11,025	11.025 kHz	Poor AM radio
22,050	22.05 kHz	Near FM radio
32,000	32 kHz	Better than FM radio
44,100	44.1 kHz	CD audio
48,000	48 kHz	Standard DVD and videotape

The higher the sample rate, the greater the quality, but the larger the file size. Also, stereo files are double the size of mono files.

- You send this videotape, DVD, or QuickTime file to a person or company that specializes in transcription.
- The tape is received and handed off to a transcriber who listens to your clip over and over while typing what they hear into a word processor.
- In some cases, the software the transcriber uses reads the timecode of the videotape or DVD and inserts it, automatically, at the start of each paragraph. Otherwise, the transcriber will insert the timecode manually at the start of each paragraph.
- This word processing file is then proofed for accuracy by someone else and formatted according to company specs. The start of each document includes the name of the speaker and an identifier, indicating the source of the file. Each paragraph starts with a timecode reference, so you can easily find a quote in the source media.
- The final, proofed, file is e-mailed back to you.
- You review the word processing file and use it to find the specific quotes you want to use in your project. As you can see, this process has many built-in delays.

For example, a few years ago, I ran a company that was sending hundreds of hours of audio files out for transcription each month. It took a team of 20 editors and transcribers to keep up with the workload, and turn-around time was 1 week to 10 days; longer if the material was technical.

Even the best manual transcripts still need to be cleaned up to get them as accurate as possible. In the case of my company, we needed our transcripts to be as perfect as possible because we sold the finished transcripts. I had a team of eight editors reviewing each transcript before release. The whole process took about three weeks to complete a transcript.

The New Way

However, for most editing purposes, you just need the transcript to be "close enough" that you can find the material you need. You don't need it to be perfect. In these situations, Soundbooth can literally save you weeks of time.

When Soundbooth creates a transcript, the whole process gets a lot easier and much faster. Here's a quick summary of the workflow:

- Open your audio or video clip in Soundbooth.
- Adjust two dialog box settings and click **OK**.
- Depending upon the speed of your processor and the length of the clip, Soundbooth cranks out a transcript in minutes. No longer do we need to wait days.
- When the transcript is complete, every word is referenced to timecode so that jumping to a particular spot in the text is as easy as clicking the word in the transcript where you want to jump in the waveform.

These transcripts are not perfect. If I wanted the same level of accuracy as the transcripts I created with my old company, I'd still need to take each transcript through an editorial and proofreading process. But, most of the time, I just need something to help me find what I've got to work with. Soundbooth is ideal for that.

Learning the Soundbooth Interface

As we learned when looking at Adobe Bridge, all the CS4 applications have a similar look and feel. Built around the CS4 concept of Workspaces, Soundbooth is no different. (For a complete discussion of the CS4 Workspace interface, please refer to Chapter 2.)

Figure 4.1 This is the default workspace that opens when you first load a clip into Soundbooth. The list of available clips is in the top left, task and effects windows are on the left, and waveforms display on the right.

Workspaces in Soundbooth

The Default workspace (see Fig. 4.1) in Soundbooth has a list of clips in the top-left corner. Similar to the Browser in Final Cut Pro, you import (**Command + I**) the clips you want to work on.

Below it are a series of panels containing Tasks, Effects, Markers, and Properties. Each panel contains specific things you can do with each clip. On the right side is the waveform of the clip itself, with a global view on the top and detail view on the bottom.

Since we are concentrating on the creation of text transcripts, let's change workspaces to something a bit more useful for this process.

There are five prebuilt workspaces (see Fig. 4.2) in Soundbooth. The one that is designed for transcripts is Meta Logging (see Fig. 4.3).

Figure 4.2 The pop-up menu at the top of the window allows you to switch between workspaces, or to create and save your own customized workspace.

Figure 4.3 The Meta Logging workspace. Notice the new tab in the lower left titled: Speech Transcript.

Getting a File from Final Cut Pro to Soundbooth

Soundbooth prefers editing audio files in one of three formats: ASND, WAV, AIF. Use ASND if you are working exclusively in Adobe applications. Use AIF for files transferred from Final Cut. The WAV files are most common on the PC.

To export a clip or sequence from Final Cut for use in Soundbooth, use **File > Export > Audio to AIFF(s)**.

There are three ways to get your audio file into Soundbooth for transcription:

1. Import it using **File > Import > Files** (or press **Command – I**).
2. Drag it from your hard disk into the Files tab of the Soundbooth workspace.
3. Open it directly from Final Cut Pro into Soundbooth.

The first two options are fairly obvious, but this last choice is both faster and easier. Here's how to configure Final Cut Pro to support Soundbooth.

First, let's assume that the clips we want to send to Soundbooth contain both video and audio. (You can also do this with audio-only clips, too, which I'll illustrate shortly.)

Open Final Cut Pro.

Choose **Final Cut Pro > System Settings > External Editors** (Fig. 4.4).

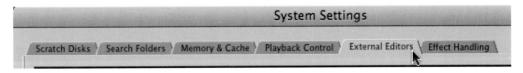

Figure 4.4 System Settings > External Editors determines what application opens a file when you select Open in Editor.

Opening Audio Files from Final Cut Into Soundbooth

As you probably guessed, changing the setting for Audio Files in the External Editor preference tab allows you to open audio files into Soundbooth as well. The procedure is the same, just adjust the Set button for Audio Files.

By default, Final Cut opens video files in QuickTime Player. To get Final Cut Pro to automatically open video files into Soundbooth, click the **Set** button for Video Files, navigate to the Adobe Soundbooth application (Fig. 4.5), select it, and click **Choose**. Your External Editors tab should now list Soundbooth next to your Video Files as shown in Fig. 4.6. (Audio linked to video travels wherever the video file goes.)

Figure 4.5 Click the Set button for video files, and then select Soundbooth from the Applications folder. This allows you to quickly open any video file directly into Soundbooth.

Figure 4.6 This tab is currently configured so that when you use Open in Editor, video files with linked audio will go to Soundbooth while stand-alone audio files will go to Soundtrack Pro. If you plan on only transcribing video interviews, this is the way your preferences should be set.

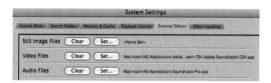

Now, to open a file from Final Cut Pro into Soundbooth, **Control-click** the file in either the Timeline or the Browser and select **Open in Editor** from the pop-up menu. As long as the video file is a format that Soundbooth supports, the file will be opened directly in Soundbooth ready for transcribing.

One downside of this approach is that, similar to Soundtrack Pro, the entire clip is opened in Soundbooth. This means that you need to manually set the In and Out points in Soundbooth to determine the range of audio you want to transcribe.

Creating Transcripts

OK. Time to get to work.

I've loaded a clip into Soundbooth. Just as in Final Cut Pro, you play, or stop, a clip using the Spacebar. The small waveform above the big waveform is called the Global View (see Fig. 4.7). It always shows your entire clip, while the larger Detail waveform allows you to zoom in and out and move around inside the clip.

My Voice-Over Script

Here's the script I used in creating this voice-over file:

Hi. This is Larry Jordan.

The new Speech-to-Text transcription inside Soundbooth CS4 can provide documentary filmmakers with a very fast, very easy way to get quick transcripts of their interviews and to locate those exact words in their media files.

Figure 4.7 With a clip loaded into Soundbooth, it's time to create a transcript.

This is a 20-second voice-over that I recorded specifically to showcase the strengths and weaknesses of Speech-to-Text transcription.

Let's resize the Speech Transcript tab by dragging the horizontal bar a bit higher (Fig. 4.8).

Once a clip is loaded, click the **Transcribe** button at the bottom of the Speech Transcript tab (Fig. 4.9).

The Speech Transcription Options window opens (Fig. 4.10). This allows us to preset the language and dialect of the clip, and determines the quality of the resulting transcript, the number of speakers, and so on.

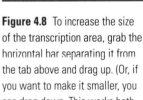

Figure 4.8 To increase the size of the transcription area, grab the horizontal bar separating it from the tab above and drag up. (Or, if you want to make it smaller, you can drag down. This works both ways.)

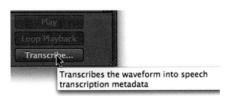

Figure 4.9 Creating a transcript starts with loading a clip and then pressing the Transcribe button.

Figure 4.10 The Transcript window allows you to properly set up your clip by telling Soundbooth the language, quality, and speakers the clip contains.

One thing I find cool is that Soundbooth distinguishes between dialects – such as British, American, and Canadian English, which you can select from the Language drop-down menu (Fig. 4.11). (I guess it's too much to hope that it would support central Wisconsinese, where I grew up...)

Next, select the Quality you want (Fig. 4.12). There is an inverse relationship between transcript quality and the time it takes to create one.

Figure 4.12 Quality and speed are linked. High quality tends to take about twice as long as Medium quality.

Figure 4.11 Soundbooth currently supports seven languages and five dialects.

Figure 4.13 A standard thermometer is displayed showing how much time is left.

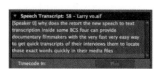

Figure 4.14 Here are the results of a high-quality transcription of the voice clip. Although not perfect, it got most of the words right.

I just did a couple of quick tests. On my MacBook Pro Core 2 Duo, a medium-quality transcript took one to two times longer than the length of the clip. A high-quality transcript took twice as long as the medium quality setting. The transcript results were about the same. Your results will vary, test to see which one works best for you. If you are in a hurry, start with medium quality as it can save you time.

Next, although Soundbooth doesn't know Fred from Ethyl, it can recognize when a speaker's voice changes in a clip and flags that point by starting a new paragraph with a speaker number at the start. While it won't hurt to leave this feature on all the time, if you only have one speaker, it isn't necessary.

Once we've made all our selections, click **OK**.

Soundbooth starts the transcription process and displays a thermometer indicating how much time is left (Fig. 4.13). In this case, I selected the Quality option as **High**.

When the transcript is done, the results are displayed in the Speech Transcript window (Fig. 4.14). If you compare the original script in the sidebar on page 71, with the results displayed here, you'll see that not every word is perfect – but most of them are.

In fact, Soundbooth displays a confidence level for each word that you can view when you select the word in the generated transcript (see Figs. 4.15 a–c). This provides a sense of whether Soundbooth thinks this is the correct word.

Generally, the higher the confidence level, the more likely Soundbooth feels the word is accurate. (Confidence levels are not displayed if you select a portion of the Timeline, only when you select the text.)

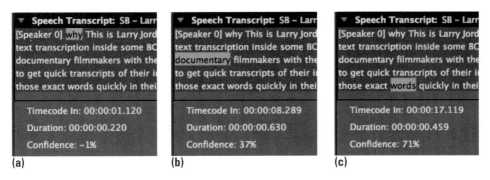

Figure 4.15 Here are three examples of confidence levels for the words (a) "why," (b) "documentary," and (c) "words. They range from −1 to 71%.

Limitations of Automatic Transcripts

The first big limitation is that Soundbooth has a lot of trouble with proper names, nouns, and acronyms. For instance, it did not get my name right, nor the words Soundbooth or CS4. Adobe tells me they are working to improve this.

Second, it doesn't know how to punctuate. It has no sense of commas or periods; when a sentence starts or stops is not indicated. While you need to do a clean-up pass on your audio, this lack of punctuation does not cause a problem if you are using the text as a very, very fast way to search for something in your media.

Third, it has problems with words that sound very similar: for instance, "Hi" and "Why" or "then" and "them."

Fourth, the quality of the recording has a direct impact on the quality of the transcript. High background noise or situations where more than one person is talking at the same time is very, very difficult to transcribe.

Since these automatic transcripts are not perfect, some have suggested that we just throw up our hands and never use the feature.

My feeling is that this is being hasty. Many times, we don't need perfection. We just need the transcript to be close and really, really timely. It's hard to complain about almost real-time automatic transcripts that don't cost any additional money.

Using the Transcript to Search

The power of using a transcript created by Soundbooth is that it makes searching for a specific word blindingly fast. Watch…

Unlike a printed transcript, where only the start of a paragraph gets a timecode reference, in Soundbooth, *every* word has a timecode reference. This means we can find any word instantly.

Transcript Time Is Processor Speed – Dependent

The time it takes to create a transcript depends upon three things: the length of the clip, the quality of the recording, and the speed of your processor. Although multiple processors will help, especially using OS X 10.6, the flat-out speed of your processors will make the most difference.

Let's say we want to find the word "documentary" in the audio waveform. In the Speech Transcripts tab, click the word "documentary." Instantly, that part of the waveform is highlighted! (In Fig. 4.16, I zoomed into the waveform to make the highlighted area easier to see. Notice that the waveform for the word "documentary" is highlighted in both the main waveform and the global view above it.)

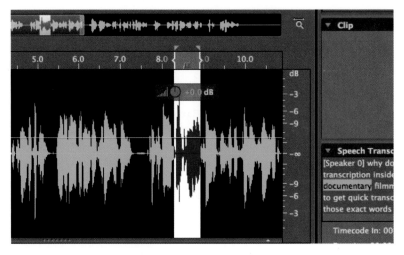

Figure 4.16 Searching is really fast. In the transcript, simply click the word you want to find and it is instantly highlighted in the waveform.

Moving Quickly between Words

 Want a fast way to move between words in a transcript? Press the **Tab** key. It jumps you to the right, from one word to the next. **Shift** + **Tab** moves you in the opposite direction. And, as each word is selected, that portion of the waveform highlights as well.

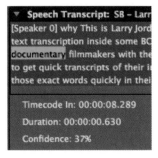

Figure 4.17 The lower portion of the Speech Transcript window displays the exact location of the selected word in the text, the timecode for the location in the audio file, the duration, and the confidence level.

You can also search transcripts in Soundbooth using **Edit > Find**. Once the word you entered is highlighted in the transcript text as in Fig. 4.17, click it to select it, and the playhead (which Adobe calls the Current Time Indicator, or CTI) will jump to that word in the waveform display.

Also, look at the bottom of the Speech Transcript tab. Three statistics are displayed: the exact location of the selected word in the waveform, duration, and confidence level.

Note, also, that the timecode is not displayed in frames, but in thousandths of a second. This means that Soundbooth will not be distracted by

Figure 4.18 Control-clicking the timecode numbers reveals a pop-up menu where you can select the frame rate the Soundbooth should use for timing your clip.

the frame rate you use to shoot your video, since Soundbooth references to portions of a second rather than frames. This is a good thing; otherwise, we would constantly need to make timing adjustments as frame rates change.

However, if you want to change the time display, right-click it and select the frame rate you want to display for your video (see Fig. 4.18).

Modifying Transcript Text

There are inaccuracies in the automatic transcript that Soundbooth created. It would be nice to fix them. We can and here's how.

Let's say we want to change a single word. In this case, the first word in the audio clip isn't "why," its "Hi!"

To change a single word, double-click the word to highlight it, then type your changes. In this case, I changed "why" to "Hi!" (Fig. 4.19)

Next, the phrase "does the retort" should be "This is Larry Jordan." (This is an example of the name recognition problem I mentioned earlier.) We can change "does" to "this" by double-clicking the word to select it and entering new text. But how do we change the words "the retort" into "is Larry Jordan"?

When you Control-click a word, you have the option to insert, delete, or merge words. The benefit to using this menu (Fig. 4.20) as opposed to directly text-editing the document is that you are able to retain the pointers that connect the word in the transcript to its place in the waveform. In this case, I'll replace "retort" with "is Larry Jordan."

We can use this technique to go through and clean up the transcript, add missing punctuation, or delete "ums" or "ahhs" that don't need to be a part of the transcript.

A Sad Note on Timecode

Audio files generally don't have timecode. But video files do. Unfortunately, Soundbooth doesn't recognize the timecode in a video clip and sets the timecode at the start of a clip to 0:00:00:00. (Unfortunately, there is no way to reset the starting timecode.) This makes referencing between the transcript and the clip more difficult. This needs to be fixed in an update to Soundbooth.

The easiest work-around for this is to change Final Cut Pro to display the alternate timecode track, which defaults to 0:00:00:00, in the Viewer while you edit.

Figure 4.19 To change a single word, double-click the word to highlight it, then make your changes.

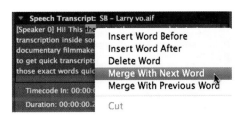

Figure 4.20 Control-click a word to merge it with the next, or previous, word.

Speaker IDs Can't Be Changed

Unlike text in the transcript, we can't change the labels that Soundbooth assigns to the different speakers.

Figure 4.21 Control-click inside the transcript and select Copy All. This allows you to paste the transcript into the word processor of your choice.

Exporting a Transcript

The bad news is that Soundbooth doesn't allow printing transcripts. The good news is that there are some simple work-arounds.

Let's assume that we want a hard copy of the transcript, so we can review it. Well, printing text is precisely what a word processor is designed to do, and the process of doing so with one of them is very easy. So we can print our transcript from a word processor.

Control-click anywhere inside the text transcript and select Copy All (see Fig. 4.21). Then, open the word processor of your choice – I decided to use Text Edit – and paste the transcript into a new document.

Voila! Instant transcript, ready to correct and print (Fig. 4.22).

However, the astute among you will notice that copying the transcript removes all the time references. Also, we've lost all the duration and confidence information that was with the transcript inside Soundbooth.

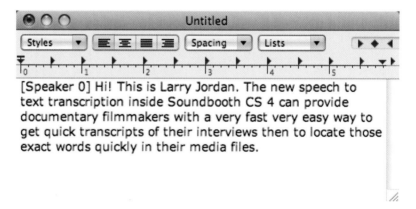

Figure 4.22 Pasting a transcript into a new word processing document allows you to make changes, improve formatting, and print the transcript.

Well, it isn't lost, but it isn't part of the Copy/Paste operation. A more complete way to keep all the information in your transcript is to export it.

Go to **File > Export > Speech Transcription XML**.

In the resulting dialog box, give the file a name and storage location.

Soundbooth automatically converts the transcript into an XML file. The good news is that this XML file contains just about everything that Soundbooth has learned about this file. The bad news is that while it is easy for computers to read XML, it isn't particularly easy for us humans, because XML closely resembles HTML in its structure.

However, as you'll see in the next chapter, this can be a beautiful thing when you can create an FLV movie of your project, post it to the Web, and make the text searchable.

This XML file contains every word in your transcript, along with lots of other neat stuff such as its location, source, and confidence value.

While I won't dwell on this, there are a few things I want to point out. In my screen shot, I've highlighted in blue all the data for the first word: "Hi!" (Fig. 4.23).

The time is expressed as minutes-seconds-thousandths of a second (MM:SS.###). To translate this number, put a period in front of the right-most three digits. So, in this example, the word "Hi!" starts 1.120 seconds in from the start of the clip.

Note, also, that every element is set off by the phrase Parameter. This makes it easy for the computer to find different elements. Soundbooth always exports the following in the XML file:

- The time location of the word from the start of the clip
- The word itself
- The source of the word
- The duration of the word
- The confidence level of the word

```
⬤ ⬤ ⬤  SB – Larry vo.xml
<?xml version="1.0" encoding="UTF-8"
standalone="no" ?> <FLVCoreCuePoints
Version="1">
<CuePoint>
  <Time>1120</Time>
  <Type>event</Type>
  <Name>Hi!</Name>
  <Parameters>
    <Parameter>
      <Name>source</Name>
      <Value>transcription</Value>
    </Parameter>
    <Parameter>
      <Name>duration</Name>
      <Value>220</Value>
    </Parameter>
    <Parameter>
      <Name>confidence</Name>
      <Value>-1</Value>
    </Parameter>
  </Parameters>
</CuePoint>
<CuePoint>
  <Time>1559</Time>
  <Type>event</Type>
  <Name>This</Name>
  <Parameters>
    <Parameter>
      <Name>source</Name>
      <Value>transcription</Value>
```

Figure 4.23 Here is the beginning of the XML export file for our transcript. I've highlighted the results for the first word "Hi!"

So, if you want a fast and easy way to print your transcripts, just Copy/Paste them into a word processor. If you need all the elements of a transcript, export them as an XML file.

By the time this book is published, I hope to see utilities on the market which can take this XML data and turn it into something readable for the rest of us.

Additional Notes on Soundbooth

Final Cut editors are generally comfortable with the idea of capture files and render files; in other words, files that Final Cut creates to do its job. Well, just as Final Cut creates work files, so does Soundbooth. In this section, I want to take a couple of minutes to share some housekeeping tips that will keep your system running smoothly.

Importing Files into After Effects

 If you import a file containing speech transcripts into After Effects, each word appears as a layer marker in the composition.

Configure and Clean the Media Cache

Soundbooth creates cache files for each audio and video file you import. These files increase performance and allow Soundbooth to support a wide variety of sample rates.

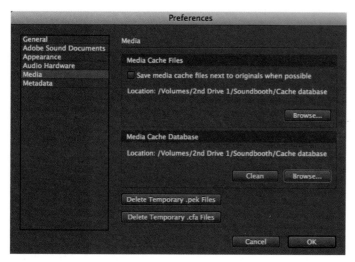

Figure 4.24 For improved performance, move your cache files and database to a second drive and clean them periodically.

You can customize this location – again, I suggest storing it to a second drive – as well as empty it from time to time, which will improve performance.

To do so, go to **Adobe Soundbooth > Preferences > Media** (Fig. 4.24).

By default, media cache files and the media cache database are stored in the user's home directory.

What I did was create a new folder on my second drive, called **Soundbooth**, and inside it I created three new folders: **Cache files, Cache database**, and **Recordings** (see Fig. 4.25).

Then, I repointed the preference settings to these folders.

Figure 4.25 To simplify file management, create a new folder on your second drive, and then put the work folders the Soundbooth needs inside it.

Benefits of Soundbooth over Soundtrack Pro

The ability to create, modify, and export Speech-to-Text transcripts is a huge benefit that Soundbooth provides and that Soundtrack Pro does not. In addition, there are several other features worth mentioning. These include:

- Tight integration with Adobe Bridge
- Ability to create musical Scores
- Its support for extensive XMP metadata

Integration with Adobe Bridge

Only Soundbooth and Premiere are able to create and display text transcripts. Adobe Bridge does not display transcribed text or metadata for a clip, although it does easily allow us to search, preview, rename, and delete audio files stored anywhere on our system.

For a more complete discussion of Bridge, please refer to Chapter 2.

Create Musical Scores

A score is a customized musical soundtrack.

Soundtrack Pro gives us two types of musical cues: loops and completed pieces of music. Soundbooth Scores are something in-between – a completed piece of music that can be customized for length and, to a degree, in instrumentation. Here's how it works.

By default, Soundbooth installs two scores:

- AquoVisit, which is a piece of music.
- CityStreet, which is an ambience sound effect.

You can add more scores by clicking **More Scores at Resource Central** in the top-right corner of the Scores tab (see Fig. 4.26). This displays the Resource Central tab (Fig. 4.27), which allows you to access more scores and other resources from Adobe's Web site.

Although there are lots of different musical styles to choose from, the process of working with a score is the same. In this example, I chose AquoVisit.

First, switch your workspace back to **Default** – either from the **Workspace** pop-up menu at the top of Soundbooth or the **Window > Workspace** menu at the top of your screen.

To listen to a score, select the name of the score, and then click the right-pointing arrow at the bottom of the Scores tab. Click it again to stop playback. Or, double-click the score to play it, double-click again to stop playback.

To modify a Score, select **File > New > MultiTrack File** (or press **Shift + Command + N**). This creates a new MultiTrack project, which is the only place Scores can be adjusted.

Drag the name of the score you want to use from the Scores tab on the left side of the workspace into the large Editor tab on the right side of the window (see Fig. 4.28).

Figure 4.26 Scores are customizable music. You can add more scores by clicking **More Scores** at Resource Central in the top-right corner.

Figure 4.27 Adobe makes lots of scores, and other audio resources, available at Resource Central, which is built into Soundbooth.

Note: The Spacebar Doesn't Play Scores

Pressing the Spacebar won't preview scores. Instead, it only plays clips located in the Timeline.

Figure 4.28 Drag a Score from the list in the Scores tab on the left into the large Editor window on the right.

Change the duration of the music by grabbing the right edge of the clip, indicated where the black of the track turns into green by a red bracket, and dragging to the duration you want (see Fig. 4.29).

Figure 4.29 Change the duration of a Score by dragging the right edge of the music. In this case, I shortened it from 2½ min to 30 seconds.

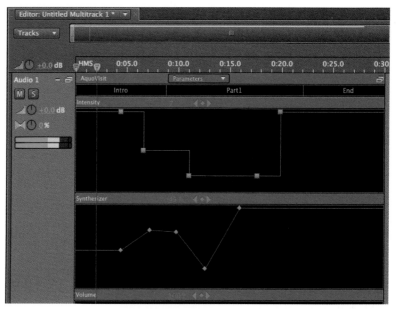

Figure 4.30 You can make specific changes in the Property tab, such as setting a precise duration or whether you want the music to have a beginning or an end.

How to Zoom the Timeline

 Unlike Final Cut, to zoom into the Soundbooth Timeline, press + (plus), to zoom out press – (hyphen). To fit the Timeline into the window, press \ (backslash). To increase the vertical height of a track, click the **Maximize Track** button (Fig. 4.31).

Or, you can make specific changes in the **Property** tab, located in the lower left box of the workspace, such as setting a precise duration or whether you want the music to have a beginning or an end (Fig. 4.30).

Here is where Scores gets interesting. In the Properties tab, click the **Keyframing** button. This allows you to set keyframes

Figure 4.31 To increase the vertical height of a track, click the Maximize Track button.

Figure 4.32 Here is an example of setting keyframes for both Intensity and Synthesizer.

to adjust the Intensity, Synthesizer, and Volume settings. If the Synthesizer parameter is not showing, click the **Parameters** pop-up menu just at the top of the Multitrack window and check the **Synthesizer** option.

To set a keyframe, as in Soundtrack Pro, click the light-green keyframe line in the Editor window. Remember to set at least two keyframes – the first is the starting position, and then drag the second keyframe vertically or horizontally to adjust (see Fig. 4.32).

Drag the playhead (or CTI) to the beginning of the clip (press the **Home** key), and press the Spacebar to play. Listen to the changes and tweak as necessary.

To export your musical masterpiece as an AIF file, select **File > Export > Multitrack Mixdown**. Give your file a name and storage location and click Save. By default, it creates a stereo AIF file, which you can use anywhere.

Cool.

Support for XMP Metadata for Audio Files

Like all the Adobe CS4 applications, Soundbooth has extensive support for metadata. Using the XMP format, Soundbooth generally stores the metadata in the clip itself so that this information can be easily shared between applications.

To view the metadata associated with a clip, **Choose Window > Workspace > Meta Logging** (Fig. 4.33). Within the Metadata panel that opens, Soundbooth divides metadata into two sections: File and Clip (Fig. 4.34).

The **File** tab displays properties for the currently selected audio clip. File metadata is stored directly in the file itself.

The **Clip** tab displays properties for a selected multitrack clip. This metadata is stored in a separate file, called a sidecar, that has the same name as the clip, but ends with the extension .xmp.

To enlarge the Metadata panel full screen, press the **Tilde** (`) key in the upper left corner of your keyboard.

Entering Metadata

There are four sets of metadata displayed by default in the File tab:

- Dublin Core
- Basic
- Rights Management
- Dynamic Media

Dublin Core provides general information and commonly used properties about the clip – including title and subject (Fig. 4.35).

A Word about Smartsound and SonicFire Pro

Soundbooth uses scores to create flexible music. But nothing equals the flexibility of the music created by Smartsound (www.smartsound.com). With over 2000 music cues to choose from, you can create music of any length, with multiple variations on the theme, and combine instruments almost at will. Smartsound is positively stunning and blows the doors off both Soundbooth and Soundtrack Pro. In addition, it recently released a new version that tightly integrates with Final Cut Pro.

Figure 4.33 Metadata (information about your media) is added using the Meta Logging workspace.

Figure 4.34 Soundbooth uses two tabs to display metadata: File and Clip.

Basic displays creation information about the clip – such as the application that created it, when it was created, last modified, and so on (Fig. 4.36).

Rights Management provides a place to enter information about license terms, security certificates, and Web links (Fig. 4.37).

Dynamic Media is the place to enter all the different technical information about the clip. Much of this is automatically filled in by Soundbooth as it reads the file. There are approximately 100 fields that can be entered in this category (Fig. 4.38).

There are actually 14 different categories of metadata, Soundbooth displays only four of them by default. If you always use one of these and never use the others, you can choose the metadata fields that Soundbooth displays by clicking the small fly-out menu icon in the top-right corner of the Soundbooth window and selecting Metadata Display (Fig. 4.39).

There are two types of fields: those you can enter data into (light gray) and those that are completed automatically (dark gray) for you by Soundbooth.

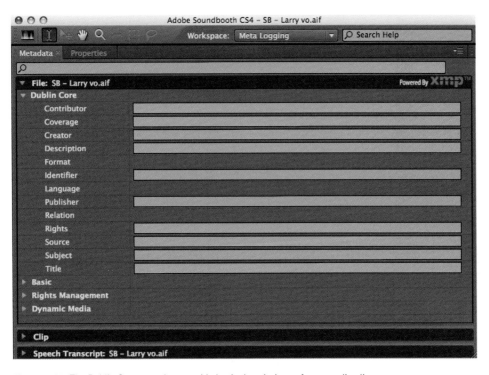

Figure 4.35 The Dublin Core metadata provide basic descriptions of your media clip.

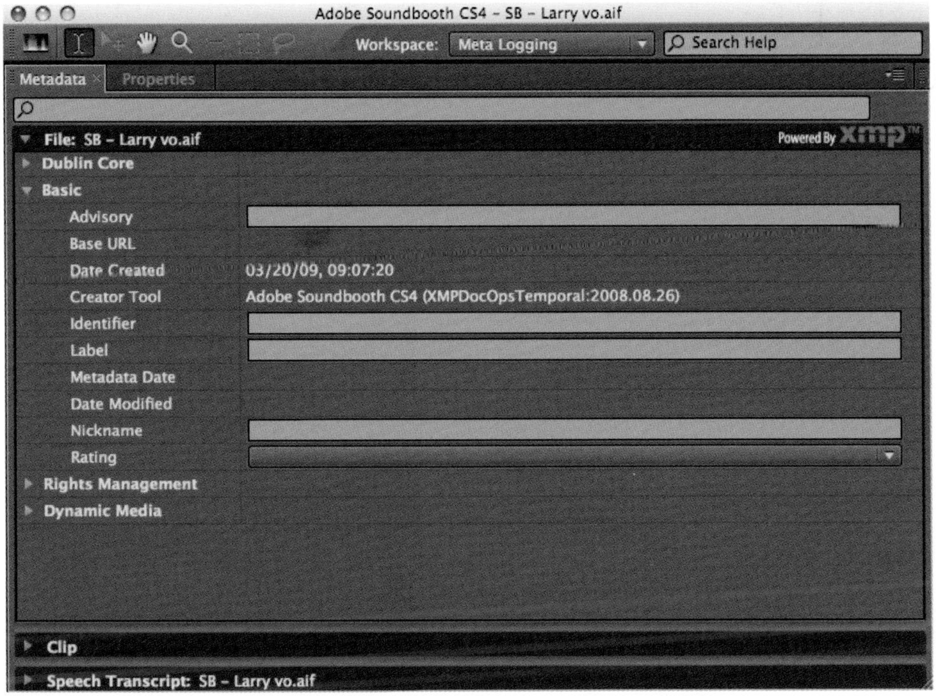

Figure 4.36 Basic metadata includes file creation information.

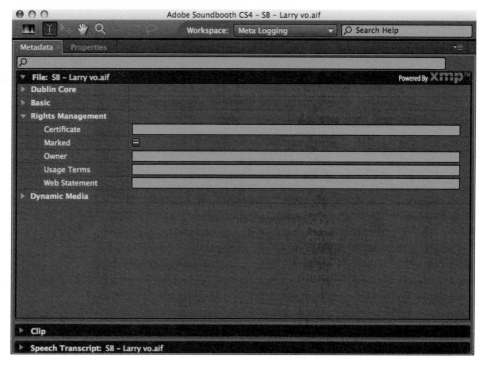

Figure 4.37 Rights information is the place to enter license and copy management data.

Figure 4.38 The Dynamic category is where you'll put most of your metadata, as this is the section designed for media clips.

Figure 4.39 To customize the metadata choices available to you, click the small fly-out menu in the top-right corner and select Metadata Display.

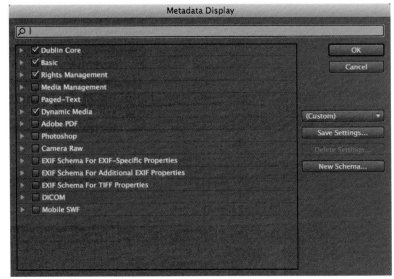

Figure 4.40 Create custom metadata displays in this window, by checking the categories you want to display. Click **Save Settings**, on the right, to save your choices.

To enter or edit metadata, simply click in the field you want to use (Fig. 4.40).

Searching Metadata

Searching metadata in Soundbooth is not the same as searching inside Adobe Bridge. In Bridge, you search across multiple files to find the files that match your search criteria. In Soundbooth, you search multiple metadata fields contained within a single clip to find the metadata that matches your search criteria.

For example, rather than try and figure out where the Description metadata field is stored, simply type "desc" (or some portion of its name) into the Metadata tab search field and press **Enter** (Fig. 4.41). All metadata fields that meet your criteria will be displayed.

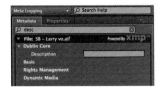

Figure 4.41 To find and display a specific metadata field, enter at least a portion of its name into the Search box and press Enter.

Saving Metadata

Metadata is stored automatically as you exit each field (for example, by pressing **Tab** or **Enter**) and is saved when you save the project. If the metadata is stored in a sidecar file, the data will be saved when you export the file; for example, when you finish your multitrack mix. Sidecar files have the same name as your clip and end with the extension .xml.

Adobe Premiere

Just as we can create transcripts in Soundbooth, we can also create transcripts in Premiere. With the 4.1 update to Premiere, it is as easy to move files from Final Cut Pro into Premiere as it is to move them to Soundbooth. (Unlike Soundbooth, Premiere Pro allows us to process files in a batch.) Moving files back and forth is the subject for the next chapter.

Since the process of creating transcripts is very similar between the two programs and the next chapter talks about integrating Premiere with Final Cut Pro, we'll take a side trip in the next chapter and show you how to use Premiere to create transcripts.

One of the advantages to using Premiere, compared to Final Cut, for your rough cut is that Premiere allows you to click a word in your transcript and instantly jump to that word in the clip. (This is the same feature that Soundboooth provides, except Premiere offers this in the context of video editing.)

However, as with Soundbooth, you'll still most likely want a printout of all your transcripts to enable you to quickly organize and review transcripts between multiple clips. This is because Soundbooth and Premiere only display the transcript for the selected clip.

Integrating Transcript Text with Final Cut Studio

The one big limitation of creating text transcripts in Soundbooth is that Final Cut Pro doesn't display them.

Then, again, Soundbooth and Premiere only show the transcript for the highlighted clip, and Bridge doesn't show the transcript at all. I can't use Bridge, for example, to find all clips where someone says: "Our problem began back in 2003." So, regardless of which application I'm working with, I'd still need to find some way to track my transcripts.

This means that in a real-world situation, the way I most often work with transcripts is that I have a sheaf of papers – all my transcripts – printed and on my desk, so I can mark them up, shuffle them, and start to figure out what clips I want to use to tell my story.

Based on this, here's my Final Cut workflow:

- Create the transcript in Soundbooth.
- Export it, retaining the Speaker ID, to a word processor.
- Manually enter the timecode at the beginning of a paragraph or relevant section.
- Clean up the text to the extent necessary. (Remember, it doesn't need to be perfect if you are only using it for finding key sections of a clip.)
- Print the transcript to paper, or create a PDF, which is searchable on the computer.
- Repeat for all necessary clips.

I would then use these printed transcripts as my key reference to figure out the clips that should be used to tell my story.

Someday soon, I'm sure, more applications will support searching and displaying transcripts. For now, Soundbooth provides a solid start.

Keyboard Shortcuts

Although you can create your own keyboard shortcuts, here are some handy default settings for Soundbooth CS4:

Shortcut	What it does
J - K - L	Shuttles playback back and forth (same as FCP)
=	Zoom into Timeline
–	Zoom out of Timeline
\	Fit Timeline in window
Mouse wheel	Zoom into/out of Timeline
~	Expand selected panel to fill screen
M	Add Timeline marker
Left/right arrow	Move to previous/next keyframe, or next video frame
Home	Move Current Time Indicator (playhead) to beginning
End	Move Current Time Indicator to end
Option + Command + X	Export Speech Transcription as XML

My Story: A Mouse Does Not Rely on Just One Hole

Jamie Talbott Hurt
ThunderFish Studios
ThunderFishStudios.com

Larry's note: *While this story doesn't directly relate to creating text transcripts, it does speak to the bigger issue of the integration between all these different applications. Chapter 7 discusses retouching video in Photoshop in detail.*

"Mus uni non fidit antro" is a favorite Latin proverb of mine that means a mouse does not rely on just one hole. It was 11:00 P.M., maybe it was 11:30, I don't remember. I do remember I was dog-tired pushing past a 16-hour work-day after a long flight and equally long hours the past few days. I'm sitting backstage in a

Figure 4.42 Jamie Hurt.

dark recess of the Grand Ballroom in hotel anywhere USA surrounded by hundreds of blinking LEDs and thousands of dollars in hardware. The show director and a few techs are shutting down their gear to go home for the night. I've got my two 17" Macbook Pro laptops with me that will be used to run presentation content and animations to the primary and secondary projection screens at the crack-of-dawn early tomorrow morning. I've got backups of all the production files, I'm ready for anything, including some long-overdue rest.

The opening keynote speaker just left the room with an entourage of 10 or more "support" staffs. There are a few changes to the main presentation content...no big deal there, but there was also a show-stopping localization error in the opening video and a scattering of other minor changes requested in the same video. The show-stopper request was to remove the logos from two buildings in the opening shots. Who knew those buildings belonged to a London-based investment banker firm that is being dragged through mud for their naive mishandling of investments in the US subprime lending markets? The other request was to make the product sequence Pop, and of course, the dreaded, "Can you make my logo bigger?" request.

Normally, none of this is a big deal to change when you have access to the original clips or Adobe AfterEffects, but I only planned to playback the "final and approved" video from a DVD. I didn't bring my multiterabyte RAID drive with all the B-roll on it, but I did bring a final, high-resolution master-mix of all the videos in a QuickTime format.

No one ever hires me to complain or say their requests are impossible, so first thing I need to solve is removing the logos on the buildings shot. My "show laptops" do not have my high-end production applications on it, but I did have FCP loaded on one of them and, of course, PhotoShop CS4 Extended (PS) on both. Photoshop Extended can open QuickTime files. It's almost midnight. I feel like the MacGyver of moving pixels and order some coffee to keep my focus on a solution.

Opening the high-resolution clip in FCP to access one of the neat shortcuts I like to use for various postproduction steps from FCP is to mark the in/out points on the Timeline and export the video without recompressing the footage. In the first case, it exported an 8-second, 1920 × 1080p, 1:1, 30 fps Apple Pro Res clip in about 4 or 5 seconds, and the file only weighs in at about 1 MB. It's a reference file and Apple's equivalent function to Adobe's dynamic linking minus some of the automation. The QuickTime engine points the file's linked resources back to the source clip, rendered effects, etc., from the original Timeline in FCP. If you set up your FCP sequence presets using an uncompressed matching format, this trick is a lossless trip out of the FCP Timeline and into whatever application you need. Good for making a quick proxy file for scoring music to a video-in-progress or as a high-resolution source file that can be used to create and re-render a replacement clip on the FCP Timeline.

Starting with the bad logo clip in PS, I selected a large soft brush for the stamp tool, and on a new layer, with just a couple clicks, I had covered up the offending logos. Fortunately, it was a fairly slow pan and nothing crossed in front of the logo, so later a couple of keyframes for a slight adjustment on the position of the top-most layer and the edit was done. I got lucky. File, Export, Render Video ... One down and it's only 12:30 A.M. I think it's just me and the security staff left in the ballroom now.

Back to FCP to see what I can do to enhance the product sequence. Well, I have a few basic filter effects and color-correction effects I could try natively in FCP, but I had a hunch I could do something tastefully unique and interesting using PhotoShop Extended. Remember, if I had my copy of After Effects with me and, of course, the thousands of dollars in plug-ins that I've purchased over the years, the solution would have been different, but I didn't and this was another way out and worked quite well, albeit a little unfamiliar.

I marked the in/out points of the product clip I needed to enhance, then I chose File, Export, QuickTime Movie, and did not select the checkbox for Make Movie Self-Contained. I opened the reference QuickTime clip just as before in PS, but this time I right-clicked on the layer and selected Convert to Smart Layer. The advantage with this crucial step is a Smart Layer that allows you to apply a nondestructive Smart Filter to the entire QuickTime sequence. Pretty cool, I mean pretty smart, huh? I duplicate the Smart Layer, and after a couple of experiments, I decided to apply one of the hundreds of built-in PhotoShop filters to the top layer. I think I used the filter called Dark Strokes and set the layer to multiply to create a nice high-contrast, almost hand-drawn cartoony effect to the video. It was a bit over-the-top, but since a Smart Filter also has the ability to be masked, I was able to use a big, fat, soft brush to paint a hole in the video effect layer and that created a nice vignette effect, allowing the unaltered product shot to really get the attention it deserved. File, Export, Render Video.... It's now 12:55 A.M., I'm inches from the goal line and barely breaking a sweat. I regret the double-tall latte I downed about an hour ago.

Now, to make the logo bigger. It's a cliche request in this business, but I guess I understand the anxiety around it. So, I am back to the Timeline in FCP to mark the in/out points on the 8 seconds of the closing logo bumper. File, Export, QuickTime Movie... But I do not select the checkbox for Make Movie Self-Contained, and I am back to PS to open the clip. This time,

I spent a bit more time to experiment with a solution that would make the animated logo bigger and still be tasteful and true to the company's brand and current marketing campaign. Using two sets of Smart Layer effects this time, I chose to apply the Spherize Smart Filter to the top layer, set to Screen, and the bottom layer to Spherize and Plaster effects on the bottom layer. It was an odd combination of layer effects and opacity keyframes to get it to look right and finish unaltered, but you'll have to trust me at 1:30 A.M., it looked awesome.

5

WORKFLOWS TO MOVE STUFF AROUND

I am wrestling with a conundrum in this book, that is, how to provide meaningful help concerning some extraordinarily deep software. Trying to explain how to use even one of the CS4 applications in 300 pages is very difficult.

To explain how **all** of them work is ridiculously impossible.

So, rather than writing a manual on how each of these applications works, I decided to show how these applications integrate. Because, as I've discovered doing my research, there are many books that do the former, and none that do the latter.

This chapter shows you how to move stuff around and, along the way, answers the question why you would want to do so.

We'll start with a discussion of Round-Tripping versus Dynamic Linking: what they are and what they do.

Then, I'll provide a fascinating workflow between Final Cut, Premiere, and the Adobe Media Encoder (AME) that allows you to edit in Final Cut, transcribe in Premiere Pro, and then post text-searchable movies to your Web site.

After that, we'll take a look at how to move files between Final Cut Pro and After Effects for effects creation, then how to bring the finished file back to Final Cut for final integration and output.

Finally, I tackle the bane of my existence: altering an Illustrator file that is part of a video sequence.

This is a very cool chapter.

Round-Tripping versus Dynamic Links

First, since both Final Cut and Adobe use the term *round-tripping*, and Adobe adds the term *Dynamic Links*, let's define these two terms.

Round-tripping is the capability to move a file instantly from within one program to another and back again, without first exiting a program, jumping to the operating system, then moving to the second application. Round-tripping exists in both Apple and Adobe products.

Dynamic Linking is an Adobe term describing the capability to make changes to a media file, then send that file from one Adobe media application to another without first requiring it to render. Dynamic Linking exists only between Adobe's video software applications such as Premiere Pro, Encore, Soundbooth, and After Effects. Thus, we can only dynamically link (that is, move video files without first rendering them) between these four applications.

As Adobe's Web site states: [The benefit is that] "Dynamic Link enables you to work faster and stay in the creative flow by eliminating intermediate rendering when you make changes to assets – whether you're editing a sequence of clips in Adobe Premiere Pro, changing a composition in After Effects, refining a project in Encore, or sweetening audio in Soundbooth."

In the Final Cut world, we round-trip in two different ways: Open in Editor or Send.

Open in Editor is used, for example, to open a source file currently imported in Final Cut Pro to its originating application, such as LiveType or any of the Adobe applications. In this case, a file is opened in one application, changes are made and saved, then the file is updated in Final Cut Pro with no re-importing necessary.

Send is used to move files between the applications in Final Cut Studio, generally without first requiring rendering.

If a file was created outside Final Cut Studio, you use Open in Editor to reopen it to make changes. If the media originated in Final Cut Studio, you use Send. In either case, final rendering is done in Final Cut Pro, rather than the original application.

A Reason to Use Both Final Cut Pro and Premiere Pro

Most of the time, Final Cut Pro is fine for editing. But, here's a reason to consider using both Final Cut Pro and Premiere Pro: to take advantage of the speech-to-text transcription feature in Premiere Pro and to create movies that you can post to the Web that are text searchable.

In a previous chapter I explained how to use Soundbooth to create text transcripts. The problem is that Soundbooth doesn't edit video or do batch processing in the background; for that, we need Premiere Pro.

In the first workflow in this chapter, I'll show you how to edit a project in Final Cut, import it into Premiere Pro to create a text transcript, then using the Adobe Media Encoder (AME) embed the dialog into a Flash movie to post online.

To do this, we are going to take advantage of two new pieces of software that were not available when Adobe CS4 first shipped: version 4.1 of Premiere Pro that allows importing from Final Cut and a link to a free Adobe media player you can post to your own Web site that allows you to search transcripts in your videos online.

Weird – but True!

Do you want another reason to use Premiere Pro? With the release of the latest version of Premiere, you can now open Final Cut Pro projects in Windows by importing them into Premiere Pro!

Workflow: from Final Cut Pro to Searchable Text on the Web

The problem with posting video and audio to the Web is that you can't search it. The only way people can find out what's in a video is to look at the title and any related keywords, if they exist. Wouldn't it be great if you could type in a search phrase and all the videos that contain that text would be listed on your screen?

I have created hundreds of hours of video tutorials. But, there's no way to know exactly what's inside them. For instance, how do you find the specific tutorial that discusses how to maintain video white levels below 100% in Final Cut. This is an important issue, but it is always covered as part of a larger tutorial on color correction. Unless you knew that, you couldn't find it.

We can easily do searches today on text articles, but not with video. And that's because there's no way to automatically convert the spoken word into a text file that can be indexed for searching.

Until now. With the release of CS4, Adobe has taken the first major steps along this path. In this workflow, I want to illustrate one way to take your videos from Final Cut to searchable text on the Web.

Overview

Here's the *Reader's Digest* version of this process:

- Edit the sequence in Final Cut Pro.
- Export the sequence as an XML file from Final Cut.
- Using the new Premiere Pro 4.1 import utility, import the sequence into Premiere Pro.
- Create the text transcript in Premiere Pro – Premiere is especially good for processing a batch of movies, which Soundtrack Pro can't do.
- Export the file from Premiere using Adobe Media Encoder.

A Special Present Just for You!

 Adobe has created a video-search kit and posted it to Adobe.com, which provides the capability to search Web videos. You can find it by visiting Adobe.com and searching for "Video Search."

Oops!

Theoretically, you should not need to use Soundbooth at all in this process. However, as Adobe was building the CS4 applications, it totally forgot to add the capability to export text transcripts from Premiere Pro. Adobe tells me it will fix this in a future update. For now, Soundbooth needs to be a part of this process.

Important Note

In order for this procedure to work, you *must* use an audio and video format that is supported in both Final Cut Pro and Premiere Pro. Although there are a wide variety of formats to choose from, not all formats are supported by both programs. Testing before getting too deep into a project is *always* a good idea.

- Open the file you exported from Premiere in Soundbooth, and export as an XML file, with an XMP sidecar. We now have the media file (FLV) and metadata file (XMP).
- Using the new media player, you can view that file, enter text to search for in the file, display all the occurrences of that text in the file, and instantly jump to any word in the transcript.

Details

Back in September 2004, I had the great pleasure of producing and editing a short documentary for Alcatel/Lucent featuring Dr. Vint Cerf, considered by many to be the developer of the key technical backbone creating today's Internet. I decided to revisit this project to see how to combine editing in Final Cut Pro, with speech-to-text transcripts in Premiere Pro, to create a searchable video that I can post to the Web. (And I'm grateful to both Alcatel/Lucent and Dr. Cerf for their generous permission to use these elements here.)

Working in Final Cut Pro

The first portion of this process is to edit our project as normal inside Final Cut Pro. Export for transcription only when all editing is complete.

In Final Cut, open the project with the sequence you want to export (Fig. 5.1).

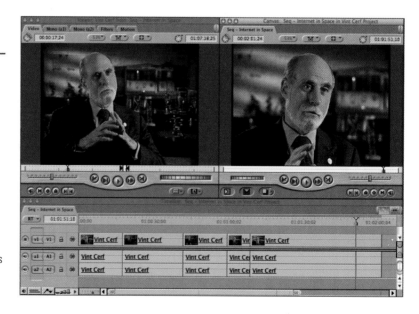

Figure 5.1 A portion of the documentary that we'll use in this example, already edited in Final Cut Pro.

Select the sequence you want to export in the Browser. (While you can export from an open sequence in the Timeline, I always prefer to do so by selecting the sequence I want to export in the Browser.)

Since we need to move this information between applications, export it using **File > Export > XML**. Adobe suggests you make sure that both checkboxes (shown in Fig. 5.2) are selected. This assures that all clip information will be exported with your sequence and that your project file saves all necessary metadata. Click **OK** when done.

Figure 5.2 Be sure both checkboxes are selected so that both the sequence and the clips it includes are exported.

A Save dialog box appears, so give the file a name and location. Final Cut automatically adds an XML extension. Click **Save**.

The Final Cut portion of this process is complete.

Repeat this process for all movies for which you want to create searchable text. In this example, we will work with just one file; however, the process of transcription and posting supports an unlimited number of batch-processed files.

Working in Premiere Pro and AME

Next, we turn to Premiere Pro, which acts as a translator – we'll see this again later in this chapter when we use Premiere to move the files between Final Cut and After Effects.

Open Premiere Pro CS4 and create a new project. (This technique requires version 4.1 or later.)

When you create a new Premiere Pro project, the Location dialog at the bottom of the first tab asks where you want project data to be stored. In my case, I created a **Premiere projects** folder on my second (media) drive, which I show in Fig. 5.3. I suggest you create and name an easily identifiable folder for your project on your second drive.

Figure 5.3 When you create a new project in Premiere, it first asks you where you want to store the project data. Be sure to put it on your second drive.

Important Note: There's No Shortcut

Premiere does not allow you to transcribe just a portion of a clip you have opened in the Timeline. You need to encode and transcribe the entire master clip stored on your hard drive. To minimize transcribing the clips you don't need, export the completed sequence from Final Cut as a self-contained QuickTime movie. Import that movie back into Final Cut and export the XML file of just that completed movie. This way no extra media gets transcribed.

What Drive Should You Use?

Premiere projects, like Final Cut Pro projects, don't contain media. Therefore, you can store them on any drive you like. I prefer to store both Premiere project files and media files on a hard drive other than the boot drive. This recommendation is essential for media, but optional for projects.

Click the Scratch Disks tab at the top and set all four scratch disks to a separate folder on your second drive. In this case, I created a folder called **Premiere scratch disks** (Fig. 5.4).

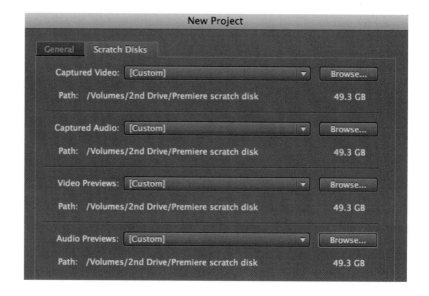

Figure 5.4 Click the Scratch Disks tab at the top, and set all four scratch disk settings to a separate folder on your second drive.

What Codecs Are Supported?

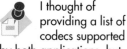 I thought of providing a list of codecs supported by both applications, but applications change codec support too quickly to put into a book. The best advice is to visit Adobe's website (www.adobe.com) then test your video before committing to this workflow.

Click **OK**.

Unlike Final Cut, Premiere generally wants to know what video format you are using before it even opens up the project. (Though, if you click **Cancel**, it opens a new, empty project with no Timeline. Although the CS4 version supports multiple sequence types in a single project, Premiere does not currently support having more than one project open at a time.)

In the New Sequence screen that opens next, click the **Sequence Presets** tab (see Fig. 5.5) and pick the video format that matches the format you were using in Final Cut Pro. Since not all video formats are supported by both the programs, spending time testing at the beginning can save a lot of headaches later.

In Premiere, choose **File > Import**, and find the XML file you created in Final Cut Pro. Premiere automatically opens it and loads it into the Project window in the top-left corner.

How Final Cut Pro Files are Named in Premiere Pro

In the Project tab, Premiere creates a folder named after the XML file. Inside this folder is a Master Clips folder containing your media and a sequence with the same sequence name you used in Final Cut.

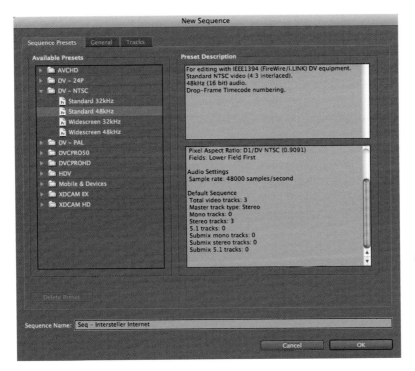

Figure 5.5 This window is where you determine your sequence settings. Match the settings you used in Final Cut Pro.

Double-click the sequence name in the Project tab to load it into the Timeline (Fig. 5.6).

Figure 5.6 The Project tab, in the upper left corner, contains the sequence and the media imported from the XML file.

Figure 5.7 Display the Speech Transcript window by choosing **Window > Metadata**.

Select **Window > Metadata** to display the workspace containing the Speech Transcript tab (Fig. 5.7).

This is a **CRITICAL** step: in Premiere's Project tab, not the Timeline, select all clips you want to transcribe to text. Selecting only the sequence won't work, you need to select the actual clips contained in the sequence. If you don't select the clips in the Browser, the rest of these steps won't work.

If multiple clips are selected in the Project tab, choose **Clips > Audio Options > Transcribe to Text**. If only one clip is selected, or if the clip is selected in the Timeline, click the **Transcribe** button at the bottom of the Metadata window.

Set the Speech Transcription Options dialog as described in the Soundbooth chapter (Chapter 4) and click **OK** (Fig. 5.8).

Figure 5.8 To transcribe a batch of clips, select **Clip > Audio Options > Transcribe to Text.**

Adobe Media Encoder (AME) launches. (Yes, I found this confusing initially, but using AME to create transcripts in the background allows me to continue editing in Premiere.) When all the clips that you want to transcribe are added to this dialog, click **Start Queue** (Fig. 5.9).

Figure 5.9 Set your transcription settings in the Speech Transcript window, then click **OK** to begin the transcription process.

The AME is preset to create a transcript, so there is nothing you need to set once this dialog opens. This encoding process can take a long time, depending upon the length of your source clips. The AME is encoding the entire source clip, not just what you have on the Timeline. Transcription time can take six times longer than real time.

Notes to Improve Accuracy

As we discussed in the Soundbooth chapter, the accuracy of text transcripts can vary widely. You can improve accuracy by making sure that audio levels are good and loud. The louder a clip is, the better — as long as it doesn't distort. Also, Adobe uses a technology called Speech Prediction to help identify the words. In fact, it will even complete the sentences for you. If a speaker doesn't finish a thought, or suddenly speaks very excitedly, the software assumes this is a new speaker. Adobe tells me it is working on custom dictionaries and other "amazing things" to improve accuracy in future versions.

Once the transcription process is complete in AME, you can view the text for a clip in the metadata panel by selecting a clip in the Timeline or Browser. Remember the transcript is from the entire source clip, not just from the clip in the Timeline.

Now, it's time to export the edited project from Premiere. To do so, select the sequence containing the clips you just transcribed in the Browser and select **File > Export > Media** (or type **Command-M**). In the Export Settings window (Fig. 5.10), be sure the format is set to **FLV | F4V** (the format for a Flash file). Give the file a name and location. The transcription data travels with the file.

Important Note

Select the *clips* to create transcripts, but select the *sequence* to export the transcripts.

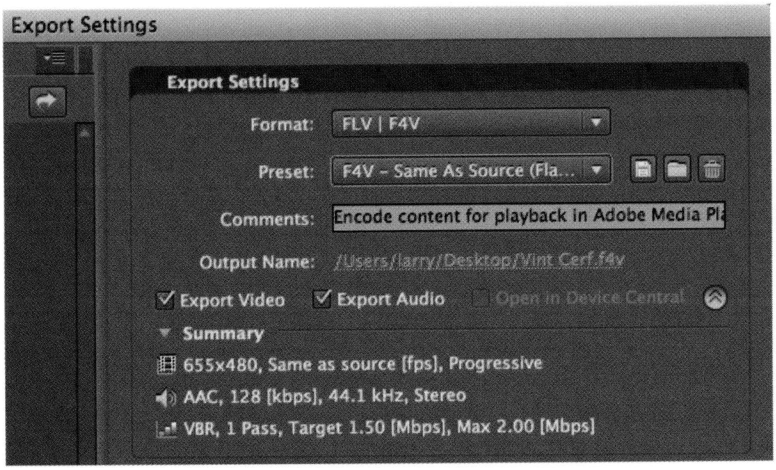

Export Settings

Export Settings

Format: FLV | F4V

Preset: F4V – Same As Source (Fla...

Comments: Encode content for playback in Adobe Media Pl

Output Name: /Users/larry/Desktop/Vint Cerf.f4v

☑ Export Video ☑ Export Audio ☐ Open in Device Central

▼ Summary

655x480, Same as source [fps], Progressive

AAC, 128 [kbps], 44.1 kHz, Stereo

VBR, 1 Pass, Target 1.50 [Mbps], Max 2.00 [Mbps]

Figure 5.10 Select the sequence to export in the Browser, select **File > Export > Media**.

We are now done with Premiere.

Now, we need to return to AME. The first time you open AME it defaults to encoding an FLV (Flash) movie. After that, it defaults to the last setting used. Since we are creating searchable Flash movies, encoding them as an FLV | F4V is fine. Remember to double-click the orange text for the Output Name dialog in the upper right of the Export Settings window to give the soon-to-be-compressed file a name and specify where you want it stored (see Fig. 5.11).

Once again, the AME starts, and your exported file is loaded into it. Click **Start Queue** to begin the compression process.

When the file is completely compressed in AME, create a folder to store all the elements of this soon-to-be-searchable media. I created one on my desktop named **Media folder**. Store your compressed file in this Media folder.

It's time to move on to Soundbooth.

Can't Get Enough of That AME

Yup, you are correct. We are making two trips through the AME. The first-time through creates the transcript, and the second-time through creates the compressed Flash media file.

Figure 5.11 The default export settings, shown in the top right corner, will create an FLV file. These defaults are for a Flash video, which is fine.

Creating Searchable XML in Soundbooth

The next series of steps creates a searchable text file that is linked to the compressed media file that we just created in AME. Although we can create text files for almost any QuickTime movie, the search engine provided by Adobe only works with Flash movies. At this point in the process, we can't see the text associated with the FLV file, but it's still there.

Using Soundbooth allows us to create an XML file with customized tags, such as cue points, that can't be created if we were just working in HTML.

Open Soundbooth, and then open the compressed Flash file; it has an .F4V extension. The text transcript opens automatically in the Speech Transcript window (Fig. 5.12).

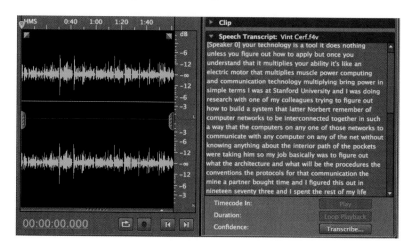

Figure 5.12 When you open the Flash movie in Soundbooth, the text transcript opens automatically in the Speech Transcript window.

Choose **File > Export > Speech Transcription** as shown in Fig. 5.13. Save this to the same Media folder that contains the compressed Flash file. (Again, it would be easier to do this directly out of Premiere – but until Adobe adds that option, we need to use Soundbooth.)

Figure 5.13 Select **File > Export > Speech** Transcription to create the searchable XML file we need for posting.

You now have two files in the Media folder: the compressed media file and the searchable XML file. These now get posted to the Web like any Flash movie. The media file will be what viewers watch and the XML file will be what they search.

Searching Your Web Files

At this point, technology is changing quickly. When CS4 was first announced, the only way to view a text-searchable Flash movie was to create your own player. In its documentation, Adobe described this process as "requiring a fundamental knowledge of object-oriented programming, particularly ActionScript 3."

Hmmm…. I checked my resume and discovered I was a little weak in this area.

However, Adobe recently showed me a new version of a media player you can post on your site that allows searching videos based on the text in the XML files. I expect it to be freely available by the time this book is released. You can learn more about it and download it here: http://www.adobe.com/products/creativesuite/production/videosearch/

Workflow: Round-Tripping a Photoshop PSD File from Final Cut Pro to Adobe Photoshop; and Back

Photoshop documents (PSD files) are essential to virtually every production. In this workflow, I'll show you an easy way to move a file from a Final Cut project to Photoshop for some adjustment and bring it back into Final Cut for inclusion in the finished project. In Chapter 6 we'll discuss how to create these images.

The reason Final Cut and Photoshop are so compatible is that both deal with images as a collection of pixels, called bitmaps, which means they can easily share files.

Notes on Metadata

If you are creating a Flash movie, the metadata (that is, the transcript) is stored inside the FLV file. If you are creating a searchable MPEG-2 file, for example, in preparation for editing HDV, the MPEG format doesn't support the inclusion of metadata, so the transcript is stored in an XML sidecar file, using the same file name as the MPEG file, but with an XML extension. Both files are stored in the same location.

According to Adobe's Web site, file formats that support writing XMP metadata directly into the file include FLV, F4V, MOV, AVI, and WMV. For a complete list, visit Adobe's Web site.

In this example, I'll work with a still image that I want to use as the title graphic for my program.

Overview

Here's a summary of how this works:

- Import a PSD file into Final Cut Pro.
- Using Open in Editor, send it from Final Cut to Photoshop to make changes.
- Save the changes in Photoshop.
- When you switch back to Final Cut, the file updates automatically without reimporting.

A Cautionary Note

Chapter 6 discusses still images in detail, however, a quick word of caution. When importing PSD graphics, Final Cut treats them as sequences, not images. This means that you must be sure that the settings in Final Cut Pro > Easy Setup match the sequence settings you edit your PSD file into. If they don't match and you've already imported the graphic, delete the graphic, reset your settings, and reimport.

Details

There are several ways we can import a Photoshop file into Final Cut Pro:

- Find it using Adobe Bridge, and then drag it into the Final Cut Browser.
- Within Final Cut, import it using **File > Import File(s)** or type **Command + I**.
- Drag it from the desktop into the Final Cut Browser. (Dragging files into the Browser is preferable to dragging directly into the Timeline.)

In this case, I used Bridge because it gave me a very fast way of reviewing over 2,000 images on my hard drive to decide which one I wanted to use. So, we'll drag the image from Bridge into Final Cut Pro (see Fig. 5.14).

Figure 5.14 Adding an image to Final Cut can be done by importing, or by simply dragging the files you need from Bridge into Final Cut Pro.

You Can Preset the Duration of Imported Graphics

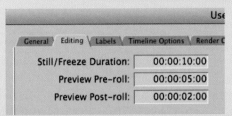

Figure 5.15

There is a little-known preference setting that allows you to set the duration of imported graphics and freeze frames. To set it, go to **Final Cut Pro > User Preferences > Editing** tab (see Fig. 5.15). The Still Freeze duration defaults to 10 seconds and controls the duration of all graphics and freeze frames. Changing this can be useful especially when you are building a graphic montage and need all your images to run the same length. Set this to the duration you want before you import your graphics. Then, when you import them, they will be the duration you want.

Because this is a layered Photoshop graphic, each layer is imported as a separate track in Final Cut (see Fig. 5.16). If a layer is invisible, it will still be imported, but set to invisible in Final Cut, as well.

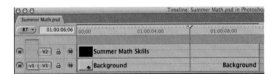

Figure 5.16 Layers in Photoshop are imported as individual tracks in Final Cut.

In looking at this, I want to see what the text would look like if it were white. Perhaps it would stand out better against the background. Then, I'll see if a drop shadow makes it more readable as well.

Here is our Round-tripping workflow:

1. To move this image back to Photoshop, open it in the Timeline, not in the Browser, **Control-click** any layer, and select **Open in Editor** (Fig. 5.17). Because the file ends in .PSD, Final Cut knows this came from Photoshop and immediately opens the file in Photoshop.

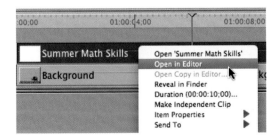

Figure 5.17 To automatically open a Photoshop file from Final Cut, **Control-click** the clip in the Timeline and select Open in Editor.

2. In Photoshop, change the text color to white and add a drop shadow (Fig. 5.18).

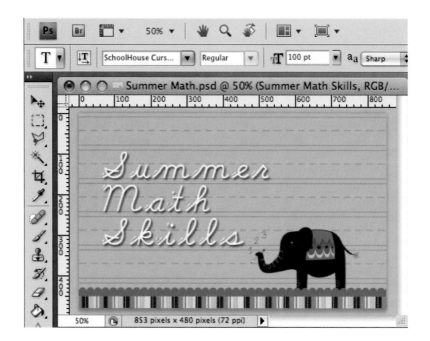

Figure 5.18 We modified the text to white and added a drop shadow.

3. Before sending the file back to Final Cut, you must make the drop shadow a permanent part of the clip because drop shadows in Photoshop are created using "layer effects." These are like a filter in Final Cut, in that they don't change the clip, they just change the display of the clip.

Select your image by making its window active and selecting **Layer > Smart Objects > Convert to Smart Objects**. A Smart Object is a layer that contains image data from raster or vector images, such as Photoshop or Illustrator files. Smart Objects preserve the source content of an image with all its original characteristics, enabling you to perform nondestructive editing to the layer.

Converting the text with drop shadow to a Smart Object turns the effect of the drop shadow into actual pixels that will import into Final Cut. Any layer effect that you apply

A Downside to Smart Objects

Once a layer is converted to a Smart Object, the text is harder to edit. Unlike a standard text layer, where you can just select the text with the text tool to edit it, once it's a Smart Object, you need to double-click the Smart Object, which opens as a .psb file. The Smart Object can then be edited as a vector. However, there is a gotcha. The Smart Object is defined by the size of its original bounding box. So, you must be careful. If you add letters to your text, for instance, you will have to increase the Canvas size to give you a larger space.

in Photoshop should be treated this way in order for it to transfer to Final Cut.

4. Now, here's the fun part. To get it back to Final Cut, all you need to do is **save** the file inside Photoshop.

5. Switch back to Final Cut and – ta-DAH! – the file is instantly updated!

Using this workflow, it becomes really easy to move files back and forth between Final Cut and Photoshop. In the next workflow, we'll take this one step further and see how we can use Illustrator to retouch a file that we are using in Final Cut Pro.

Workflow: Modifying an Adobe Illustrator File from Final Cut Using Photoshop

As we said in the last workflow, all video files use bitmapped pixels. This means that every frame is composed of pixels that are fixed in size and position. All Final Cut Pro images are bitmapped.

However, Adobe Illustrator describes every line, shape, and piece of text using a different method, mathematical equation called a "vector".

The benefits of using bitmapped pixels are that calculations are fast and pixels can be displayed easily. However, video file sizes are huge, and the resolution of the image is fixed.

The benefits to using vector graphics are that file sizes are very small and the resolution can be scaled to any size for any form of output. Meaning, you don't lose resolution if you enlarge the size of your image.

Graphic artists love the flexibility of vectors, whereas video editors are totally immersed in the world of pixels. Naturally, moving between these two worlds can be a challenge.

In this example, we are given an Illustrator file that has background colors that need to be adjusted to match the overall look of the video project.

Overview

Here's a summary of how this works:

- Before importing any Illustrator file into Final Cut, save it as a Photoshop PDF.
- Import the PDF file into Final Cut Pro.
- To modify the file, Control-click the file in the Browser or the Timeline and select Open in Editor.
- In Photoshop, select **Layers > Smart Object > Edit Contents**.
- Edit the image in Illustrator.
- Save the image in Illustrator.
- Save the image in Photoshop.
- It automatically updates in Final Cut (weird, but true!).

Why Not Just Update the Image Directly?

Theoretically, you could just switch back to Photoshop, change your image, and save it, which would update it automatically in Final Cut Pro. However, sometimes you'll get caught by the operating system, which says the file is already open and won't allow you to save it using the same name. To prevent this problem, get in the habit of using Open in Editor.

Why Not Open an Illustrator File in Illustrator?

Yes, you can save your Illustrator image as an Adobe PDF using Illustrator. The problem with this is that there is no way to round-trip between Final Cut and Illustrator. When you select Open in Editor, Final Cut opens the PDF in Acrobat Reader, not the Illustrator. By first saving the file as a Photoshop PDF, this tells Final Cut to open the file in Photoshop when selecting Open in Editor.

Details

First, when creating images in Illustrator, they should be sized the same as you would in creating PSD or TIFF images. Chapter 6 discusses this in detail.

For this example, let's assume the Illustrator file your client gave you needs a background color modified to fit the look of a project. Although I am not an Illustrator wizard, I've learned over time how to make simple changes so that I don't need to reinvolve a graphic artist to get my projects finished.

While Final Cut will allow us to import an Illustrator file and place it on the Timeline, this does not give us as much flexibility in editing as we would like. Instead, though it seems counter-intuitive, we will open the file in Photoshop first.

When you open the file in Photoshop, you may see a dialog asking for import settings. If so, set the Crop to **Media size** and set DPI to **72**.

Photoshop opens the image to the same size as it was created in Illustrator. This is one of the benefits of using CS4 – the Save As PDF dialog was improved so that PDF files can be more easily edited.

Here are the specific steps of this technique.

With the Illustrator file open in Photoshop, select **File > Save As,** and from the format pop-up, select **Photoshop PDF** to link it to Photoshop.

In the Save Adobe PDF window (Fig. 5.19), set the Adobe PDF Preset to **High** Quality, set Compatibility to the highest level the pop-up displays (in this case **Acrobat 8**), and make sure Preserve Photoshop Editing Capabilities is checked "on." This creates a

Something Is Lost

 When we convert an Illustrator file to PDF, text cannot be edited, nor can many other elements be changed. If you need to make continuous changes to an Illustrator file, you are better-off creating a master file in Illustrator then outputting TIFFs or PNGs to move into Final Cut. However, at that point, you lose the ability to round-trip the TIFF or PNG with Final Cut Pro.

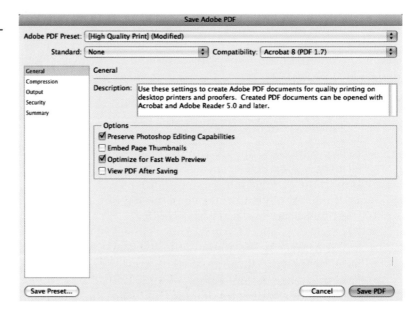

Figure 5.19 When saving a file as a PDF, set your settings to match this window.

high-quality, highly editable PDF that we can use in Final Cut for our project.

Import the PDF into Final Cut Pro and edit as you would any other still image (Fig. 5.20).

Figure 5.20 The image we are starting with, displayed in the Viewer.

1. If a change needs to be made, Control-click the PDF in the Browser and select **Open in Editor** (Fig. 5.21). In this case, we want to change the background color from magenta to a more deep-space-like dark blue. This automatically opens the PDF in Photoshop and sets it as a **Smart Object**. This is the key step to making this easy to work with in Illustrator.

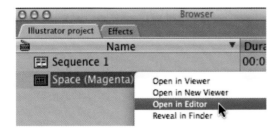

Figure 5.21 Control-click a PDF in the Final Cut Pro Browser to automatically open it in Photoshop as a Smart Object.

2. Without making any changes to the file in Photoshop (the program is actually just serving as a transfer utility), select **Layer > Smart Objects > Edit Contents** (Fig. 5.22), and the file opens in Illustrator, ready for editing.

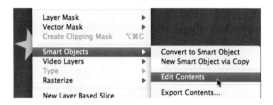

Figure 5.22 Select Layers > Smart Objects > Edit Contents to open the PDF for editing inside Illustrator.

Figure 5.23 Select the image in Illustrator and click the small wheel in the center of the toolbar to open the Recolor Artwork dialog.

3. In Illustrator, select the image by clicking in the center of it, then click the small gray wheel button in the center of the toolbar. The yellow tooltip says **Recolor Artwork** (Fig. 5.23).
4. Click the Edit tab to display the color editor window (Fig. 5.24).

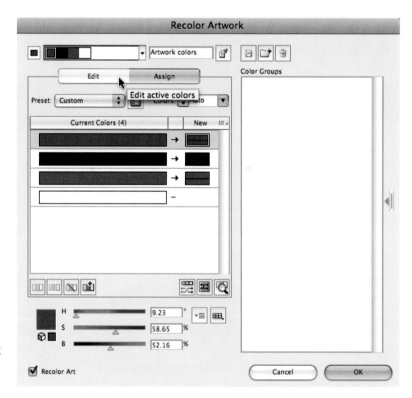

Figure 5.24 The Recolor Artwork window allows you to change the colors of the selected object. Click the Edit tab to display the color editor window.

5. Click the almost-too-small-to-see chain icon button labeled **Link harmony colors** (see Fig. 5.25). This links all your colors together so that when you change one, they all change together to keep their overall relationship. This is a *really* powerful feature, because it means you don't need to understand color theory to make pleasing color changes.

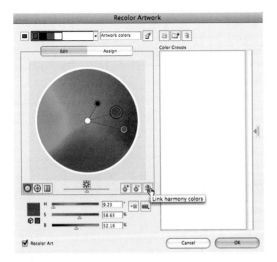

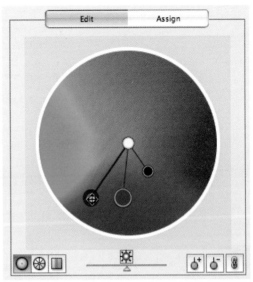

Figure 5.25 Click the Link harmony colors icon to link all the colors in the document together, so color relationships are maintained.

Figure 5.26 Once the colors are linked, drag any color to change all the colors.

6. Grab and drag any of the color handles in the color wheel and drag until you get the results you need. In this case, I'm dragging the handles around toward the left to change the background color from magenta to dark blue (Fig. 5.26). Click the **OK** button when you are satisfied with your changes. In the example shown in Fig. 5.27, we went from magenta to dark blue (Figs. 5.27a and b). Now, here's the very, very cool part.

(a)

(b)

Figure 5.27 (a) The starting image is on the left. (b) The corrected image is on the right.

7. Save your file in Illustrator. (If a dialog box appears about legacy files, just click **OK**.)

Figure 5.28 Save the file in Illustrator, save it again in Photoshop, switch to Final Cut, and the file is instantly updated.

8. Switch to Photoshop. After a few seconds of processing, the corrected file is updated and displayed. You don't need to change anything, just save it, again, in Photoshop (Fig. 5.28).
9. Switch to Final Cut, and the file is instantly updated, again.

Ta-DAH! Done.

Workflow: From Final Cut Pro to After Effects

In this workflow, I'll use Final Cut to build the basic structure of my effect, send it to After Effects for all the actual effects work, export the file from After Effects as a high-quality QuickTime movie, and bring it back into Final Cut. Although creating your effect first in Final Cut is not required, it often helps in terms of thinking through what you want to do.

In addition, as a bonus, in After Effects I'll show you a neat effect that we can't do in either Final Cut or Motion to animate a still image.

Overview

There are two ways the files can be moved from Final Cut Pro to After Effects, and both require an intermediary: the first uses Premiere Pro and the second uses Automatic Duck.

Here's a summary of the workflow using Premiere Pro:

- Assemble the clips for your effect in a sequence in Final Cut Pro.
- Export your project from Final Cut Pro as an XML file.
- Import your project into Premiere Pro. (Importing XML requires version 4.1 or later.)
- Save your imported file as a Premiere Pro project.
- Import the Premiere Pro project into After Effects.
- Add your effects.
- Render the finished video from After Effects as a QuickTime movie.
- Import the finished QuickTime movie into Final Cut.

Here's a summary of the workflow using a third-party utility called Automatic Duck (http://www.automaticduck.com):

- Assemble the clips for your effect in a sequence in Final Cut Pro.

Premiere Is Good for More than Editing

Both After Effects and Premiere Pro are included in the Adobe Production Premium bundle. So, even though you are not using Premiere for editing, you can still use Premiere Pro to move files around between the applications.

- Export your project from Final Cut Pro as an XML file.
- From within After Effects, select **Import Using Automatic Duck**.
- Add your effects.
- Render the finished video from After Effects as a QuickTime movie.
- Import the finished QuickTime movie into Final Cut.

Details

Final Cut Pro is built on a foundation of XML, which provides a very flexible language to move files from one application to the next. We'll take advantage of this technology in this workflow. This means that whether you are exporting a single clip or a whole sequence of clips, the process is the same.

Let's say I want to create a short effect for my upcoming children's special. It's the climatic moment where the fearsome dragon first lands atop the dreaded mountain range.

I have this great still image of a fire-breathing dragon, but it needs to animate. This is something that neither Final Cut nor Motion can do, but After Effects can – using the Puppet Tool.

This gives me a chance to show how to move files around between the applications, in addition, show you a killer effect inside After Effects.

1. To get started, I've created a new Final Cut project and two-layer sequence (Fig. 5.29). While not required, it is often helpful to build the effect you want to move to After Effects in its own Final Cut sequence to simplify the moving between applications. In this case, our sequence is 4:3 DV. On V1 is the background image of a mountain range and on V2 is the fearsome dragon (see Fig. 5.30). So, maybe this isn't the most fearsome dragon ever, but just wait! Since the dragon doesn't move, your initial fear probably subsided too quickly. We need to animate its head and wings to increase the fear factor! It's time to move this to After Effects!

> **Note: After Effects Export Tool Coming Soon**
>
> Adobe has announced, but not yet shipped, a Final Cut export tool for both Premiere and After Effects. Once this ships, you'll be able to export from both programs to Final Cut, while keeping all your clips intact, rather than consolidating them into a single QuickTime movie.

Figure 5.29 Here's what the sequence looks like.

Figure 5.30 The initial composite of our deadly dragon.

2. Select the sequence(s) you want to export and choose **File > Export > XML**. If you don't select a sequence in the Browser first, this command will export all your Browser sequences! The Source line at the top of the XML dialog box indicates how many sequences and clips are being exported in the XML file. In the Format pop-up, always select the highest level XML that your Final Cut Pro version supports (see Fig. 5.31).

Figure 5.31 The Source line at the top of the XML dialog indicates how many sequences and clips are being exported.

3. In the resulting Save dialog, give the file a name and location. Be sure **Include Master Clips** is checked. This option is useful when exporting to make sure all clips are properly included in the XML file.
4. Because After Effects doesn't import XML files directly, open Premier Pro and select **File > Import** (Fig. 5.32).

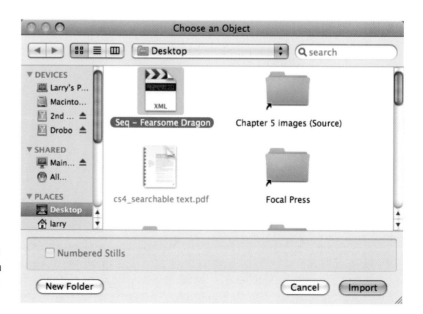

Figure 5.32 Premiere Pro uses a different interface for importing a file. Highlight the file(s) you need and click OK.

5. If Premiere Pro has any problems importing an XML file, it displays the Translation report dialog. Click **OK** (Fig. 5.33). To read this error report, go to the Project tab in the upper left corner, twirl down the folder representing all the clips and sequences you exported, and double-click the **FCP Translation Results** (see Fig. 5.34). In this case, After Effects said that it ignored a distortion setting on the still image in the background. Each report will be different, depending upon the elements in your project.

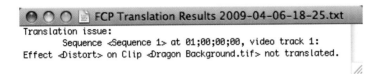

Figure 5.33 If Premiere has any problems during import, it displays this dialog. In our example, note that effects placed in Final Cut don't export into Premiere Pro.

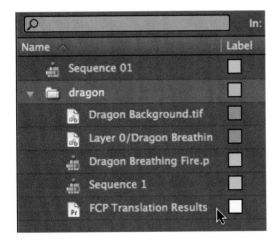

Figure 5.34 If Premiere Pro has a problem importing a Final Cut Pro sequence, it lists all problems in the FCP Translation Results report.

6. If any other sequences were created when you first started Premiere, you can delete them in the Project tab. We are only interested in the one sequence we imported.
7. Without making any other changes to the imported sequence, select **Save As** to give the project a name and save all the imported files as a Premiere Pro project. (You could use Save, but it would not allow you to rename the project.)
8. Open After Effects, and select **File > Import > Adobe Premiere Pro Project** (see Fig. 5.35). The Premiere Pro Importer dialog opens, allowing you to select the sequence

you want to import. The default setting is **All** Sequences (see Fig. 5.36). Double-click the composition you want to work on and begin creating your effect.

Figure 5.35 To open a Premiere Project in After Effects, select File > Import > Adobe Premiere Pro Project.

Figure 5.36 The Premiere Pro Importer dialog allows you to select the sequences you want to import.

At this point, your importing is complete. We don't need Premiere any more, it just served to convert the file from a Final Cut Pro XML into an After Effects composition.

Creating a Puppet Effect

The Puppet effect is an easy way to get a still image to move. And I don't mean a simple horizontal move from side to side or zooming in or out, but, in the case of our dragon, by bending its head and flapping its wings!

Let me show you how this works.

Double-click the composition to load it from the workspace Project tab into the Canvas (to use a Final Cut term; Fig. 5.37).

Figure 5.37 Double-clicking a composition loads it into the Composition window.

Select the track you want to animate by clicking the name of the track located to the left of the Timeline (Fig. 5.38).

Figure 5.38 Select the track you want to animate by clicking its name.

Select the Puppet Tool by clicking the small pushpin in the toolbar. (It turns yellow when you roll over it.) The keyboard shortcut is **Command + P** (Fig. 5.39).

Figure 5.39 Select the Puppet Tool by clicking the small yellow pushpin at the top in the toolbar.

Click the pushpin on the image where you want to set "joints," that is, points around which the image will bend (see Fig. 5.40).

What this tool does is map your entire image using a mesh – you can see it if you click the **Mesh: Show** checkbox immediately to the right of the Pin tool. This mesh allows the entire image to be deformed (bent) based on changing only a few of the control points set by the Pin (Fig. 5.41).

I've set puppet pins at the neck, the nose, where the wings meet the body, the tops of both wings, and where the leg joins the body (Fig. 5.42).

Figure 5.40 Click the image with the pushpin to set "joints," that is, where you want the image to bend.

Figure 5.41 What the Puppet Tool does is wrap your image in an interactive mesh.

Figure 5.42 The small yellow circles indicate the "joints" in the image, which are set using Puppet pins. The pin at the top of the right wing is selected.

Now the fun starts. Hold down the **Command** key. This tells After Effects you are about to set keyframes in real time. Then, click one of the control points – in this case, the one at the front of his nose – and drag it to move the head of the dragon in a very dragonly manner. (I didn't plan that pun, but I'm going to leave it in here anyway.)

Messing Up the Mesh

You can set multiple keyframes as you make multiple passes through the animation, moving a different pin each time. However, if you totally mess up and just want to restart, look for the track labeled "Mesh 1." Highlight the name and delete it. Everything goes back to normal, and you try again with no permanent harm done.

When you let go of the mouse and the Command key, the playhead (After Effects calls it the Current Time Indicator) jumps back to the beginning of the Timeline. Repeat this process for everything you want to move. In the case of my dragon, I animated the head and the tops of both wings.

To view the effect, without waiting for everything to be rendered, create a RAM Preview by choosing **Composition > Preview > RAM Preview** (Fig. 5.43).

Figure 5.43 To preview an effect without waiting for it to be rendered, select RAM Preview. This is similar to what LiveType does to display an effect.

Hmmm… I have a problem. The lower leg keeps moving, when it should be stationary on the rock. To solve this, go back to the **Puppet Tool** and select **Puppet Starch Tool** (Fig. 5.44). Then, click a few control points in the body part that you don't want to move. In our case, that will tend to hold the leg still.

Once you are happy with your effect, its time to export the movie back to Final Cut Pro. This is just a wildly cool effect!

Figure 5.44 Using a few starch pins keeps an object, like the leg of the dragon, from moving.

Exporting a Movie from After Effects

Unlike Final Cut, where we export to create a finished file of our edit, with After Effects, it's a two-step process: add the file to the Render Queue, then render (export) the movie.

Although there is an export option in After Effects, you will always be better served by the Render Queue instead, because it has more options and higher quality. Another huge benefit of using the Render Queue is that you can load in a bunch of different files, then process them all as a batch, for instance, overnight.

Here's how.

With your sequence selected and open in the Timeline, choose **Composition > Add to Render Queue**. Adding a composition to the Render Queue switches the Timeline to display the Render Queue tab.

The Timeline switches to display the contents of the Render Queue tab (Fig. 5.45). The Render Queue has three settings windows:

- Render Settings
- Output Module
- Output To

To open any settings window, click the orange text next to the corresponding white label.

Render Settings (Fig. 5.46) determines the quality, size, and format of the clip you are about to create. The cool thing about

Figure 5.45 Adding a composition to the Render Queue switches the Timeline to display the Render Queue tab.

Figure 5.46 Render Settings window.

this is that since you created your project in Final Cut and exported it to Premiere, After Effects is preset with all the correct settings so that most of the time you won't need to touch this.

Output Module (Fig. 5.47) controls the video format of the clip you are about to export. Again, all these settings are generally

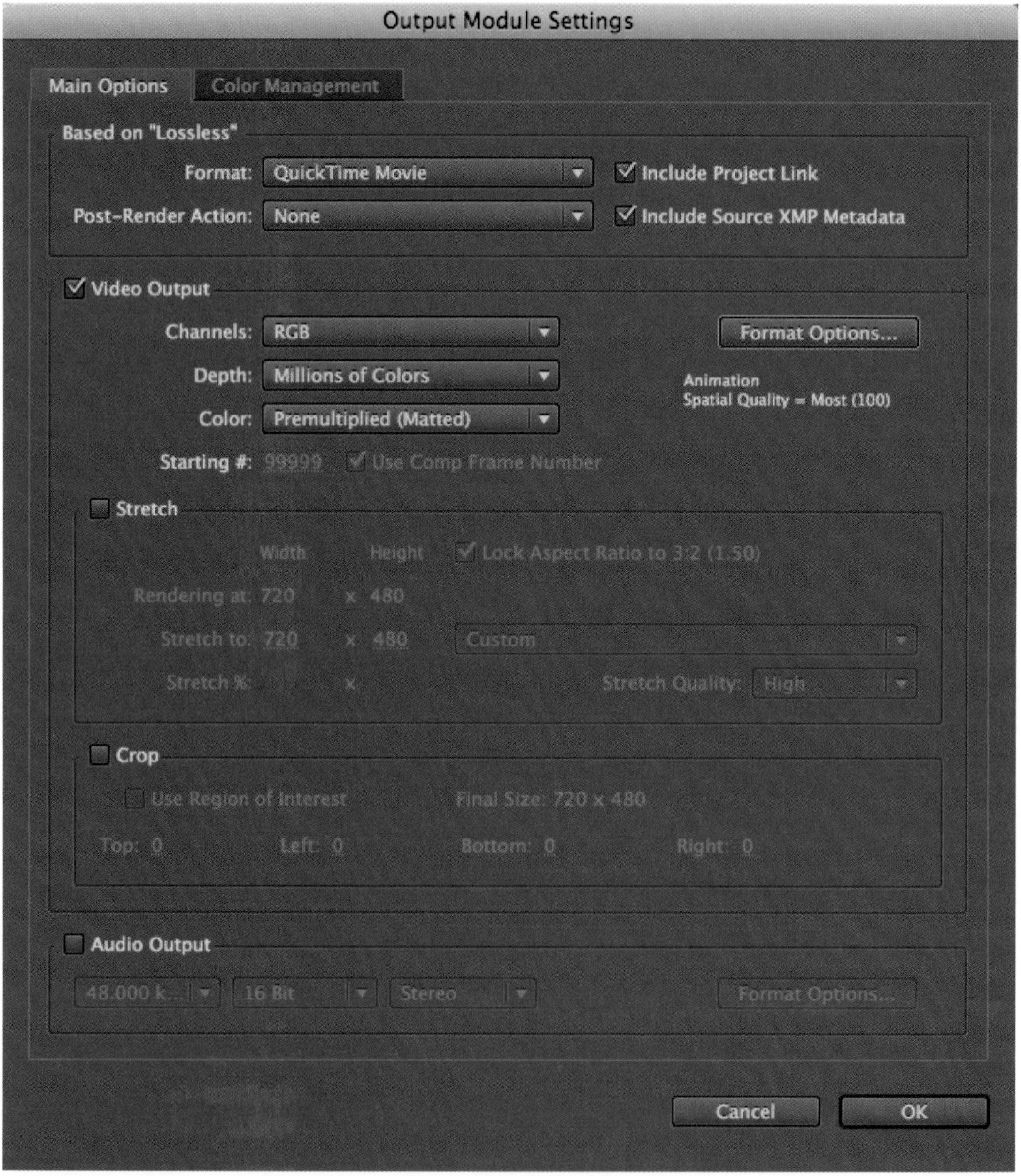

Figure 5.47 Output Module controls what video format you'll create when you export. The Format Options button is critical and must be set prior to output.

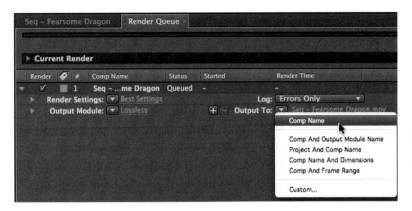

Figure **5.48** Back on the main Render Queue screen, Output To determines what to call your exported file and where it will be stored.

correct – except Format Options, which we will discuss in a minute.

Output To (Fig. 5.48) determines the file name of the soon-to-be-created file and where it will be stored.

Picking the Output Format

In general, you won't need to adjust Render Settings. And creating a file name and location for Output To is straightforward. The trick is to properly set the Output Module. And here's my suggestion.

If you are creating a finished effect that will simply be played back in Final Cut, and you want to avoid any additional rendering, then set the Format Options to match your Final Cut sequence (i.e., DV NTSC 4:3).

If, on the other hand, you need to retain the transparency of a clip, then set the Format Options to **Animation** if you are using Final Cut Pro 6, or **ProRes 4444** for if you have Final Cut Pro 7. (ProRes 4444 provides higher-quality, with smaller file sizes, than Animation.)

ProRes 4444 and Animation files can't, generally, be played in real-time, and they always need to render inside Final Cut. But, they provide absolutely the highest-quality. Again, you don't need to select this option unless you need transparency, because Final Cut is going to render the clip again.

If, instead, you want real-time playback, extremely good quality, plan to do additional effects or rendering in Final Cut Pro, and don't need to retain transparency, use ProRes 422 HQ. This new codec does everything that Animation does, except provide transparency, in a smaller file size with real-time playback. And it's supported in both Final Cut Pro 6 and 7.

Here's how to set the Format Setting:

- Click the orange text for **Output Module**.
- Click the **Format Options** button.

- From the Compression Type, select the video format you want to use.
- The other options are generally good, so click **OK**.

Figure 5.49 To begin the output process, click the **Render** button on the far right side of the Render Queue window.

To begin outputting your files, click the **Render** button on the far right side of the window (Fig. 5.49). An orange line extends along the top of the Render Queue tab showing the status of the output. The **Stop** and **Pause** buttons allow you to, yup, stop or pause the output.

When the file is complete, a cheerful tone beeps to let you know After Effects is done.

Simply import the finished file into Final Cut and continue editing your project.

Thoughts on Using Automatic Duck

Automatic Duck (www.automaticduck.com) is a very clever, reliable, third-party utility that allows you to move files easily between Final Cut Pro and a variety of other applications. The benefit of using Automatic Duck is that it takes the XML file that you export from Final Cut and allows you to import it directly into After Effects without first loading it into Premiere Pro.

Another benefit is that Automatic Duck preserves Motion tab settings, including opacity, transitions, and filter settings, provided that the same filter runs on both Final Cut Pro and After Effects.

If you only occasionally move files from Final Cut to After Effects, using Premiere Pro is a perfectly fine way to work.

However, if you are regularly moving files between the two programs, the speed and flexibility that Automatic Duck provides will more than pay you back for its cost.

Summary

This chapter concentrated on moving files between Final Cut Pro and a variety of Adobe Production Premium applications. What you do with them once they arrive is limited only by your imagination.

My Story

Mark Spencer
Freelance editor and motion graphics artist
Day Street Productions
www.daystreet.com
www.applemotion.net

Larry's note: This whole chapter talked about the benefits of moving files from one application to another. This story, from Mark Spencer, is a great illustration of why you should use the right tool for the job.

Every freelancer knows that when opportunity comes knocking, you open the door, even if your hands are full.

A new client contacted me about creating an opening-animated sequence for a video that (of course) needed to be completed immediately. I was slammed with work, but I said I'd be happy to take a look.

Figure 5.50 Mark Spencer (um, on the right).

Thankfully, they had existing artwork that they wanted to animate: a poster of an upcoming conference. Even more thankfully, it was created in Photoshop, and they had the source file. One of my favorite ways to work is combining Adobe Photoshop with Apple Motion – and here was the perfect opportunity.

Often, I don't receive a separate file with any layers or I'm working from a flat photograph, and I need to use Photoshop's selection tools to break out elements, and then use the cloning tools to fill in the holes behind the separated layers. This takes some time. Luckily, this artwork was all created in Photoshop with layers, so no selections or cloning would be needed. The Photoshop file contained dozens of layers, including type, shapes, blend modes, and layer styles. I spent a few minutes consolidating some layers together and converting layers with layer styles applied to Smart Objects – this way the layer styles would appear in Motion, but the Photoshop file would still be editable.

I brought the file into Motion as "all layers." Every layer appeared with the same name they were given in Photoshop – and the blend modes were all intact, as were the layer styles applied to the Smart Objects. I adjusted the anchor points of each layer to the center of the composition, added a camera, and then used the Heads Up Display to spread the layers away from each other in z-space while automatically scaling them to compensate so that they look unchanged from the camera's perspective.

I decided to tweak the fonts and layer styles, so I opened the Photoshop file back up and made a few adjustments. In Motion, the file updated automatically. This ability to go back and forth between applications and make changes anywhere in the process is critical to my workflow.

From there I set two keyframes to lock the camera's beginning and ending positions and then pushed and rotated the camera straight through the layers on the first keyframe. These keyframes created a smooth pullback that revealed each layer flying away from the camera as they arranged themselves perfectly to form the final image. Watching the animation in real time, I adjusted the keyframe interpolation for a nice, smooth landing, exported the final movie, and uploaded it for the client.

Total time involved: about an hour. Client: thrilled. Me: on to the next project!

6

WORKING WITH STILLS

Probably nothing in video editing causes more confusion than working with still images. Whether prepping scans of images for a video montage, or exporting still images from Final Cut for use on the Web, stills are a mess.

This is all due to the sad fact that computers display their images as a collection of square pixels, whereas video displays the images using a wide variety of rectangular pixels (see Fig. 6.1). Even in HD, there's no consistency in pixel shape. Some formats, like RED or HDCAM SR, use square pixels. Other formats, like HDV, use a variety of differently shaped rectangles. Consequently, the pixel shapes don't match between computer and video images.

Sigh . . . its enough to drive us all nuts.

This chapter has six main sections:

- Explaining this whole pixel mess
- Single-layer images with no transparency
- Single-layer images that you want to do moves on
- Photoshop images (PSD) that contain transparency
- Correcting freeze frames exported from Final Cut into Photoshop
- Thoughts on the differences between computer and video images

Explaining This Whole Pixel Mess

You've probably heard more than once about the differences in pixel shape (also called the pixel "aspect ratio") between video and computers: video uses rectangular pixels, whereas computers use square pixels (see Fig. 6.1). Results of this mismatch are imported still images that look stretched in video. The problem is figuring out how to fix it.

Here's a good place to start: don't confuse the shape of the image with the shape of the pixels inside it. For instance, as Fig. 6.2 illustrates, I can fill a 4:3 shape with 12 square pixels or 15 rectangular pixels.

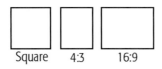

Square   4:3   16:9

Figure 6.1 This is the cause of the problem: computers create images using square pixels, whereas NTSC 4:3 video uses thin rectangles, and 16:9 NTSC video uses fat rectangles. (Shapes are exaggerated for dramatic effect.)

If we wanted everything to be consistent, we'd use square pixels everywhere. But, video has a bigger objective: keeping file sizes down. By adjusting the shape of the pixels that make up an image, they can decrease the number of pixels needed to create an image, which decreases file size.

In and of itself, this isn't bad. What makes this difficult is that different video formats use different shapes, and almost none of them match the square pixels of the computer.

For instance, both NTSC and PAL use rectangular pixels, but the shapes of the rectangles are different. 4:3 NTSC uses tall/thin pixels, whereas 4:3 PAL uses short/fat pixels. 16:9 NTSC uses short/fat pixels, whereas 16:9 PAL uses even shorter and fatter pixels. HD uses 12 different pixel shapes—from stretched rectangles to squares!

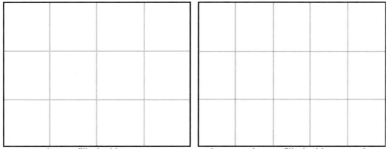

An image filled with squares.   The same image filled with rectangles.

Figure 6.2 If we take the same shape and fill it with pixels, the number of pixels is determined both by the size of the shape and the size of the pixels. The shape on the left uses 12 square pixels (4 × 3), whereas the same size shape on the right uses 15 rectangular pixels (5 × 3). In other words, the total number of pixels doesn't match, even though the size of the shape is the same.

For Those Who Want to Know

 For those who want to know how we got ourselves into this sorry state, Chris Meyer of ProVideo Coalition wrote a blog recently that describes the reasons for different pixel shapes. You can read it here: provideocoalition. com/index.php/ cmg_keyframes/story/ par_for_the_course/

Here's an example of why we need to care about this problem. The image size of 4:3 NTSC video is 720 × 480. If, in Photoshop, we draw a perfect circle contained in a 720 × 480 image, it looks beautiful. However, when we save this image as a PNG, and import it into Final Cut, the square pixels which Photoshop used to create the image get converted to the rectangular pixels which DV NTSC uses.

As Fig. 6.3 illustrates, our perfect Photoshop circle is now an egg. In fact, when we compare it with a perfect circle created in Final Cut, as shown in the image on the right, the problem becomes completely obvious: still images need special treatment to look good in video.

The confusion caused by these different aspect ratios can lead to heavy drinking if not dealt with correctly!

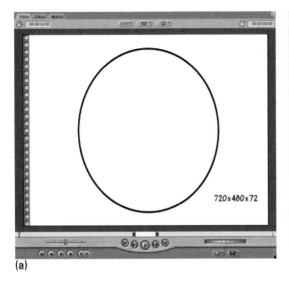 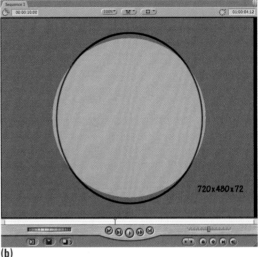

(a) (b)

Figure 6.3 (a) The image on the left is a PNG file, created in Photoshop, containing a perfect circle, then imported into Final Cut. (b) The image on the right compares the circle created in Photoshop with a circle created in Final Cut. The shapes should match, but they don't.

Using Photoshop's Film and Video Presets

Recent versions of Photoshop have attempted to solve this problem through the use of presets. Now, when you create a new image, changing the preset from **Custom** to **Film & Video** allows you to select a wide variety of presets for popular video image sizes.

This is not a bad solution—if you are in a hurry, use them.

However, these presets have two fairly significant problems: first, Apple and Adobe used different math to figure out what these ratios should be. This means that the circles you create in Photoshop will be close to circular in shape, but still "egg-shaped" when you import them into Final Cut Pro. Second, these presets don't account for all the different video formats out there. In a few pages, Table 1 will provide specific image sizes you can use to create properly sized still images for Final Cut.

For now, however, here's how these presets work:

To select a specific preset when creating a new image, select **Film & Video** from the Preset pop-up menu (see Fig. 6.4). This determines the shape of the pixels used by the video format.

Next, select the image size from the **Size** menu (Fig. 6.5). (You can see already that only a limited number of video formats are available, because no one would expect Photoshop to support all the video formats that Final Cut Pro supports.)

Using these presets simplifies compensating for the differences in shape between computer pixels and video pixels.

Figure 6.4 When creating a new graphic in Photoshop, selecting a Film & Video preset allows you to configure the pixel aspect ratio to match the video format you are working with.

What to Do When Your Widescreen Image Isn't

When you use a Photoshop preset to create an anamorphic (16:9) single-layer graphic, Final Cut may not automatically set the Anamorphic flag correctly. This means that your imported images look very squished. To fix this, before editing the clip to the Timeline, before editing the clip to the Timeline, select the offending graphic in Final Cut's Browser, then scroll to the right until you see the Anamorphic column and put a check mark in the column. It resizes your graphic so that it looks correct (Fig. 6.6).

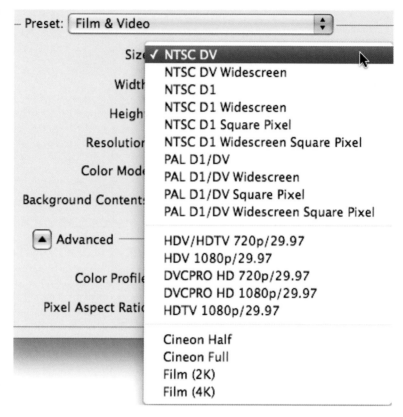

Figure 6.5 Select the correct pixel aspect ratio from the Size pop-up menu.

Figure 6.6 Sometimes, Final Cut does not set the imported graphic to anamorphic when you use a Photoshop preset. To fix this, check the Anamorphic column for that file in the Browser.

Does Anyone Use a Square Pixel besides Photoshop?

Well, yes. RED, some AVCHD formats and HDCAM SR all use square pixels. There will probably be others in the future – why should anything be consistent?

So, here's the summary: if you want a fast solution, which is reasonably close, use the Photoshop Film & Video presets. If you want to be absolutely sure your images import with correct aspect ratios, keep reading.

When Does DPI Matter?

DPI matters for printing, but not for video.

All video images have a fixed resolution. This means that regardless of how big, or small, your TV set is, the number of pixels it displays remains the same. This is not true for computers. As a computer monitor gets bigger, it is able to display more information.

Here's the easiest way to think of this: if computer monitors worked like video monitors, the bigger the TV set, the greater the resolution of your image. In other words, you could switch to viewing HD just by buying a TV set with a bigger screen.

Sadly, this isn't true. Regardless of the size of the video monitor, all video images in the same video format have the same size and number of pixels. Because this resolution is fixed, we sometimes say that video has a 72-DPI resolution. A more accurate way of expressing this is that video only counts the total pixels across by the total pixels high. The DPI is meaningless.

There are three main categories of video images:

- Standard-definition (SD)
- High-definition (HD)
- Images used for high-resolution digital intermediate CGI work, like 2K, 4K, or greater.

This book looks at the first two categories, which is the principal domain of video and Final Cut Pro.

Picking the Right Image Size

Within SD video, we have three video formats, each with 4:3 and 16:9 aspect ratios:

- NTSC DV
- NTSC SD
- PAL

Within HD, we have a wide variety of formats, but two principal image sizes, both with a 16:9 aspect ratio:

- 1920 × 1080 (called 1080)
- 1280 × 720 (called 720)

Just as we have multiple video formats, we also have two types of images:

- Images without transparency in them—photographs and scans
- Images with transparency in them—Photoshop documents

Most often, images without transparency consist of a single layer, stored as a TIFF, PNG, or JPEG. Images with transparency consist of either a single layer, like a company logo with an alpha channel, or a multilayer extravaganza. These images are most commonly stored as a PSD.

Sizing Single-Layer Images without Transparency

Just when things seem most bleak, there is an easy way to size single-layer images without transparency: create your single-layer image in square pixels at a size that compensates for the differences in pixel shape.

Before Your Object

 Although it is true that more than PSD files contain transparency, for this chapter, we will make the following assumption: when we are discussing images without transparency, we are referring to JPEG, TIFF, and PNG formats. When we are discussing images with transparency, we are referring to PSD documents. The reason for this distinction is that Final Cut Pro handles these image types differently, as you are about to see.

If you create your stills in Photoshop according to Table 1 your circles will remain perfectly round when you import them into Final Cut.

Here's the key step: when you create your image in Photoshop, set the Preset to **Custom** (see Fig. 6.7). This tells Photoshop to use square pixels when creating your image, then, from Table 1 below, find your image format and the aspect ratio for your sequence. The far-right column contains the pixel dimensions you need to enter into Photoshop when you create your image.

Figure 6.7 When creating a new image in Photoshop, set the Preset to Custom to configure your image using square pixels.

Here's the table that makes sizing single-layer, full-frame images easy.

Table 1: Sizing Full Screen Images

Video format	Aspect ratio	Create your image at size
DV NTSC	4:3	720 × 540
	16:9	853 × 480
SD NTSC*	4:3	720 × 547
	16:9	853 × 486
PAL	4:3	768 × 576
	16:9	1024 × 576
HD 720	16:9**	1280 × 720
HD 1080	16:9**	1920 × 1080

Because all video images are fixed in resolution, it is common practice to set the DPI of your image in Photoshop to 72. DPI is relevant in printing, but not for video. The only important numbers in video are the total number of pixels across and the total number of pixels down.

*NTSC has two image sizes: one for DV and the other for broadcast (also called D1). All consumer cameras shoot a DV image size. If you are shooting and editing a broadcast video format, such as Beta SP or DigiBeta, use the SD NTSC image size.

**While there are a wide variety of HD video formats, regardless of which HD format you are using, you create your graphic size based on the final output size of your HD sequence.

Choosing a Still Image File Type

All images created in digital video are bitmapped; so are still images taken with a digital camera. Bitmapped images are created from pixels, and do not scale well. You can make these images smaller, but not larger, than 100% in size. Increasing their size beyond 100% makes the image blurry, filled with strangely colored artifacts, and unpleasant to look at.

Because Photoshop was designed to work with bitmapped images, it is the ideal tool to use in conjunction with Final Cut.

I mentioned at the beginning of this chapter that the easiest way to think about your images is to divide them into two categories: images that contain transparency and those that don't.

And the reason for this is that Final Cut imports nontransparent images as graphic files, whereas it opens PSD images with transparency as sequences. And there is a significant difference between how Final Cut Pro handles graphics vs. sequences.

While there are a variety of image formats to choose from, I recommend saving your nontransparent images as either TIFF or PNG images. Both are uncompressed formats that work perfectly with Final Cut. (I use TIFFs for my projects. However, since TIFF files tend to be larger, many editors prefer to use PNGs.)

Try to avoid using JPEG (also called JPG) images. These are highly compressed files and often have artifacts, or image glitches, which degrade the image. Although Final Cut Pro handles JPEG images with no problem, it is generally considered good practice to avoid them where possible.

Since JPEG images are all over the Web, sometimes using them can't be avoided. Also, you don't need to resave a JPEG image as a PNG; Final Cut handles them just fine. However, prior to import into Final Cut, you should size all images according to Table 1 above.

Although Final Cut Pro prefers bitmapped images, you can also import PDF files and Adobe Illustrator files. Both these files store their images as vectors, which video doesn't support. So, Final

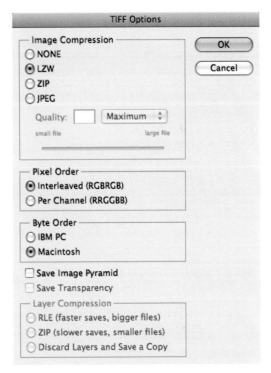

Figure 6.8 Recommended settings when saving a TIFF file.

How to Save TIFFs

Ever wonder which setting to choose when saving a TIFF (Fig. 6.8)? I generally use LZW—it creates smaller files than None. While current versions of Final Cut Pro support ZIP-compressed TIFFs, earlier versions didn't. So, I got in the habit of using LZW. Although the file sizes are smaller, don't use JPEG compression. (This may be why many editors prefer PNG; they don't have to worry about these choices.)

Why Not Vectors?

Since vector images, such as those created by Adobe Illustrator, describe an image as a mathematical equation rather than as a pixel, they can scale to any size with no loss in resolution at all. The fonts on your Mac are vectors, also.

While vectors sound great, the problem is that video doesn't know a vector from a potato. So, it can't use them. This is why Final Cut converts all vector images into bitmaps during import, which solves this problem.

When Should You Not Be Sharp?

While the folks at the National Association of Photoshop Professionals recommend using Bicubic Sharper for scaling operations, you may find that scaling images with gradients, like sunsets or facial close-ups, may look better when scaled using just Bicubic. Still, my first try is always Bicubic Sharper.

Cut just converts them to a bitmap that matches your current Easy Setup settings during import.

Scaling Digital Photographs

If you want to import a digital photo into Final Cut, everything I've already talked about is still true. But, there is one more thing I want to mention and that is how to scale the image.

Never scale a bitmapped image larger than 100%. You can make images smaller with no problem, but scaling an image larger decreases the resolution, and the image looks worse the larger you make it. To zoom into an image, create it larger in the first place.

So, bring your image into Photoshop and crop it to match the image sizes listed in Table 1; unless you want to do pans and zooms on the image, in which case, Table 2, still a couple of pages away, provides the sizes you need to use.

Photoshop's scaling is far superior to Final Cut Pro's scaling. So, I suggest doing as much image manipulation as you can in Photoshop.

And here's a secret I learned from the National Association of Photoshop Professionals: when resizing an image in Photoshop using **Image > Image size**, always select **Bicubic Sharper** (see Fig. 6.9). The default setting is Bicubic. Bicubic Sharper improves the perception of edges and focus without degrading your image. Whether you are increasing an image size (which is rare) or decreasing it (which is frequent), always use Bicubic Sharper.

So, here are the workflow steps to properly prep a digital still image for Final Cut Pro. For this example, we will create a 16:9 DV NTSC graphic:

1. Open your digital photo in Photoshop.
2. Select the **Crop** tool (press **C**) and, in the toolbar at the top, set the Width to **853**, the Height to **480**, and the DPI to **72** (see Fig. 6.10).
3. Press **Enter** to resize your image.
4. Save the image as a PNG, or TIFF, file.
5. Import the image into Final Cut Pro.
6. Edit it into your Timeline.

Setting the Correct Color Profile

Prior to Snow Leopard (OS X 10.6), our Macs will use a different midpoint gray setting than video uses. This gray-scale setting is called *gamma*. Macs display images lighter, using a gamma of 1.8. Video uses a darker gamma of 2.2. This means that an image that looks perfect on your computer monitor may look light and washed out in video.

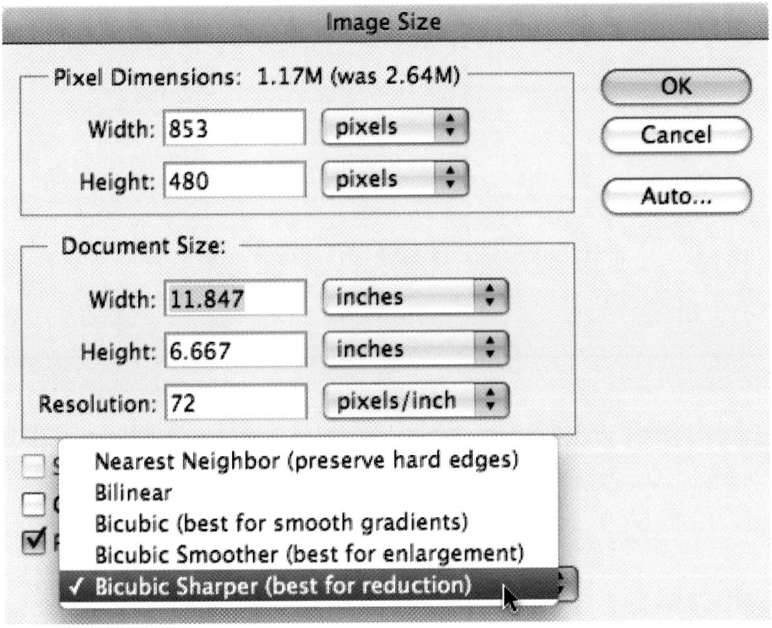

Figure 6.9 When resizing an image, change the scaling setting in Image > Image Size to Bicubic Sharper.

Once Snow Leopard ships and we all upgrade to it, our Macs will change to a gamma of 2.2, which is the same as video, and this gray-scale problem goes away.

Until then, we need to prevent this gray-scale shift. To do this, we need to assign a different color profile to any still that is destined for video:

1. Open the still image in Photoshop.
2. Choose **Edit > Assign Profile**.

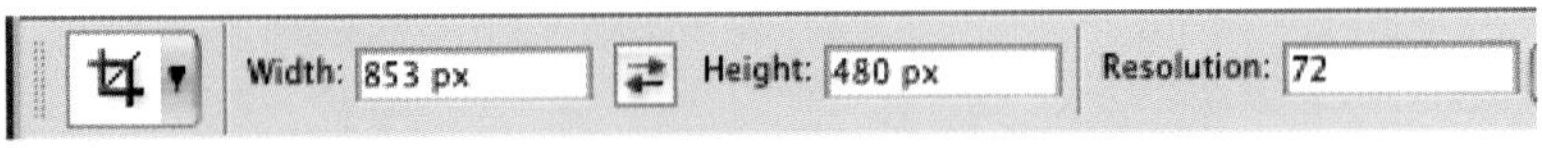

Figure 6.10 To crop an image to a specific size, select the Crop tool, then enter the image size you need. This is an example of a 16:9 NTSC image.

When Should You Change the Size (Rescale) of an Image?

There has been a lot of discussion on the Web about when is the best time to scale a single-layer full-screen image—in Photoshop before importing into Final Cut or after it is imported into Final Cut. Based on the testing I've done, my recommendation is to create your image in Photoshop at the sizes I've outlined here, and import them into Final Cut. Some have written about doing a second scaling step inside Photoshop to create a "presquished" graphic to match the video aspect ratio before importing. I have not seen any significant improvement in quality by doing so; it is an extra step, creating another image master that needs to be tracked. I don't recommend the process for nontransparent images. However, I do recommend it for PSD files. More on that in a minute.

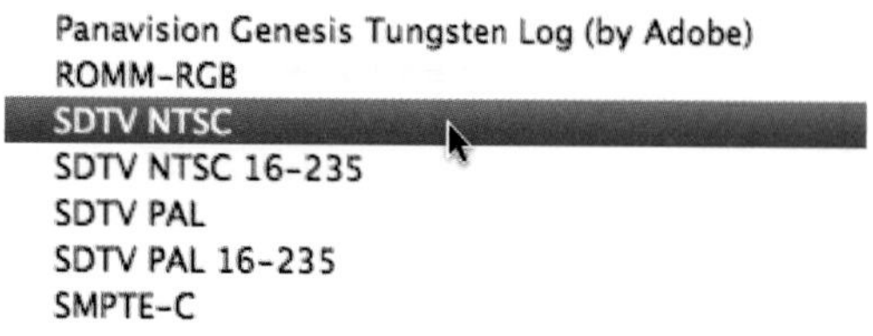

Panavision Genesis Tungsten Log (by Adobe)
ROMM–RGB
SDTV NTSC
SDTV NTSC 16–235
SDTV PAL
SDTV PAL 16–235
SMPTE–C

Figure 6.11 When working with SD video, be sure to set the Color Profile to SDTV NTSC or SDTV PAL, depending upon the video format you are using.

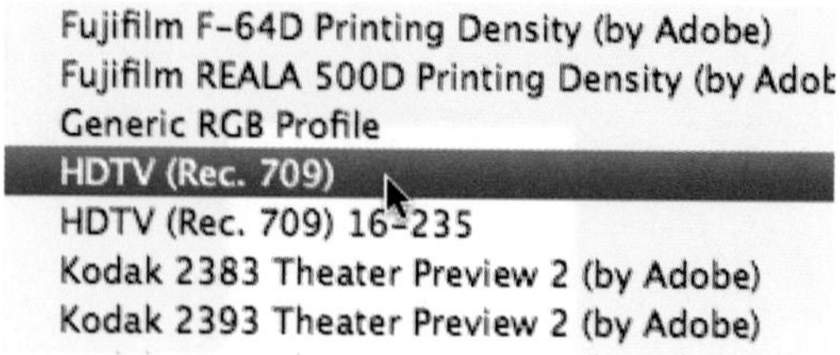

Fujifilm F–64D Printing Density (by Adobe)
Fujifilm REALA 500D Printing Density (by Adobe
Generic RGB Profile
HDTV (Rec. 709)
HDTV (Rec. 709) 16–235
Kodak 2383 Theater Preview 2 (by Adobe)
Kodak 2393 Theater Preview 2 (by Adobe)

Figure 6.12 When working with HD video, set the Color Profile to HDTV (Rec. 709). Be careful not to pick HDTV (Rec. 709) 16-235.

3. If you are working in SD NTSC, set the Color Profile to **SDTV NTSC**. For PAL, use **SDTV PAL**. If your version of Photoshop doesn't have those profiles, use **sRGB** or **SMPTE-C** (see Fig. 6.11).
4. If you are working in any flavor of HD, set the Destination Space Profile to **HDTV (Rec. 709)** (Fig. 6.12).

This assigns a Color Profile that Final Cut recognizes to make sure the image you adjust in Photoshop looks the same once it gets into Final Cut.

Still Images Have Durations

Whenever you import an image into Final Cut, the imported image is given a default duration of 10 seconds and a length of 2 minutes.

There are several ways you can change the duration. If you are making it shorter than 2 min, simply load the image into the Viewer and set an In and Out, the same as any other clip.

However, if you need the image to run longer than 2 min, you have several options:

- In **User Preferences > Editing tab**, change the **Still/Freeze Duration** to the length you need. This is a good option if you have a number of images to import and you want them all to be the same length.
- In the Browser, display the **Length** column and type in the value you need.
- Load the clip from the Browser into the Viewer; in the Duration box in the top-left corner, change the duration to the length you want before editing it into the Timeline.

However, this technique doesn't work once you edit a clip into the Timeline, then load it back into the Viewer.

Changing the duration of an image allows you to create really long clips, for instance, to superimpose a logo over an entire sequence.

What's the Difference between Duration and Length?

 Duration is the time between the In and the Out.

Length is the time from the start of the clip to the end of the clip, regardless of where the In and Out are set.

By Default, the Length Column Is Hidden

Just to keep you on your toes, Final Cut hides the Length column. To display it, Control-click the header in any Browser column, except the Name column. In this illustration, I'm clicking the In column. Select Show Length, and it is displayed to the left of the column you clicked (Fig. 6.13). You can change the length of any graphic image that hasn't been edited to the Timeline.

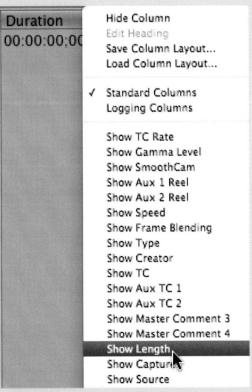

Figure 6.13 Length column.

To change a duration, either load each clip into the Viewer and add an In and an Out or in the Browser, enter a new value in the Duration column. While this change needs to be made individually for each clip, here's a fast way to change the default setting, so all your imported images have the correct length.

Go to **Final Cut Pro > User Preferences > Editing** tab. In the top-right corner, change the **Still/Freeze Duration** to the duration you want. (Remember, duration is the time between the In and the Out) (see Fig. 6.14).

	Name	▼ Length	Duration
	Seq – Montage	00:00:00:00	00:00:00:00
	Caliente-poppies.jpg	00:05:00:01	00:03:00:00

Figure 6.14 Changing the duration is a fast way to change the duration of all imported graphics to the same amount.

Creating Still Image Montages Set to Music

I use this technique to change the Still/Freeze Duration when creating a montage of still images set to music. Because the music has a consistent beat, I calculate the time between downbeats and change the import duration to match that time. Then, all my clips automatically end on the downbeat, which reduces the amount of setting Ins and Outs and trimming that I need to do.

Sizing Still Images for Movement

The most common single-layer image is a digital photo or a scan of an old photograph. In such a file, all the image elements are on a single layer. Most often, we simply import this into Final Cut and edit it into our sequence as is. However, sometimes, we want to do some moves on the image using the keyframes available in the Motion tab.

Keep in mind that all digital photos use square pixels, so you'll still need to prep them to compensate for the differences in aspect ratio. However, now you have two choices:

- To keep the image full-screen with no movement
- To move around inside the image

If you don't want the image to move, size it according to Table 1 that I provided earlier. This allows you to make sure all the elements you need to see are framed properly.

However, if you want to do moves around the image, including zooms, keep reading.

Prepping to Move Inside a Single-Layer Image

Fortunately, everything we've already talked about with still images is still true. Remember earlier in this chapter that I mentioned the best an image will look is when you keep its size to 100% or smaller?

Well, here's where that becomes an issue. To move around inside an image requires that the image be bigger than your video frame. (Making it bigger than the video frame means that as we move the image around, we won't scoot off the edges.)

This means that we need to create the image to compensate for the differences in pixel shapes and make the image bigger than the screen size. In the past, we just used multiples of the original dimensions. The problem I had with this is that all too often Final Cut would get confused and convert an oversize DV image into HDV. At which point, resetting it back to DV became a real pain.

So, instead of multiplying each dimension by 2 or 3, which caused all this confusion, I decided to multiply each image dimension by 2.5. This creates image sizes that are unique to each video format, with no confusion between the formats.

This means that it's time for another table.

By creating the images at the sizes listed here, you can pan, tilt, or zoom into an image up to 2.5× without revealing an edge or magnifying the image more than 100%.

Table 2: Sizing Images for Moves

Video format	Aspect ratio	Create your single-layer image at size
DV NTSC	4:3	1800 × 1350 × 72
	16:9	2133 × 1200 × 72
SD NTSC	4:3	1800 × 1368 × 72
	16:9	2133 × 1215 × 72
PAL	4:3	1920 × 1140 × 72
	16:9	2560 × 1140 × 72
HD 720	–	2560 × 1440 × 72
HD 1080	–	3840 × 2160 × 72

Another Way to Do Moves on Stills—PhotoMotion

Creating movement in Final Cut Pro is done by loading a clip into the Viewer and setting keyframes in the Motion tab. This technique has not changed for many versions of Final Cut, and many books and tutorials discuss how to do it.

However, the process is time-consuming and, depending upon the move you are creating, it can be frustratingly difficult to get to look right.

There are a number of programs that create moves on stills, including iMovie, iPhoto, and Moving Picture. However, each has their limitations.

Recently, at the NAB Show (the trade show of the National Association of Broadcasters), a new piece of software—called PhotoMotion—was released from Gee Three Software (www. geethree.com) that makes creating moves on still images, a piece of cake.

Because this fills a gap between what Photoshop can do and what Final Cut can do, I want to quickly showcase it here. PhotoMotion installs two generator plug-ins for Final Cut—one that creates moves on a single image and the other that creates image montages.

After purchasing and installing the PhotoMotion software, open Final Cut. In the Viewer, go to the lower right corner, and in the Generator menu, select **Slick FX > PhotoMotion** (Fig. 6.15).

Is Any Image Too Big for Final Cut Pro?

 Yes. Final Cut prefers that all images be smaller than 4000 pixels on a side. Final Cut 5 crashed if you imported an image greater than 4000 pixels. Final Cut is no longer crashing, but caution is still called for. Remember, DPI is not important. What is important is the total number of pixels across by the total number of pixels down.

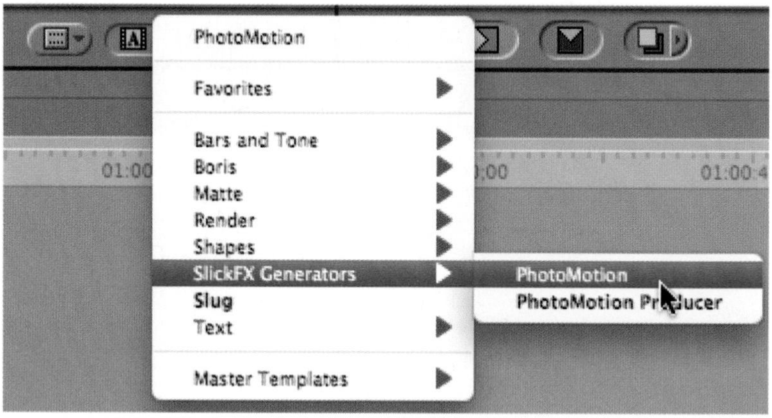

Figure 6.15 PhotoMotion is a generator. To animate a still image, select SlickFX > PhotoMotion from the Generator menu in the lower right corner of the Viewer.

- Edit the resulting clip from the Viewer to the Timeline and adjust it to the length you want.
- Double-click the clip to load it back into the Viewer.
- Click the **Controls** tab, then click **Configure** to enter the PhotoMotion interface (Fig. 6.16).

Figure 6.16 This is the PhotoMotion interface. The starting position of the image is shown in the left window, and the ending position is on the right.

By default, PhotoMotion displays the contents of your Pictures folder. You can drag other image folders from the desktop into PhotoMotion. (If Final Cut is blocking your view of the desktop, press **Command + H** to hide Final Cut.)

Drag the image you want to animate from the display of images on the left into the dark area on the right. By default, the image you select is displayed so that the entire image fills the frame (see Fig. 6.17).

Figure 6.17 In this example, we are zooming from the wide shot to a closer view of the tree. Note that I am not zooming past 100%, as indicated by the top line of the box on the right. This allows me to maintain the highest image quality.

While PhotoMotion works with nonstandard image sizes, I cropped the ones used for this illustration according to Table 1 above.

The image on the left shows the starting position of the image. One of the benefits of using PhotoMotion is that if you are adding transitions, you are able to see the entire image, without the transition getting in the way; handles are added automatically.

By adjusting the sliders under each image you can control how far to zoom in, or out. By dragging the image in the window, you control where the pan or zoom is going to begin and end. In this case, I'm doing a slow zoom-in to the tree on the right side of the frame.

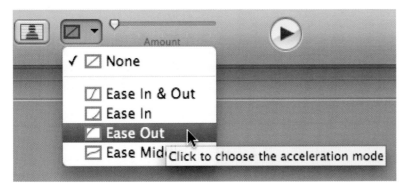

Figure 6.18 Each move can start slowly (i.e., increase in speed), end slowly, or slow down in the middle.

From the pop-up menu at the bottom (see Fig. 6.18), you can quickly add an Ease In (slow start), Ease Middle (slow in the middle of the move), or Ease Out (slow ending) to your move. By adjusting the Amount slider, you can control how much acceleration you want to add.

Click **OK**, and your animated image is loaded into the Timeline, ready for preview and rendering.

While there are many more features to PhotoMotion, this covers the highlights. After spending countless hours creating movement using keyframes in Final Cut, this is a much faster and more flexible way to animate stills. (It even has a built-in flicker-reduction filter that works remarkably well.)

Working with PSD Files Containing Transparency

The process of preparing single-layer still images works great—as long as the entire image fills the frame and is saved as a PNG or TIFF. (You can also save images as JPEGs, but the quality isn't as high.)

Things go awry when we start working with PSD files that contain transparency, either single-layer logos or multiple-layer graphic masterpieces.

When Final Cut imports a PSD file, it always turns the file into a sequence. Because of this, it doesn't compensate for the

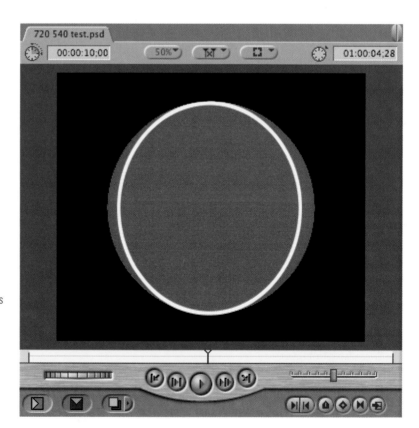

Figure 6.19 The white circle was created in Photoshop as a 720 × 540 × 72 single-layer image and saved as a PSD file. However, it doesn't match the red circle, which was created in Final Cut when imported into a 4:3 NTSC DV sequence.

differences between pixel shapes the same way it does for graphic images. It does something entirely different.

This means we are back to the circles-becoming-eggs problem, as Fig. 6.19 illustrates (Deep, depressed, sigh).

For images imported as sequences, we must use a different approach I call "presquishing."

Presquishing involves creating the image, saving the image, then changing the size of the image in Photoshop before importing it into Final Cut, to compensate for the differences in pixel aspect ratio.

"But wait a minute!" I hear you exclaim, "Why not do this for every image?" Well, you can. But, I don't like this approach mainly because it involves extra steps and multiple files—a master file and a copy—which I then need to track. I like keeping things simple. But, in the case of PSDs, that's not possible.

Here are the steps to make this technique work:

- Create your image at the size indicated in Table 3 below. If you are given a PSD file at the wrong size, create a new image at the correct size, then copy and paste the graphic into this properly sized file.
- Finish all graphics work and save the file as a **PSD**. This becomes your image master file, in case future changes are necessary. (And they almost always are, clients being who they are.)
- Go to **Image > Image size**, uncheck Constrain Proportions, which allows changing the size of one dimension, such as height, without adjusting the other (Fig. 6.20).

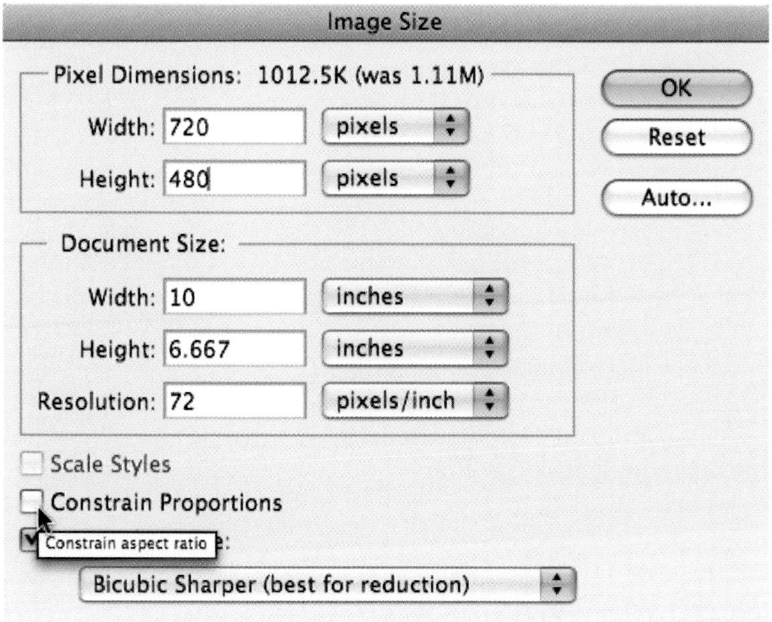

Figure 6.20 To presquish an image, go to Image > Image size and turn off Constrain Proportions.

- Change either the width or the height to match Table 3, below.
- Click **OK**. Now, your image should look egg-shaped (see Fig. 6.21).

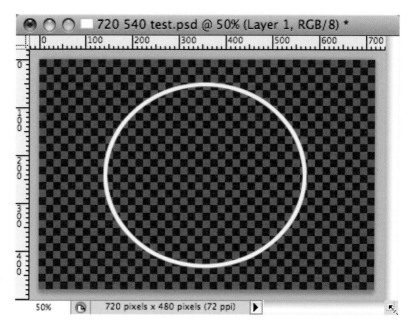

Figure 6.21 When you squish an image in Photoshop, it looks egg-like. That's OK, because when you bring it into Final Cut, it will look fine.

- Save the squished file also as a PSD and give it a name to identify it as your presquished image. I tend to use the name of the master file, followed by "(squished)."
- Here's the critical next step. When importing a PSD, Final Cut treats it as a sequence, not as a graphics file. So, open Final Cut, then, *before* you import the image, check **Final Cut Pro > Easy Setup** to make sure the active setup matches the video format of your sequence. Final Cut uses the sequence settings to determine how to shape the pixels of the incoming PSD file.
- Then, import the squished file into Final Cut Pro. It imports the file as a new sequence and loads it into the Browser.
- At this point, you can open it into the Timeline.

What I most often do, when working with multilayer PSD files, is to open each PSD file into its own sequence, then copy and paste the individual clips that I need from the PSD sequence into my main sequence for editing.

When you follow this approach, as Fig. 6.22 illustrates, your images will be in perfect shape. Ta-DAH!

If you need to make changes, don't make them to the squished file. Instead, make your changes in the master file you created,

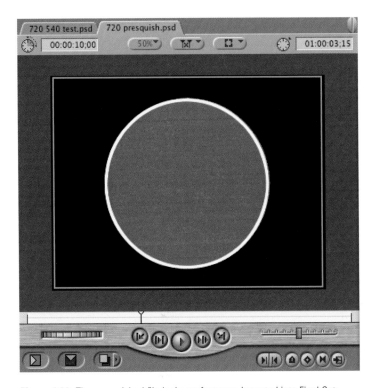

Figure 6.22 The presquished file looks perfect once imported into Final Cut.

and then create another squished file with the same name so that the old file is replaced with the new file.

This is why I don't like this technique—I end up with two versions of the same file: the master and the squished. But, after experimenting with a lot of different techniques, this is the easiest and consistently delivers the best results.

As I was writing this chapter, I was hoping that just as we have a simple pair of image sizes for HD graphics, we would have the same simplicity for HD PSD files. But such is not the case.

In testing for this chapter, I discovered that we need to squish our HD images to match the pixel aspect ratio of each specific HD format. So, although Table 3 below is a list of popular sizes, with new codecs being released every week, this is not a complete list. To determine the image size for your camera, if one of these settings doesn't work, check the manufacturer's Web site for the actual pixel dimensions of the video image created by your camera.

Here's how to use Table 3:

- Find your video format and the aspect ratio.
- Create your master file to the dimensions in the Master image column.

- Squish your images to the dimensions in the Squished image column.
- Import into Final Cut, after making sure Easy Setup and your sequence settings match.

Table 3: Sizing PSD Images

Video format	Aspect ratio	Master image size	Squished image size
DV NTSC	4:3	720 × 540 × 72	720 × 480 × 72
	16:9	853 × 480 × 72	720 × 480 × 72
SD NTSC	4:3	720 × 547 × 72	720 × 486 × 72
	16:9	853 × 547 × 72	720 × 486 × 72
PAL	4:3	768 × 576 × 72	720 × 576 × 72
	16:9	1024 × 576 × 72	720 × 576 × 72
HDV 1080	16:9	1920 × 1080 × 72	1440 × 1080 × 72
HDV 720	16:9	1280 × 720 × 72	1280 × 720 × 72
DVCPROHD (P2) 1080	16:9	1920 × 1080 × 72	1280 × 1080 × 72
DVCPROHD (P2) 720	16:9	1280 × 720 × 72	960 × 720 × 72
AVC 1080*	16:9	1920 × 1080 × 72	No squishing necessary.
AVC 720*	16:9	1280 × 720 × 72	No squishing necessary.
RED 1080	16:9	1920 × 1080 × 72	No squishing necessary.
XDCAM HD 1080	16:9	1920 × 1080 × 72	1440 × 1080 × 72
XDCAM HD 720	16:9	1280 × 720 × 72	No squishing necessary.
XDCAM EX 1080	16:9	1920 × 1080 × 72	No squishing necessary.
XDCAM EX 720	16:9	1280 × 720 × 72	No squishing necessary.

*As of this writing, the entire family of AVC formats is transcoded into ProRes 422. So, use those sizes when creating your graphics.

Whether you are creating a single-layer image or a multilayer image, the process of importing it into Final Cut is the same. I'll cover that in the next section.

Importing Images into Final Cut

When it comes to importing images, the process is easy:

Select **File > Import > File(s)**, or type **Command + I**, to import a single file or a selection of files. As you would expect, files in the Browser are named after the file names in the Finder.

Select **File > Import > Folder** to import the contents of an entire folder. This creates a new Browser bin, named after the folder in the Finder, with all the images inside.

And that's it!

Final Cut automatically determines what kind of file it is and enters all the appropriate data into the Browser columns automatically.

Final Cut Pro also sets the duration of all imported clips to match the settings in **Final Cut Pro > User Preferences > Editing** tab.

What Doesn't Import

When you save your Photoshop file as a PNG, or TIFF, all elements are converted to a bitmap, which is what Final Cut expects.

However, when you save your Photoshop file as a PSD, not all elements are converted to a bitmap, which means that Final Cut Pro won't see them. This is true for all layer effects, like drop shadows, and text.

To solve this problem you need to rasterize, or convert, the layer to a bitmap in Photoshop before you save it for Final Cut.

To do this, select the layer that contains the effect you need to bring into Final Cut. Go to **Layer > Rasterize** and select what you need to convert (Fig. 6.23).

As an alternative, you can convert the layer into a Smart Object (**Layer > Smart Object > Convert to Smart Object**). That can often be faster.

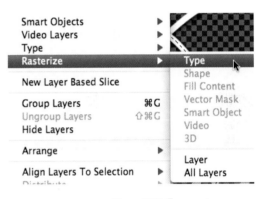

Figure 6.23 To convert a Photoshop layer effect into something that Final Cut can display, select the layer in Photoshop and choose Layer > Rasterize.

Exporting Freeze Frames from Final Cut Pro

Just as we can get still images created in Photoshop into Final Cut using importing, so also we can get stills out of Final Cut by exporting. Final Cut calls the still images generated from video "freeze frames."

And, as you might expect from our discussion earlier in this chapter, we need to convert the images from rectangular pixels into square pixels, so everything looks correct when that image is printed or posted to the Web.

Creating a Freeze Frame

You create freeze frame, that is, a still image created from a frame of moving video, in the Viewer, the Canvas, or the Timeline. Whichever window you decide to use, put your playhead on the frame you want to freeze and select **Modify > Make Freeze Frame** (or press **Shift + N**).

Freeze Frame Durations Can Be Adjusted

By default, all freeze frames have a 10-second duration. This can be adjusted, as we discussed earlier during importing, by going to Final Cut Pro > User Preferences > Editing tab and changing the Still/Freeze Duration to the time you want. This preference remains in force until you change it.

Instantly, a still frame appears in the Viewer with a default duration of 10 seconds.

Even though you've created a freeze frame, it acts just like a clip:

- If you want to save the freeze frame for use later, drag it from the Viewer into the Browser.
- If you want to edit the freeze frame back into your Timeline, put the playhead where you want it to appear and edit it in, just like a clip.

However, since this section is called "Exporting Freeze Frames," I'm going to stop playing with my freeze frames in the Timeline and export them.

Here's how:

1. To export a still frame, you don't need to create it first! All you need is to put your playhead on the frame you want to export. If it is in the Viewer, be sure the Viewer is selected (see Fig. 6.24). If it is in the Timeline, be sure the Timeline is selected.

Special Trick

Tom Wolsky suggests the following: here's a trick that I think looks a little better on clips with motion. If you make a freeze frame, do not insert it back into the Timeline where the playhead is. Rather move forward one frame then insert it. In many cases, this will look smoother.

Figure 6.24 Here's the still frame of Andrew and Lisa we want to export to promote this movie on our Web site. (Um, we'll remove the green background "in post.")

2. Go to **File > Export > Using QuickTime Conversion**. Although I don't normally recommend this option for exporting a movie, it is the best choice for exporting a freeze frame. Give the image a name and a location (Fig. 6.25).

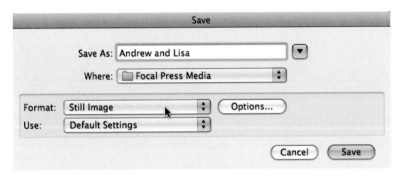

Figure 6.25 Give the freeze frame a name and a location. Then, change the Format to **Still Image**.

3. Then, from the **Format** pop-up menu, change it from the default setting of QuickTime Movie (which outputs your entire sequence) to **Still Image**, which outputs only the frame your playhead is parked on (Fig. 6.26).

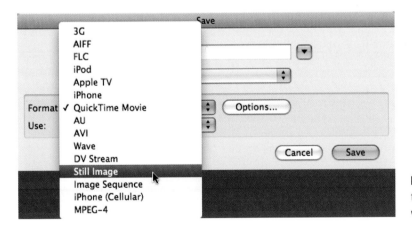

Figure 6.26 Be sure to change the Format to Still Image, or you will export your entire sequence.

4. By default, this outputs a PNG file. This is perfectly OK. However, if you want to change it, you can select different output options from the Options button. Again, avoid JPEG, due to its lower quality.

With that, your work in Final Cut is done. Now, we need to move to Photoshop to finish our work.

Cleaning Up a Still Frame in Photoshop

To bring a still frame into Photoshop, all you need to do is open Photoshop, go to **File > Open,** and select your image file.

Note how stretched both Andrew and Lisa are (Fig. 6.27). That's because we need to convert this image from rectangular to square pixels. This pixel aspect thing works in both directions.

Figure 6.27 Andrew and Lisa in PS. See how squished they look. We need to convert this image from rectangular to square pixels.

Once you have the image open in Photoshop, the process of cleaning up the still frames has three basic steps:

1. Deinterlace the image if you are shooting NTSC, PAL, or any HD format that ends in the letter "i," such as 1080i.
2. Apply any filters and adjustments you want to the image. For instance, Levels or Color Balance.
3. When the image is finished, the last step is to resize it to correct the pixel aspect ratio.

I strongly recommend you follow these steps in this order. Because step #2 is as varied as all the filters in Photoshop make possible, I will illustrate just steps 1 and 3.

Deinterlacing a Still Frame

Interlacing was invented at the dawn of television to solve two technical problems: how pictures were displayed to the picture tube of a television set and how video was sent over a broadcast television transmitter. That was back in the late 1930s, and we still live with interlacing today.

Interlacing displays every other line of an image (i.e., all the even-numbered lines) first, then, a fraction of a second later, it displays the remaining lines. The problem is in that "fraction of a second later." If you are photographing something that doesn't move, that time delay is not important. But, if you are photographing something that moves—which is a common occurrence—that time delay creates thin horizontal lines radiating off all moving edges. Very distracting.

Deinterlacing is the process of removing those horizontal lines. There are a number of ways this can be done. For instance, we could remove every other line and duplicate the lines that are left. This is very fast, but tends to blur the image. Or, we could remove every other line and calculate new lines to take their place. While the math behind this process is very complex, selecting the right option is not. This is the best choice, because Photoshop deinterlaces much better than Final Cut Pro.

We can either deinterlace the entire image or just the portion of the image that's moving.

To deinterlace the entire image, select **Filter > Video > De-Interlace** (Fig. 6.28). In most situations, the default settings of this filter are best.

In the resulting De-Interlace dialog, "Interpolation" means that Photoshop is calculating new lines to replace the lines it removed. This is always the best choice. Deinterlacing almost always causes a drop in image quality, especially if something is moving.

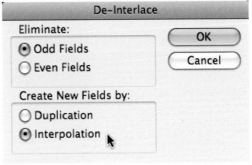

Figure 6.28 To deinterlace, select Filter > Video > De-Interlace.

However, if everything in the image is stationary, except something small in a portion of the frame, we can select just the moving object and deinterlace that portion of the image. This tends to maintain the overall image quality.

There are dozens of ways to select something in Photoshop. But, as we don't always need to be precise, here's a fast way.

With your still frame open in Photoshop, select the Lasso tool (Fig. 6.29).

To soften the edges ("feather") of your selection, go up to the toolbar and in the Feather dialog for the Lasso enter a number from 15 (not too soft) to 50 (quite soft), as shown Fig. 6.30.

Draw around the object you want to deinterlace (see Fig. 6.31). In this case, Andrew was moving and Lisa was not, so I want to deinterlace just Andrew so that I don't lose the detail in Lisa's hair.

Choose **Filter > Video > De-Interlace**, and only the selected area is deinterlaced.

Figure 6.29 To draw an area around something to select it, choose the Lasso tool.

Figure 6.30 To soften the edges of a selection, add a little bit of feathering. In this case, I used 20 pixels.

Figure 6.31 Here I'm selecting just Andrew, because he was moving. This retains the fine detail in Lisa's hair, which might otherwise be lost if I deinterlaced the entire image.

Important Note

 If you plan to clean up a freeze frame in Photoshop, then reimport it back into Final Cut, don't deinterlace and don't resize. Otherwise, the image quality of your still frame will suffer compared with the video elements surrounding it on the Timeline.

Remember, in general, you only need to deinterlace if you are shooting an NTSC, a PAL, or an HD format that ends in "i." Shooting an HD format that ends in "p" does not require deinterlacing. (Um, unless it does. Some progressive formats actually use interlacing. Weird, but true.)

In the next chapter, I'll show you a variety of techniques we can use in Photoshop to retouch still images and video. For now, I want to finish the process of working with freeze frames.

Resizing a Freeze Frame in Photoshop

After exporting your image and cleaning it up in Photoshop, you still need to resize the image before it is ready to print or post to the Web. (It's those pesky pixels again.)

The reason I deinterlace first is that any filters or corrections are being done on the actual pixels of the final image. The reason I resize last is that I don't want to change the shape of any pixels until all my other image processing is done.

And, this is as good a time as any to introduce the last table in this chapter. Regardless of what size the image was exported from Final Cut, resize the image based on this table for best results.

Table 4: Resizing Freeze Frames in Photoshop

Video format	Aspect ratio	Resize image to size
DV NTSC	4:3	640 × 480 × 72
	16:9	640 × 360 × 72
SD NTSC	4:3	640 × 480 × 72*
	16:9	640 × 360 × 72*
PAL	4:3	768 × 576 × 72
	16:9	1024 × 576 × 72
HD 720	–	1280 × 720 × 72
HD 1080	–	1920 × 1080 × 72

*Theoretically, SD video should be resized to 640 × 486 or 640 × 366; however, those extra six lines were never designed to be seen. A better alternative is to crop the image in Photoshop to remove those six lines, then resize to the specs in this table.

To resize an image, do the following:

Choose **Image > Image Size**. In the Image Size window, uncheck Constrain Proportions. This allows you to change the width without changing the height (see Fig. 6.32).

In the Width and Height data entry boxes, enter the appropriate numbers from the table above. In this example, I was shooting 16:9 DV, so I enter **640 × 360**. As always, I set the DPI to **72**.

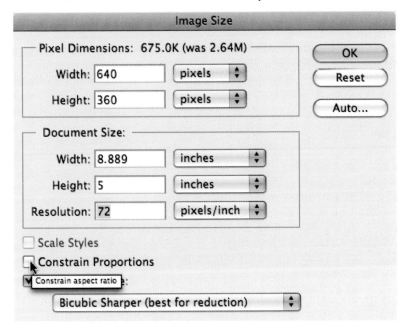

Figure 6.32 Key to resizing is to uncheck Constrain Proportions. This allows changing the width without changing the height.

Click **OK** to make your changes (Fig. 6.33).
Our people look human again!

Figure 6.33 Our finished, and resized, image.

Thoughts on the Differences between Computer Images and Video Images

For the technically inclined, I want to digress a moment to discuss the differences between computer and video images. We've already talked about the differences in pixel shape, but the differences go deeper than that. Here is an excerpt from an article I wrote for my Web site (www.larryjordan.biz) that provides more detail.

Video is really, really good at showing motion and emotion. However, it's not so good at displaying details or text.

One of the discouraging facts of life is that we create all these great graphics on our computers only to see them destroyed when they get transferred to video. (Well, OK, maybe not destroyed, but significantly changed due to lower resolution and color space.)

Is there anything we can do to change this situation? Well, um, no. But, there are things you can do to improve the look of your graphics and text when they are displayed on video. And that's what this section is about.

First, I'll explain how video and computers are different, then wrap up with a series of specific suggestions you can use to improve the look of your text.

In the Beginning

Video was invented about 40 years before computers, which means that computers were able to improve on the lessons we learned during the development of video. Because of this, there are eight major differences between graphics on video and graphics on the computer. Keeping these in mind will help you improve the look of your text.

The following are the eight differences:

- Video resolution is fixed, computer resolution varies by monitor size.
- Video most often records interlaced images, computers use only progressive images.
- Video gamma is different from computer gamma (this changes in Snow Leopard).
- Video white is grayer than computer white.
- Video bit-depth is more limited than computer bit-depth.
- Video uses Y'CbCr color space to describe its colors, which is more restrictive than the computer's RGB color space.
- Video colors are not as precise as computer colors.
- Video pixels are rectangular, the computer pixels are square.

Let's take a look at each of these and see what problems they cause.

Fixed Resolution

Regardless of the size of a video monitor, all SD NTSC video is 720×480 pixels (720×486 for NTSC broadcast and 720×576 for PAL). If you do the math, this works out to about 0.3 megapixels per frame—a far cry from even a cheap digital still camera's 4, 6, or 8 megapixels.

This limited number of pixels means that your image quality varies by screen size. The bigger the screen, the grainier the image. Also, because there are so few pixels, lines that are nearly horizontal or vertical show serious "stair-stepping," in a way that the same line angle on the computer does not.

This means that, graphically, we need to avoid using very fine detail or lots of thin or swirly lines. Video just doesn't have enough pixels to draw the image accurately.

This improves slightly in HD. However, even a 1080p image is just barely a 2-megapixel image. Both 720p and 1080i are less.

Interlacing

NTSC, PAL, and some HD formats are interlaced. This means that while we see many complete images each second, each image, or field, is not complete in and of itself. Instead, the video monitor displays the image in two parts—in the case of NTSC video, first the even (lower) lines are displayed, then the odd (upper) lines.

This means that in the United States, we are not seeing 30 images per second, but, instead, are seeing 60 half-images per second. These "half-images" are called "fields." (PAL displays 25 images per second, composed of 50 half-images, or fields.)

Essentially, interlacing means that the vertical resolution of our image is instantly cut in half, because we are only seeing half the image at any given instant.

The result of using fields is that we have even less image data to work with. Thin lines flicker wildly because they are in one field, and not the other. Curved lines look even more stair-stepped. A moving object has weird horizontal lines radiating out from each edge that you can see on the computer, but not on the video monitor.

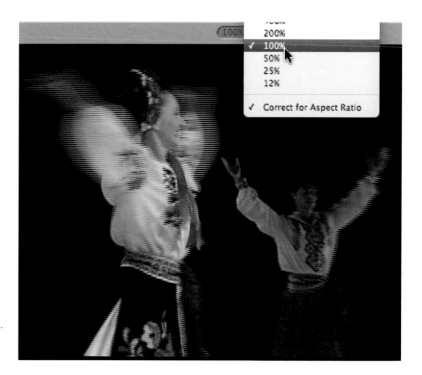

Figure 6.34 Interlacing is only displayed when the Final Cut Viewer or Canvas are set to 100%. See the horizontal lines radiating from her rapidly moving arms.

Final Cut Pro suppresses displaying interlace lines unless you show your image at 100% size in either the Canvas or the Viewer. Figure 6.34 illustrates what interlacing looks like; see the horizontal interlace lines radiating from her arms.

Video Gamma Is Different from Computer Gamma

Have you ever noticed that stills exported from Final Cut look darker than you expected?

This is because the mid-tone gray level (called "gamma") is not the same for your Mac and video. Each uses a different gamma setting. The standard gamma for the Mac is 1.8. The standard gamma for video is 2.2, which is darker than 1.8. You can compensate by loading your stills into PhotoShop and setting the

Color Profile to SDTV NTSC for NTSC video, SDTV PAL for PAL video, or HDTV (Rec. 709) for HD video. However, don't change the gamma setting on stills you want to reimport into your Final Cut Pro project, or they won't match your existing footage. (Note, these differences in gamma are fixed in Snow Leopard.)

TV White Is Actually Gray

Video was invented in an analog world—computers are digital. Consequently, they don't use the same black-and-white points.

Digital black is displayed at 0% on Final Cut Pro's Waveform monitor. Digital white is displayed at 109%.

However, digital black to white is too great a range for analog video, which includes broadcast, cable, and DVDs. When you are creating graphics or text for video, set your black level to zero on the Waveform monitor, but keep your white levels to 100% or less.

This is called keeping your white levels "broadcast safe." You can also clamp your white levels to the correct value by applying the Broadcast Safe filter (**Effects > Video Filters > Color Correction > Broadcast Safe**).

Figure 6.35 In Final Cut Pro View > Range Check > Excess Luma displays a green checkmark if your white levels are broadcast safe. The yellow warning indicates white levels that are too hot.

You can tell if your white levels are too hot by selecting either the Canvas or the Viewer and choosing **View > Range Check > Excess Luma** (see Fig. 6.35). If you see a yellow warning triangle, your white levels are too hot. A green checkmark means they are OK.

You can see this, as well, by looking at your video on the Waveform monitor. If any white pixels are above the 100% White line, your white levels are too hot.

Excess white levels cause white text to shimmer, tear, or break up. It can also cause a buzz in the audio. It also means that your video will be rejected for broadcast, as well as by most cable outlets and duplication facilities. You'll need to reduce your white levels and re-output.

Shooting and editing using DV, then outputting to the web is all digital—and doesn't require clamping, or restricting, your white levels to 100%. However, if you then compress your file for DVD or broadcast, you'll find that the process of compression converts your images into a broadcast safe format, which may, or may not, give you the expected results.

Video Can't Display as Many Colors as Your Computer

Computers use an RGB color space, whereas digital video uses Y'CbCr (analog video uses YUV). Both video color spaces are more restrictive than the computer. In other words, you can easily create colors on the computer that can't be displayed in video. Saturated yellows, reds, and blues come instantly to mind.

You can tell if your chroma levels are too hot by selecting either the Canvas or the Viewer and choosing **View > Range Check >**

Excess Chroma. If you see a yellow warning triangle, your white levels are too hot. A green checkmark means they are OK. (These symbols look remarkably similar to the white level symbols I just discussed—that's because they are.)

You can see this, as well, by looking at your video on the Vectorscope. If you connect the tops of the six targets, representing the six primary and secondary colors, if any white pixels exceed the boundaries of that rectangle, your chroma levels are probably too hot (see Fig. 6.36).

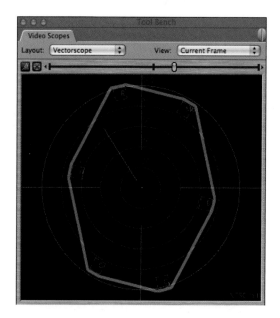

Figure 6.36 As a general rule, keep your chroma levels inside a boundary connecting the tops of your Vectorscope targets.

Excess chroma levels, like excess white levels, cause colors to tear or bleed into adjacent color areas. It can also cause a buzz in the audio. It also means that your video will be rejected for broadcast, as well as by most cable outlets and duplication facilities. You'll need to reduce your levels and re-output.

Video Provides Less Bit-Depth than Computers

In general, bit-depth determines how accurately we can reproduce reality digitally. Most popular video formats, such as DV, HDV, and XDCAM EX, use eight-bit depth. Higher quality formats, such as HDCAM and ProRes 422, use 10-bit depth. Photoshop works at 12-bit depth.

This means that subtle colors and gradients that look great in Photoshop look grainy or less subtle when transferred to video.

Video Colors Are Not as Precise as Computer Colors

Through a process called "color-sampling," the colors of adjacent video pixels are averaged to reduce the file size. The problem with color sampling is that the quality of your image is often degraded. Worse, it gets harder to pull a clean chroma-key, or to do good color correction because colors are blended between pixels.

The key issue with color sampling is that we don't have the same precision with color in video that we do with the computer. This is, generally, not an issue when we are shooting pictures, but becomes a significant concern when doing compositing effects, color correction, chroma-key, or adding text.

For example, high-quality video uses 4:2:2 color sampling. That's as good as it gets for video, though some high-end capture formats can use 4:4:4. NTSC DV has 4:1:1 sampling, which is not as good as 4:2:2. HDV uses 4:2:0 color sampling, which I would argue is not as good as DV.

Video Pixels Are Rectangles

We spent much of this chapter discussing this issue. While I don't need to go over old ground, I do want to stress that compensating for the differences in pixel aspect ratio separates images which look "weird" from those that look great.

Tips to Improving Your Looks

So, given all these constraints, it's a wonder we can create anything on our computers that displays properly on video. But, we can. And here are some tips that can help.

- If all you are doing is shooting digital stills, you won't have any problems moving between Photoshop and Final Cut Pro, provided you follow the guidance in this chapter.
- If you are doing green-screen work, try to shoot 4:2:2 video.
- If you are doing lots of compositing, try to shoot 10-bit video.
- If you are shooting for the Web, shoot progressive images.
- DPI is not as important as total pixels across and total pixels down.

Finally, give yourself time to experiment. Nothing is worse than trying to fix a bad situation on a deadline, when a little planning at the beginning could have made all the difference.

Summary

This chapter discussed how to convert still images between the computer and the video. The biggest problem is that they don't use the same-shaped pixels. Once you understand the differences, it is easy to set up a consistent workflow that guarantees consistent results.

My Story: Sometimes, It's the Little Things

Ryan Hasan Design
www.ryanhasandesign.com

Figure 6.37 Ryan Hasan.

There's no other tool on earth that I like editing in more than Final Cut, but I must confess that the way it handles still images drives me crazy. Perhaps, the most frustrating thing is the inconsistent way it handles the pixel aspect ratios (depending on the file type, whether it's layered or not, and a combination thereof), but there's plenty more hair-pulling where that came from.

However, Premiere Pro is…well, just plain more agreeable, even helpful. For starters, you can create a new Photoshop file that exactly matches your current sequence settings right from within Premiere (**File > New > Photoshop File**). Once you save the newly created file, it is automatically placed inside your Premiere project. Regardless of how you get still images into Premiere, however, it handles pixel aspect ratio in a way that is much more sane (it's based on the image's aspect ratio) and is almost always correct.

Other key advantages to working with stills in Premiere as opposed to Final Cut are as follows: you actually have a *choice* of whether you want to import a layered file as a sequence or not; even more importantly, Premiere recognizes Photoshop layer styles without you having to flatten them first. In addition, you can add, delete, and rename layers at will (without fear of repercussions), and you've got a whole new ballgame.

That's great, you say, but what if you need to do the rest of the project in Final Cut? How would you get your stills out of Premiere and into Final Cut, and—more importantly—would it even be worth it?

The answer to the first question is to simply export a QuickTime movie out of Premiere that matches your Final Cut sequence settings (sadly, Premiere doesn't seem to have an option to only export a reference movie). The answer to the second question is, of course, more subjective.

If you are merely creating a fairly basic sequence using still images and still images only, then it's probably worth it (I think so), but there's still a fair chance that you'll find it to be a wash. However, if you need to combine still images with video, and are creating something more advanced, you might find yourself needing to go back and forth between your editing program and your motion-graphics program. If this is the case, and you prefer to do your motion-graphics work in After Effects then I would say that it's definitely worth it: After Effects integrates much more tightly with Premiere than it does with Final Cut, after all.

So, there you go, the best of both worlds: do the bulk of your editing in Final Cut, but—when you need to do that homage to Ken Burns or Guy Ritchie—don't pull your hair out. Instead, fire up Premiere and enjoy being pampered, until it's time to go back home to Final Cut.

7

RETOUCHING VIDEO IN PHOTOSHOP

Nothing is more ingrained in my consciousness than "Photoshop is for stills, Final Cut is for video."

Sigh . . . How things change.

Starting with the release of CS3, Photoshop began supporting video. Not for editing, but for retouching and cleanup; something Photoshop has always been famous for with still images.

In the first part of this chapter, I'll show you how to quickly and easily move video clips from Final Cut Pro to Photoshop, how to play them in Photoshop, and then how to export them to get them back into Final Cut.

Then, in the second half of this chapter, I'll give you a variety of techniques you can use in Photoshop to make your videos look great.

Moving Video Clips from FCP to Photoshop

Here's a clip from Standard Films of an intrepid snowboarder about to hurtle skyward (Fig. 7.1). Except . . .

In the lower left corner is the shadow of the guy taking the picture. Now, I am not a snowboard aficionado, but it seems to me we have two wild and crazy people here: the guy on the snowboard about to leap into the sky and the guy, sliding sideways along the edge of the cliff while looking through a 16-mm film camera. I'm not exactly sure which of the two is crazier.

But, I digress.

This first image would be a great deal more powerful if we could make the shadow of the camera-person disappear. That way, the viewer's eye would not be distracted from the excitement of the jump.

We can't do this in Final Cut, but we can do this in Photoshop.

Figure 7.1 The two different portions of the same clip that need cleanup: removing the shadow on the left and removing some white dots on the right.

Getting the Settings Right

Before we start moving files, we need to configure a setting that tells FCP which application to use when sending files.

By default, when you use Open in Editor on a media file, it opens in QuickTime Player. In this case, we want it to open in Photoshop. Here's how:

1. Go to **Final Cut Pro > System Settings > External Editors** tab.
2. Click the **Set** button, navigate to your Application folder, and select **Adobe Photoshop CS4**. Be sure to select the application itself, not just the folder that contains the application (Fig. 7.2).
3. Click **OK** to save these changes.

You only need to change this setting once.

Figure 7.2 From Final Cut Pro > System Settings > External Editors tab, click the Set button and point it to Adobe Photoshop CS4.

Moving a Clip from FCP to Photoshop

Once this preference is set, whenever you want to open a clip in Photoshop, Control-click (or right-mouse-button-click) the clip itself – either in the Timeline or the Browser – and select **Open in Editor** (see Fig. 7.3). Keep in mind that Photoshop does not

understand audio. While you can listen to audio when playing a clip in Photoshop, any audio in your clip will be ignored on export.

If Photoshop is already running, the clip quickly opens in the application (Fig. 7.4). Otherwise, Final Cut first launches Photoshop, and then loads the clip into it.

A Problem with Timecode

While the ability to retouch video is a huge benefit to using Photoshop, there is a significant downside: timecode. All In and Out points set in FCP are ignored. When you use Open in Editor, you will get the complete clip loaded into Photoshop. There is no reference or relation to the clip in Final Cut, nor, perhaps even more importantly, is there any relation whatsoever to timecode. All clips begin at 00:00:00:00 in the Photoshop Animation window. Although Photoshop does support drop-frame timecode, relating your Photoshop media to your actual clips in the Timeline can be tricky.

Figure 7.4 Ta-dah! Our video file is loaded into Photoshop.

Video clips load automatically as Smart Objects. You can tell whether a layer is a Smart Object based upon the "Smart Object" icon in the lower right corner of the layer's icon in the Layer menu (see Fig. 7.5).

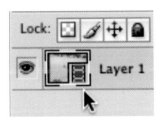

Figure 7.5 The little filmstrip icon in the lower right corner of the layer icon in the Layer palette indicates that this is a Smart Object.

Understanding Smart Objects

There's a new image type in Photoshop called a "Smart Object." As the Adobe manual states: "Smart Objects are layers that contain image data from raster or vector images, such as Photoshop or Illustrator files. Smart Objects preserve an image's source content with all its original characteristics, enabling you to perform nondestructive editing to the layer." Video files are raster (bitmapped) images, so they open automatically as Smart Objects.

However, there's a big limitation to a Smart Object. You can't alter pixel data – such as cloning – unless you convert that layer to a regular layer. However, the benefit of using Smart Objects, especially for video, is that all the changes we make are not permanent until we export the file.

The ability to use Smart Objects is another reason why keeping a master copy of your PSD file, separate from the files you import into Final Cut, makes sense.

Photoshop Does Not Support All Video Formats

While Photoshop supports virtually all known graphics formats, its support for video formats is more limited. All video must be in QuickTime format with one of the following extensions: MPG, MPEG, MP4, M4V, MOV, AVI, or FLV. MPEG-2 is supported if you have Compressor or the MPEG-2 Playback Component installed on your system. (For an updated list of supported formats, visit Adobe's Web site: www.adobe.com.)

Also, you must be using Photoshop Extended, not just Photoshop, to work with video files.

Back to our clip that just opened in Photoshop. It's here. This is great! Except, um . . . There's no way to *play* the video.

Bummer.

This is because you don't know the "secret technique" that is only taught to the very few. Like you.

With your video clip loaded, go to **Window > Animation** to display the Animation Timeline. Sha-ZAM! (He said, continuing with his seriously dated television allusions.) You are now looking at something very few people have ever seen: a timeline controller in Photoshop (Fig. 7.6). Cool.

Press **Spacebar** to play, and then again press Spacebar to stop. Drag the Playhead – Adobe calls it the CTI – to reposition it quickly.

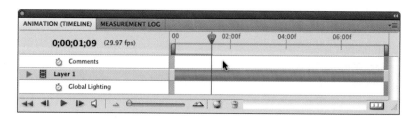

Figure 7.6 Photoshop's timeline controller – Spacebar to play or stop. Grab the playhead (Adobe calls it the Current Time Indicator [CTI]) and drag to the position you want.

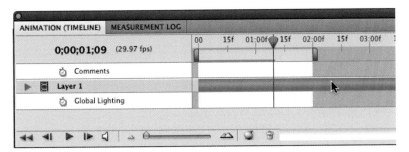

Figure 7.7 The vertical blue bars indicate a Play Range. In this case, it starts at the beginning of the clip and continues for 2 seconds. Change the Play Range by dragging one of the blue bars.

If your clip is long, and you only want to work with a portion of it, create a Play Range (see Fig. 7.7), which loops over and over as you are making your adjustments.

To create a smaller playback range, grab one of the blue bars and drag it where you want it to go. For instance, in this example, the Play Range starts at the beginning, where the photographer's shadow appears and stops about 2 seconds in, when his shadow disappears.

By default, the Play Range starts at the beginning of a clip and continues until the end – this is indicated by those two small blue bars at the beginning and end of a clip.

To change the Play Range, drag the blue bars.

To move the Playhead, either drag it or click-hold-and-drag the timecode numbers in the upper left corner of the Timeline.

To see a Thumbnail of your clip, Control-click the timecode numbers in the upper left corner and select the thumbnail size you want to view (see Fig. 7.8).

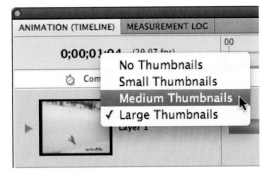

Figure 7.8 Control-click the timecode numbers to display a small thumbnail on the left side of your Timeline.

The control buttons are located in the lower left corner of the Timeline (see Fig. 7.9). From left to right they are

Figure 7.9 The buttons, in the lower left corner of the Timeline, allow you to control the playback of your clip.

- Move Playhead to the beginning of Timeline
- Go back one frame

Monitoring Video from Photoshop

If you have the right capture card, you can monitor your video directly from Photoshop, just as you can from FCP. For instance, the Blackmagic Design DeckLink card displays video directly from Photoshop. To turn this feature on, select **File > Export > Send Video to Device**. If you don't have the correct card, choosing this will have no effect. You can learn more about how Blackmagic supports Photoshop playback by visiting their Web site (www.blackmagic-design.com).

To avoid confusing your hardware for video playback, don't run both Final Cut and Photoshop at the same time.

- Play/Stop
- Go forward one frame
- Turn on/off audio playback (Photoshop supports audio playback, but not audio export.)
- The two small "mountain" symbols allow you to zoom in, or out, of the Timeline
- The slider adjusts horizontal scaling
- Toggle onion skins on/off (this will be discussed in the next section)
- Delete keyframes

Exporting from Photoshop

Assuming that all your changes are complete for your file, you need to export it to get it back into FCP.

Now I realize that, normally, you would actually *do* something to the image before exporting it. But in this case, I want to establish how to move files between the two applications first, and then spend the latter portion of this chapter discussing various Photoshop techniques that I've found useful for video.

Saving the Photoshop file is like saving a Final Cut project. It saves the *instructions* of how you want to edit your project. As in Final Cut, it isn't until you export that an actual video file is created.

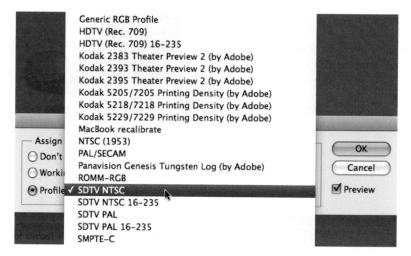

Figure 7.10 To prevent unwanted color changes when working with video, assign a color profile that matches your video format by choosing Edit > Assign Profile.

To export your clip, go to **File > Export > Render Video**.

While the Render Video window (see Fig. 7.11) has been known to frighten small children, here's the key point: the export settings you

Render Video

Location

Name: Track – Jump.mov

(Select Folder...) Macintosh HD:Training Files:...:Media:Snowboard:

☐ Create New Subfolder:

File Options

◉ QuickTime Export: QuickTime Movie ▼ (Settings...)

  Animation (Best Quality, RGBA 32 bits)

○ Image Sequence: JPEG ▼ (Settings...)

  Starting #: 0   Digits: 4 ▼   Ex: File0000.jpg

Size: Document Size ▼ 720 x 480

Range

○ All Frames

○ In Frame: 0   Out Frame: 225

◉ Currently Selected Frames: 0 to 62

Render Options

Alpha Channel: Straight – Unmatted ▼

Frame Rate: Document Frame Rate ▼ 29.97 fps

(Render)

(Reset)

Figure 7.11 The Render Video window looks intimidating. However, you only need to make a few changes before exporting.

select depend upon what you are going to do with the clip once it gets back into FCP. I'll show you the steps later, but here's the summary:

- If the clip is complete, with no additional effects applied to it, export it to match your Final Cut sequence settings.
- If the clip is going to have additional effects applied to it – whether a title key, color correction, or other processing – so that it will need to re-render in Final Cut, export it using either the Animation codec for FCP 6, or the ProRes 4444 for FCP 7 and later.
- If you need to retain alpha channel (transparency) information, export it using either the Animation codec for FCP 6, or the ProRes 4444 for FCP 7 and later.

You determine key export settings in the Movie Settings Window (see Fig. 7.12). I'll show you how to configure these shortly.

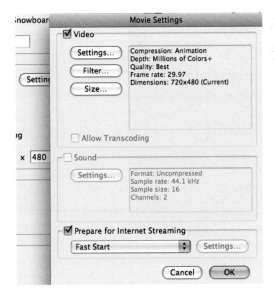

Movie Settings

☑ Video

(Settings...) Compression: Animation
(Filter...) Depth: Millions of Colors+
(Size...) Quality: Best
  Frame rate: 29.97
  Dimensions: 720x480 (Current)

☐ Allow Transcoding

☐ Sound

(Settings...) Format: Uncompressed
  Sample rate: 44.1 kHz
  Sample size: 16
  Channels: 2

☑ Prepare for Internet Streaming

Fast Start ▼ (Settings...)

(Cancel) (OK)

Figure 7.12 The Movie Settings window allows you to determine the kind of video you want Photoshop to create. To display this click the Settings button in the Render Video window.

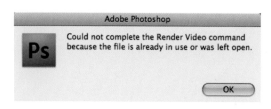

Figure 7.13 You may see this error message if you are trying to replace a clip that Final Cut currently has open in your project.

Note

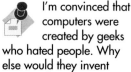

I'm convinced that computers were created by geeks who hated people. Why else would they invent terms such as *gamma* setting, *alpha* channel, or, worst of all, *rendering*? Sheesh!

Let's quickly define alpha channel, so we can put the term to work. The alpha channel simply determines the amount of transparency that each pixel contains. (It would have been a whole lot easier to call it the "transparency" channel – but then, that wouldn't have intimidated anyone, would it?) Every video clip has four channels: red, green, blue, and transparency (or "alpha").

Naming Your Clip

If you name the clip the same as the source file and replace the source file, when you switch back to FCP, FCP will automatically load the new clip into the Timeline, and Browser, with all your changes.

If you give it a new name, or new location, you'll need to import it into Final Cut before you can use it.

The benefit to using the same name is that the clip automatically links back into Final Cut. The downside to replacing the old clip with the new one is that if, by some wild permutation of fate you happen to make a mistake, you've lost the ability to go back to your original clip and start over.

Also, you may see an error message saying that the clip is already open (see Fig. 7.13). This is because Final Cut is using it in the current project. To solve this, quit Final Cut, then save your file. The clip will be updated the next time you open your project in Final Cut.

Setting the Video Format

All video is compressed to varying degrees using a codec. Common ones are DV, HDV, uncompressed 10-bit, and so on. You control the settings for these codecs in the Movie Settings window.

To adjust these codec settings:

- Click **Settings** in the File Options section of the Render Video window. The Movie Settings window opens, and the right side of the window displays a summary of the current export settings.
- Click **Settings** in the Video section. The Standard Video Compression Settings window opens.
- Click the **Compression Type** pop-up. A discouragingly long list of indecipherable acronyms appears (Fig. 7.14).

If you plan to create additional effects inside Final Cut, select **ProRes 4444** (select **Animation** if you are using FCP 6 or earlier). ProRes 4444 is a great codec, whose principal advantages are extremely high quality, smaller file size than Animation, and support for alpha channels (transparency) within the clip. If you want high quality, but don't need

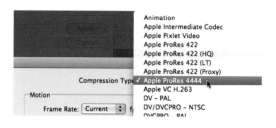

Figure 7.14 This pop-up menu determines what codec to use when exporting your video.

alpha channel support, ProRes 422 HQ is a better choice, with the benefit of even smaller file sizes. Both versions of ProRes will need to render once imported into Final Cut, depending upon your sequence settings.

If the clip in Photoshop is complete, with no additional effects applied to that clip inside FCP, select the video format that matches your Final Cut sequence settings.

For instance, if you are working with a 16:9 DV NTSC sequence in Final Cut, you would select **DV/DVCPRO – NTSC**.

If you are working with a 16:9 PAL sequence, you would select **DV – PAL**.

If you are working with a 1080i HDV sequence, you would select: **HDV 1080i/60** for NTSC countries, or **HDV 1080i/50** for PAL countries.

- Once you've selected the Compression Type (which is the most confusing part of this whole export business), set:
  Frame rate to **Current**
  Keyframes to **Automatic** (if it isn't grayed out)
  And the rest of the settings are fine.
- Click **OK** to approve these settings

Adjusting Additional Movie Window Settings

- In the Movie Settings window, **Sound** is grayed out because Photoshop does not support exporting audio.
- Uncheck **Prepare for Internet Streaming** whenever you send video back to FCP.
- Click **OK** to approve the Movie Settings window.

What you've just done determines what kind of video you are going to export.

Lower in the Render Video window, **Document Size** determines the pixel dimensions of your video. Photoshop reads this from the file itself, and almost all the time, it will be accurate.

If you want to export the entire video, click the radio button for **All Frames**. If, on the other hand, you've set a Play Range, Photoshop recognizes that and turns on **Currently Selected Frames** and presets the **Play Range** values.

Including Alpha Channels, or Transparency, in Your Clip

Finally, Render Options is grayed out for almost all video formats – except the Animation and ProRes 4444 codecs. Both allow you to include an Alpha, or transparency, channel in your video. This allows you to pregenerate your composite in Photoshop.

This can be extremely helpful in creating layered effects. Going into detail on alpha channels is more than I have time to cover. If you want to learn more about this feature, you can read about it in either the Adobe Photoshop or the After Effects manuals – they both share this feature.

Figure 7.15 To include transparency information in your clip, be sure the Compressor Depth is set to **Millions of Colors+**.

Keeping Track

Just to keep this clear – you save images and you export clips.

However, by default, exporting alpha channels is turned off. Here's how to turn it on.

In the Standard Video Compression Settings window, where you selected the codec, be sure **Compressor > Depth** is set to **Millions of Colors+**. (The plus is what tells Photoshop to include the alpha channels (see Fig. 7.15).)

Also, I don't recommend Photoshop for changing frame rates. There are much better tools for doing so. Always output at the same frame rate as your source video clip to avoid problems.

Once you are done establishing these settings, click **Render** and go get a cup of coffee. This may take a bit.

Helpful Photoshop Techniques

In this section, I want to share a variety of techniques I find helpful when working on video in Photoshop. This list is by no means inclusive – rather, I want to share some ideas, so you can continue learning on your own. (By the way, the section on cloning describes how to get rid of the photographer's shadow, and the section on spot healing shows how to get rid of the white dots.)

Many of these effects can also be created using After Effects. However, if you already know how to use Photoshop, this may be a faster way to achieve what you want.

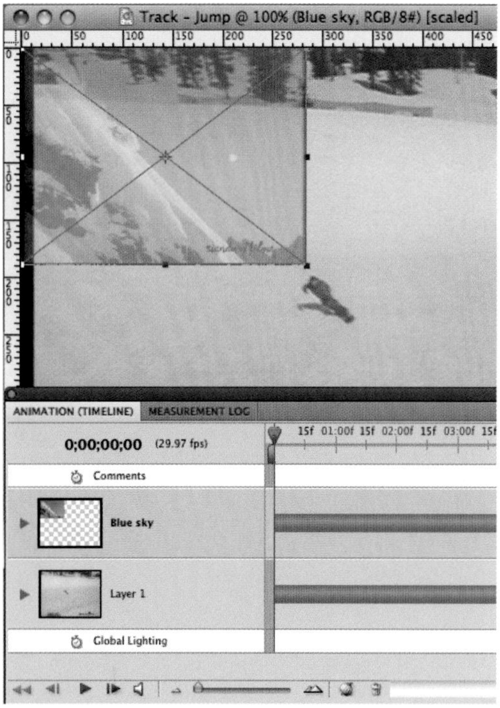

Using the Place Command

The Place command (**File > Place**) allows us to add an element as a second layer to our video. Similar to putting one image on a higher track in the Final Cut Timeline.

The benefit to doing so in Photoshop is that it allows you to composite (combine) multiple images using all the tools in Photoshop, which are more extensive than in Final Cut itself.

Here, for instance, are two video clips (Fig. 7.16). The one on top was decreased in size, moved to the upper left corner, and reduced in opacity. Note that the Animation Timeline shows two tracks. (By the way, I cheated here. Open in Editor only allows sending one file at a time. In this case, I opened each file separately in Photoshop using the Place command.)

The Place command allows us to create layers of video, running each layer in sync with all the others. As well, it retains both video clips as video, unlike **Edit > Paste Into**, which converts the pasted clip to a freeze frame.

Figure 7.16 Using the Place command, we can add multiple layers of video, called compositing, into our Photoshop document.

If you used **File > Open**, each image would open in its own window. Since we want to combine them, we used the **Place** command.

While this effect of picture-in-picture can be easily created in FCP, here's one that would be harder: using both Paste and a QuickMask.

Using Masks

A mask is a shape that allows us to control how much of the foreground image and the background image we see.

A mask has areas of transparency, which allow us to see the background image, and opacity, allowing us to see the foreground image. Some masks also allow feathering, or soft edges, which smoothes the transition from foreground to background (see Fig. 7.17).

Both Final Cut and Photoshop use the same colors to denote a mask: the opaque foreground is always displayed as white and the transparent background is always displayed as black. The foreground image automatically appears wherever there is white, and the background image always appears wherever there is black.

A mask, in Photoshop, allows us to control how much of the foreground image we see.

Figure 7.17 Here, for instance, I have placed one image above another, and then drawn a QuickMask to soften the edges of the foreground image. The problem is that QuickMasks don't work for Smart Objects.

Be Careful of QuickMasks

Photoshop has the ability to create QuickMasks. While these are very fast and useful for still images, a QuickMask only supports video on the background layer.

This is an example of what I am talking about. Let's composite (remember, that means to "combine") two video clips, and then soften the edges. Here's how:

1. Open the background video clip. This creates a Smart Object and places it on the background layer (Fig. 7.18)

Figure 7.18 This is our placed image, reduced in size and tucked into the corner.

What Gets Placed

Photoshop always loads the entire clip; which means that it ignores any Ins or Outs placed in Final Cut.

2. Using **File > Place**, add a second video clip. Grab the video clip's corner and drag to resize. Hold the **Shift** key down to constrain the aspect ratio. Press **Shift-Option** to constrain the aspect ratio and scale the image from the center, similar to Final Cut. In this example, I put the image in the top-right corner.

3. Press the **Enter** key to lock the placed image in position. Until you press Enter, you can move and resize the image as much as you want.

4. In the Layers palette, select the image you want to mask – most often it is the top-most layer.

5. Click the mask icon at the bottom of the Layers palette (Fig. 7.19). This turns on a special kind of paint brush that allows you to "paint away" portions of an image.
6. In the lower portion of the Photoshop Tool Palette, click the small white/black chip (or type **D**) to set the default colors (Fig. 7.20). By default, the foreground color is white, and the background color is black. The problem is that these colors are backwards when you want to create a mask.
7. Click the small, curved double-arrow next to the white/black chip to reverse the colors, making black the foreground color. You know you've done it right when the larger black chip is on top of the white chip.
8. Photoshop automatically selects a circular brush shape. Go up to the toolbar, click the **Brush** menu (Fig. 7.21), and adjust the size and softness to suit. In this case, my brush is **50** pixels wide, with a hardness of **51%**, which creates fairly soft edges. There is no magic number here – every situation is different.
9. Using the brush, paint along the edges of your foreground picture and watch what happens! See how, as you paint, the brush "erases" part of the foreground image (see Fig. 7.22). You can create all kinds of wild effects this way.
10. Click the **Play** button in the Animation Timeline and watch both videos play together. Although FCP can create masks, it can't easily create masks of irregular soft-edged shapes.

Figure 7.19 Click the layer mask icon at the bottom of the Layers palette to create a mask that works with Smart Objects.

Figure 7.20 Click the small white/black chip to reset Photoshop's colors to their default settings.

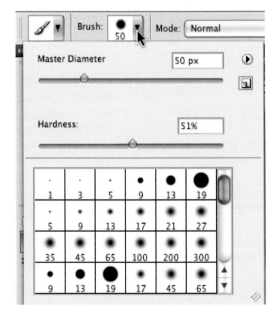

Figure 7.21 Click the brush control menu, in the top toolbar, to select the brush size and edge softness. Experiment with different settings and see what works for you.

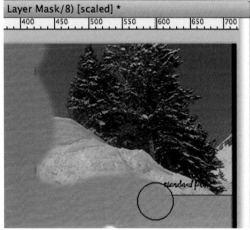

Figure 7.22 By painting with the mask brush, you can erase portions of the foreground image to create wild and crazy shapes.

The Limitations of Placing

Photoshop doesn't have any way to slip clips. All clips start at the same point, and it always loads the entire clip. So, if you want to do extensive compositing, you are much better off doing so in Motion or After Effects. Think of Photoshop as more a retouching tool rather than an editing tool.

Figure 7.23 The three stained-glass windows. The yellow border indicates a 4:3 aspect ratio. (The yellow border is simply for illustration and not required for this procedure.)

Using Content-Aware Scaling

Content-Aware Scaling, new with CS4, allows us to change the size of an image, without changing the size of the important visual content. Although this can only be used for still images, not video clips, the effect is almost magical.

This is a useful technique when you adjust the size of your images to fit into a video format. Here's how it works.

I'd like to scale this 16:9 image to fit into a 4:3 shape, but I don't want to scale the stained-glass windows (see Fig. 7.23). I could move all the images manually, but where's the fun in that?

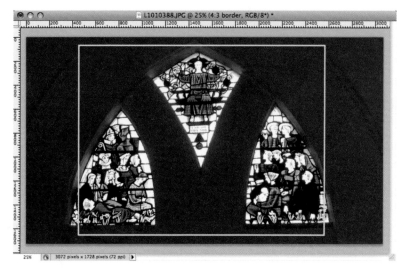

Instead, we are going to use Content-Aware Scaling. There are several ways to do this; in this technique, we will select the specific content we want to protect. Here's how:

Using the Marquee tool, draw a border around an object you want to protect so that it doesn't scale. In this case, because I'm dealing with triangles, I used the Polygonal selection tool (see Fig. 7.24).

Hold the Shift key down and draw borders around any additional shapes you need to protect. The goal is to select only the most important portion of the image; otherwise, if you protect everything, nothing changes in size. (Drawing a marquee is also called "selecting.")

Click the **Channels** tab – it shares space with the Layers palette – and click the **Save Selection as Channel** button at the bottom (Fig. 7.25). This tells Photoshop what to save. Note that a new channel appears at the bottom of the channel list, called **Alpha 1**.

Now that you've told Photoshop what to protect, you can scale the image.

Make sure the layer that contains your image is selected in the Layers palette.

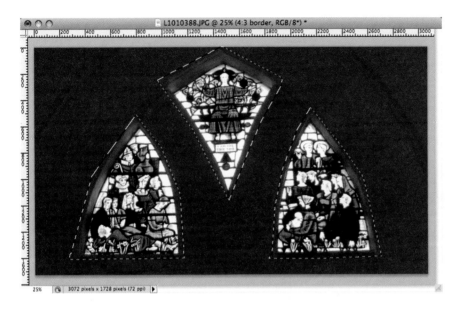

Figure 7.24 Using the selection tool of your choice, draw borders around that part of the image you want to protect from scaling.

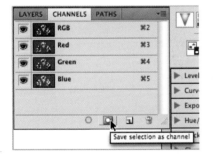

Figure 7.25 Go to the Channels palette (it shares a pane with the Layers palette) and click "Save Selection as Channel" at the bottom.

Figure 7.26 Drag a control box on a corner or along an edge, to resize the image.

Important Note

If your image is on the background layer, type **Command + A** to select the entire image. If your image is on a layer, this step is not necessary.

Go to **Edit > Content-Aware Scale**.

Grab one of the control squares on the corner, or middle of an edge, and drag until your image resizes to the size you need (Fig. 7.26).

If you make a mistake, press **Escape** to cancel the effect. Or, if the image looks the way you want, press **Enter** to record your changes. Photoshop does some processing, and then displays the rescaled image (Fig. 7.27).

(Again, in this example, I was using the yellow border as a guide to making it a 4:3 shape. The yellow border was added by me, and is not necessary for this technique.)

This is very, very cool.

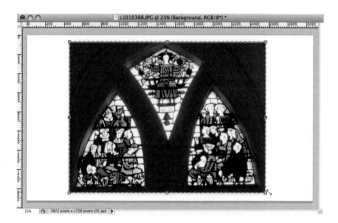

Figure 7.27 This is my completed image, scaled from 16:9 to 4:3 with the stained-glass windows still looking perfect. It fits perfectly within the yellow guide we created.

Creating an Alpha Channel Using Quick Selection

In this section, we want to make a portion of a clip transparent. The problem is, we didn't shoot it in front of a green screen, and there are different colors in the portion we want to remove. Worst of all, it is an odd shape.

Fortunately, Photoshop has a tool that makes this easy. It's called **Quick Selection** and here's how it works. (While we can't use QuickSelection on upper layers of video, we can use it on the background layer.)

1. Load the image or clip you want to work with. In this case, I want to remove the blue sky and background mountain from this image (Fig. 7.28).
2. From the Tool palette, select the **Quick Selection** tool (Fig. 7.29). You can adjust the brush shape from the Brush menu in the top toolbar. I'm going to use a medium-sized circle.

Figure 7.28 In this example, we want to remove the blue sky and background mountain. Chroma key and geometric masks won't work.

3. Click the brush anywhere in the section you want to remove – I started in the blue sky – and drag until everything you want to remove is selected (Fig 7.30).

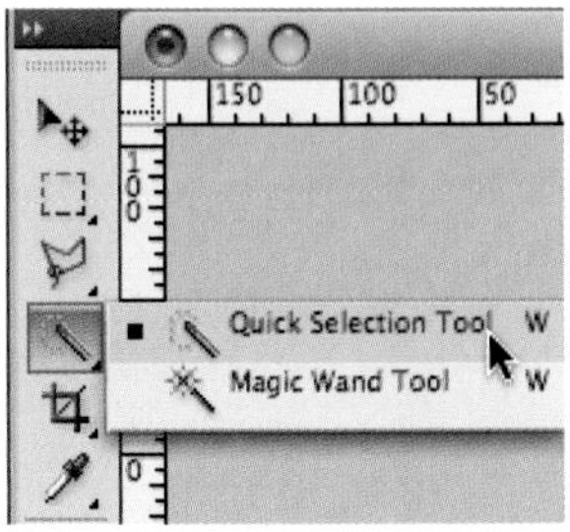

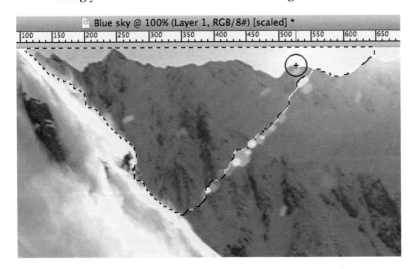

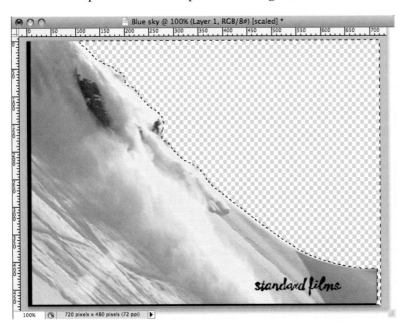

Figure 7.29 From the Tool palette, select the Quick Selection tool.

Figure 7.30 Put your brush anywhere in the area you want to remove and keep dragging until the entire portion you want to remove is selected.

4. Once you have the area selected, press the **Delete** key and – poof! – instant vaporization (Fig. 7.31)!

Figure 7.31 Once you have selected the area you want to remove, press the Delete key and its gone.

If this is a still image, save your work.

If this is a clip, you need to do this for every frame in your clip – but this is a whole lot faster than trying to draw masks. Export your clip (**File > Export > Render Video**), follow the export instructions we discussed earlier, and you're done.

Figure 7.32 Here's the problem: the shadow of the photographer, in the lower left corner, is distracting the viewer from watching the snowboarder.

Figure 7.33 Using the rectangular marquee tool, draw a selection rectangle around the area you want to work on.

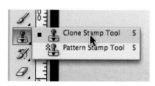

Figure 7.34 From the Tool palette, select the Clone tool: it looks like a rubber stamp.

Retouching Using Cloning

Cloning is one of the most powerful features in Photoshop, and the good news it works just as well for video as it does for stills. First, though, let's define the term. Cloning is the process of copying pixels from one part of an image to another. This makes an exact copy, hence the term *clone.* However, if we do it right, no one will notice.

With that as a definition, let's turn our attention back to our intrepid snowboarder and the photographer's errant shadow (Fig. 7.32).

You can just see his shadow in the lower part of the frame. If this were a still image, we could just clone that out.

Well, that's exactly how it works with video – except with more options.

Note that the edges of the frame are bordered by a thin, black line. This is part of the video format and is perfectly normal. However, I want to restrict the area to which the cloning will apply so that I don't overwrite the black line.

Here's the fastest way to fix this shadow problem, and then I'll show you some options that you can take advantage of in your own work.

1. Select the rectangular marquee and draw a selection rectangle around the area you want to fix (see Fig. 7.33). You can use any selection tool you want, I just find the rectangular marquee is the fastest. What the marquee does is only allow changes inside the border. This prevents you from messing up other parts of the image, which don't need changing.
2. From the Tool palette on the side, click the tool that looks like a rubber stamp, which is the Clone tool. You can also press the letter **S** (Fig. 7.34).
3. Then, and this is the important part, move the Clone tool over a portion of the image that you want to copy. In this

What Pixels Are Selected?

When you use a selection tool, pixels under the blinking lines (also called "marching ants") are included in the selection.

case, I want to copy a portion of the edge of the cliff that doesn't have a shadow, to the portion of the edge of the cliff that does have a shadow. Hold the **Option** key and click to select the source image.

As you hold the Option key, the cursor turns into a target, indicating it is ready to set the source (Fig. 7.35).

Figure 7.35 Option-click the section of the image you want to use as the source to "load it" into the tool. In this case, I want to copy a clean portion of the edge of the cliff to replace the portion with the shadow.

4. Let go of the Option key and move the cursor, which turns into a circular brush, over to where the shadow touches the edge of the cliff.
5. Hold the mouse button down and drag. The pixels under the brush shape will be replaced with the pixels from the source image (Fig. 7.36). A small cross-hair will move over the source section of the image to show you the pixels that you are copying. The marquee border prevents you from cloning outside the selected area.
6. If you drag without letting go of the mouse, you'll replace all the pixels with the source pixels. A better technique, however, is to let go of the mouse button periodically so that the new pixels don't exactly mirror the other portion of the image.

Figure 7.36 Hold the mouse button down and drag to replace the pixels under the mouse with those from the source.

This technique takes a little practice to make sure that edges are not too obvious, but once you master it, you'll wonder how you ever lived without it.

This screen shows the finished image with the shadow removed (Fig. 7.37).

The downside to cloning is that we need to make these changes to each frame. If the frame is a locked-down shot, we need to be very careful making changes as they will be very obvious as we play from frame to frame. Also, interlacing can sometimes cause problems as we clone from one area to another. If you are doing very precise work with interlaced images, moving to After Effects or other high-end video retouching software would be a better choice.

Figure 7.37 The finished image with the shadow removed.

A Little Softness Goes a Long Way

In general, adding some softness to your brush, from the **Brush** menu in the top toolbar, helps a lot in blending between the new and old pixels when cloning. There's no magic amount that works for every image, so allow a little bit of time to experiment. Generally, you don't need a lot.

Use the Timeline to Advance Frames

When you are done cloning a frame, use the Timeline to move to the next frame. Because the image changes from frame to frame, we can't use copy/paste; instead, we need to correct each frame individually using cloning.

In this case, however, because the camera is tracking very quickly as the photographer slides along the top as the other snowboarder gets ready to jump, each frame is changing so radically from the earlier frame that we don't need to be too accurate in this cleanup.

However, it's nice to know that we can be very precise if we need to be.

Cloning Options: The Clone Source Pane

Because we can use cloning for everything from cleaning up shadows to removing wires or stray microphones to adding elements that weren't there to begin with, let's explore some of the other tools we have available.

The Clone Source panel can be used for both the Clone Stamp and Healing Brush tools. It allows us to set up to five different sample sources, without needing to resample each time. For video, it allows us to specify the frame relationship between where we select video and where we put it. In other words, we can take video from frame 23 and put it on frame 25.

In this image, let's use some additional cloning tools that arrived with CS4. We can add some more trees and remove the white dots from the blue sky (see Fig. 7.38). Think of removing the white dots as similar to retouching a person's face containing skin blemishes.

1. Either select the Clone Stamp tool or go to **Window > Clone Source** to reveal this pane (Fig. 7.39). Notice that across the top of the pane are five buttons, which allow us to sample up to five different source pixels. In the case of this example, we are going to use two.

2. Click the button on the top left so it is depressed, and then Option-click a clean portion of the blue sky that is near one of the white dots you want to remove (see Fig. 7.40). The key is to get as reasonably close as you can to the area you want to change, to minimize any glaring color shifts.

3. Click the second source button and Option-click where the set of three trees meets the snow (Fig. 7.41).

4. Now, when you want to replace blue sky, select the first clone source. To add more trees, click the second clone source.

Figure 7.38 In this image, let's add some more trees and remove the white dots from the blue sky. (Why? Because we can.)

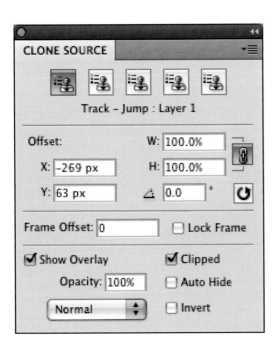

Figure 7.39 The Clone Source pane allows us to select between five source locations, as well as clone pixels from one frame to another.

Figure 7.40 To avoid unwanted color shifts, be sure to select your source pixels to be as close as possible to the pixels you want to replace.

Figure 7.41 Option-click the trees you want to add from one frame to the next.

But the Clone Source pane does even more. It allows us to clone pixels from one frame and copy them to a different frame. This is a great way to remove a wire, or other object, which is in one frame, but not another.

We do this using Frame Offset. Here, I'm cloning pixels from one frame earlier onto the current frame, so I enter (−1) as shown in Fig. 7.42.

This is also powerful if you have a dropout or video glitch to fix where the frame before or after the bad frame is good. For instance, in this example, I have a bad glitch that I want to correct (see Fig. 7.43).

The easiest way to get rid of it is to use the Clone Source Frame Offset to clone from the frame before – which has a clean blue sky with no dropout.

Here's how.

1. Go to the frame with the bad video you want to replace. Move the cursor until it is positioned on the bad section of image. Press the **Option** key and click on the bad portion of the time. This enters the cursor position into the Clone Offset window (see Fig. 7.44). Note how the X and Y Offset

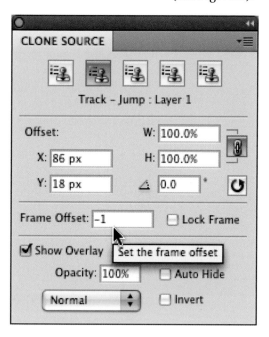

Figure 7.42 It is easy to clone pixels from one frame onto a different frame using Frame Offset. Here I'm cloning pixels from one frame earlier onto the current frame (−1).

Figure 7.43 This dropout (which I've enhanced so you can see it more easily) is very jarring.

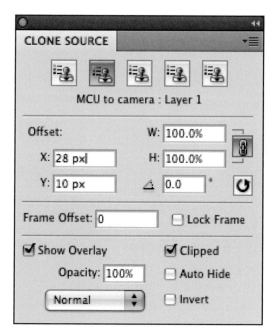

Figure 7.44 Position your cursor to the point where the bad section of image starts and note the X and Y Offset numbers.

settings change as you move the cursor around the image. These offsets indicate your current cursor position compared to where you Option-clicked.

2. Now that we know the location of the bad portion of the image, use the Animation Timeline to go to a frame that has a clean background. This is often within one or two frames of where you were.

3. Move the cursor around the image until the X and Y Offsets equal **0**. This indicates that your cursor is in exactly the same place on the clean frame as the problem section of the bad frame. Then, Option-click that spot to set the Source to these clean pixels.

4. Move back to the frame with the video you want to replace.

5. Click and drag the mouse to replace the bad pixels with the good ones.

The advantage to this technique is that lighting and color rarely change that dramatically between adjacent frames so that your repair should be virtually invisible.

One More Option: Onion Skinning

Onion skinning is the ability to display faint images of previous or next frames on the current frame. This allows you to match positions of objects between frames. While especially useful in cell animation, onion skinning also has a value when cloning.

Before I show you how to display onion skins, we need to configure them. To do so:

1. Display the Animation Timeline. In the top-right corner is a small fly-out menu. Click it and select **Onion Skin Settings** (Fig. 7.45).

2. Although the default settings generally work fine (see Fig. 7.46), sometimes you need to tweak, especially the blend mode. Setting it to **Multiply** at the bottom of the window tends to make your images darker (Fig. 7.47).

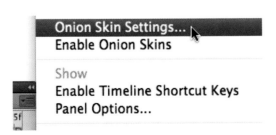

Figure 7.45 Click the fly-out menu in the top-right corner of the Animation Timeline and select Onion Skin Settings.

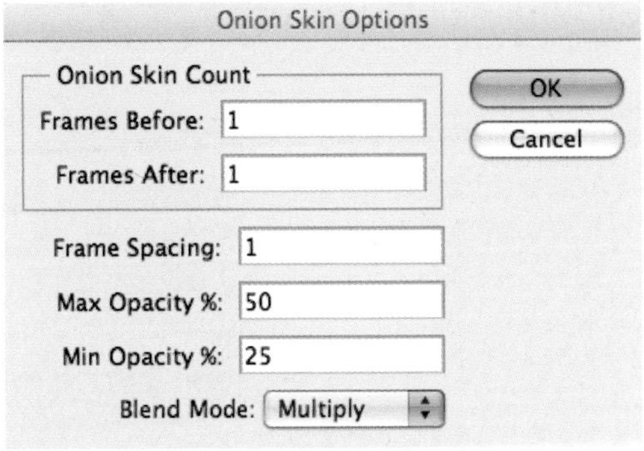

Figure 7.46 These are the default settings for onion skinning. Most of the time, they work fine.

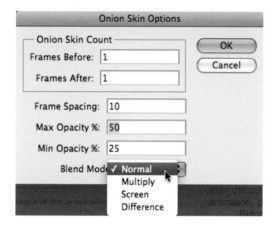

The default settings say that onion skinning will display the frame exactly one frame earlier and one frame later than the current frame – all in the same image. The earlier and later frames will be somewhat transparent.

In this case, I tweaked the settings to make the image lighter (Normal) and displaying the frame 10 frames earlier and 10 frames later (see Fig. 7.47).

Onion skinning is especially helpful when you are trying to place the position of an object, like a logo, in a frame and want to see where it came from and where it is going (Fig. 7.48).

Figure 7.47 The intensity of the onion skin effect is controlled by the Blend mode. Multiply makes it darker, Normal and Screen make it lighter.

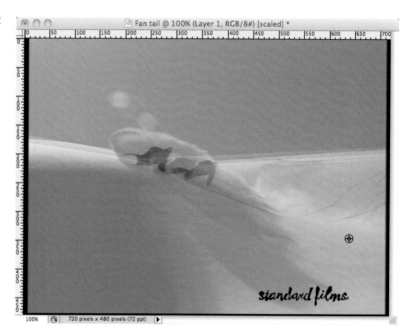

Figure 7.48 The result of the onion skin settings.

Using the Spot Healing Brush

Like the Clone tool, the Spot Healing Brush is wonderful – but for a different reason. It's a very fast way to clean up skin blemishes. For instance, the subject of this photo asked whether the brown spot on his forehead could be removed (Fig. 7.49).

This kind of cleanup is easy. Here's how.

Open the video clip or image you want to improve.

From the Tool palette, select the Spot Healing Brush tool (see Fig. 7.50).

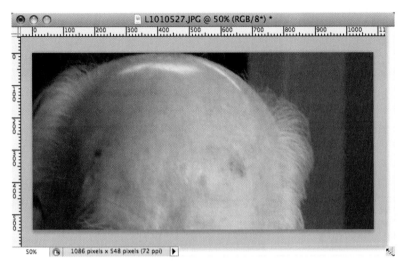

Figure 7.49 Here's an example of removing a skin blemish to improve the look of the video.

Adjust the brush width so that it is somewhat wider than the blemish you want to remove.

First, click directly on the blemish. If that doesn't provide enough correction, drag the brush across the blemish, starting somewhat before and ending somewhat after the blemish (see Fig. 7.51).

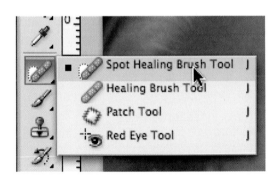

Figure 7.50 The Spot Healing Brush is perfect for removing blemishes.

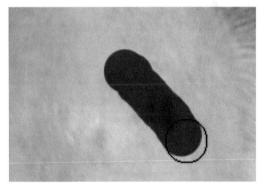

Figure 7.51 Drag the brush from somewhat before and after the blemish you want to remove. If you don't like the results, drag the brush from a different direction.

Poof! Gone (Fig. 7.52). Dragging from different directions will affect the final result. Keep trying until you get the look you want.

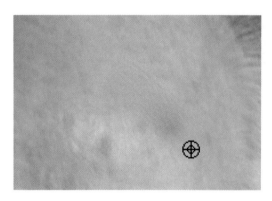

Figure 7.52 The blemish is significantly reduced.

Using Level Controls

The Level Controls have been in Photoshop for many years, but they are still incredibly useful in working with still images.

While I do not recommend using Photoshop Levels for adjusting video clips – the **Color Corrector 3-way** filter in FCP is far better for video – most digital still cameras tend to mess up levels and need to be adjusted.

Many digital cameras shoot pictures that have elevated, or washed-out, black levels and extended highlights. In other words, the pictures look "foggy" as seen in Fig. 7.53.

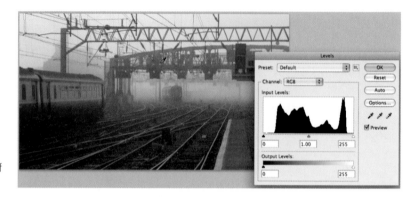

Figure 7.53 Many digital cameras shoot pictures that have elevated, or washed-out, black levels and extended highlights. This is an exaggerated example of washed-out black levels.

Here's a quick tip on getting your image exposures to look better.

Before bringing your picture into Final Cut, correct the exposures in Photoshop.

Open your image – again, don't do this with video – in Photoshop.

Select **Image > Levels** (or type **Command+L**).

Ignore the slider on the bottom, for a minute. Drag the slider on the left under the histogram (the black level) to the right until it just reaches the left edge of the clump of pixels in the histogram. What you've done is to tell Photoshop: "Adjust the gray scale of every pixel in this image so that they keep the same relationship to each other, but the darkest ones start at pure black."

Then, drag the slider on the right (the white level) until it just reaches the right edge of the histogram. What you've done now is to tell Photoshop: "Adjust the gray scale of every pixel in this image so that they keep the same relationship, but the lightest ones start at pure white."

Lowering black levels enhances the richness and vibrancy of an image. Raising the white levels adds sparkle and "life" (see Fig. 7.54).

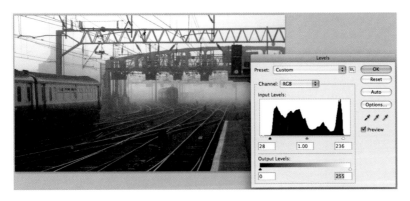

Figure 7.54 The corrected black-level setting and the result.

Straightening an Image

With CS4, Adobe moved one of my favorite tools for straightening an image. So, since I often need to straighten a poorly done scan, here's the process.

1. Open your image in Photoshop. Here, the church is leaning to the left (see Fig. 7.56). This is not good.
2. From the Tool palette on the right, click and hold the icon for the **Eyedropper**. From the fly-out menu that appears, select the **Ruler** tool (Fig. 7.57).

But Wait a Minute!

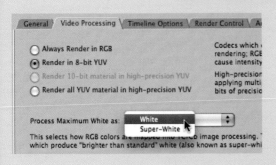

Figure 7.55

Isn't there some rule that says white levels in video can't exceed a certain amount and doesn't making this adjustment violate that rule?

Um, yes. This is true. Digital images have a higher white level than video images, and if you don't adjust for them, all your video will be screwed up.

However, the good news is that FCP automatically adjusts the white levels of all still images when you import them. So, you can make these adjustments inside Photoshop with a clear conscience, FCP will keep your video levels safe.

For those who insist on making sure, you will find the white-level setting by loading a sequence into the Timeline and selecting the sequence. Then, go to **Sequence > Settings >Video Processing** tab and make sure **Process Maximum White as** is set to **White**; which is the default.

Figure 7.56 Here's an example of a church that shouldn't be leaning.

Figure 7.57 The Ruler tool is hidden under the Eyedropper.

3. In your image, locate an edge, or line, that should be either horizontal or vertical. In this case, I used the vertical stone work in the stained-glass windows. Click one end of the horizontal or vertical edge and drag to create a very, very thin line – so thin, it is impossible to display in a screen capture. But it's there.

4. Go to **Image > Image Rotation > Arbitrary** (Fig. 7.58). When the dialog opens, it is preset with the amount and the direction you need to rotate the image to straighten it (Fig. 7.59).

5. Click **OK** and the image will now be perfectly straight (see Fig. 7.60).

Figure 7.58 The secret is to draw the ruler line before opening this dialog.

Figure 7.59 When you draw the line first, this dialog presets with the correct values to straighten the image.

33.33%   1133 pixels x 1464 pixels (72 ppi)

Figure 7.60 The finished, rotated image. Note how the entire frame has been rotated. Use Crop to make the white edges disappear.

Summary

Photoshop has a wealth of tools that will make image and video retouching a breeze. This chapter just touches the surface. However, using the techniques outlined in this chapter will put you far ahead of the average editor who is depressed because their stuff looks awful and they don't know how to fix it.

Your projects, on the other hand, will be done faster and look great!

My Story: Prepping Photos

Dan Shellenbarger
Executive Director, Ohio Channel
Sr. Lecturer, The Ohio State University
http://www.DVplace.com

Figure 7.61 Dan Shellenbarger

I do all my photo prep for Final Cut in Adobe's Photoshop. Much like there is never any video we shoot that does not get color-corrected in some way, I never use a photo in Final Cut that has not been touched up at least a little bit. Usually, it is nothing more than increasing the contrast a bit (under **Image > Adjustment > Levels**). I am always making my "blacks black and my whites white." The clone tool is my second favorite and for photos I am usually grooming my subjects a bit, here and there, removing pimples and whatnot, a digital dermatologist.

Scaling is the second thing I do to almost every photo/graphic in Photoshop. I was told to always keep the dimensions of my photos less 4000 × 4000 when using in Final Cut to keep my sequences working smoothly. I usually do that but now with our HD productions, I frequently bring in photos bigger than that. If I need to zoom in on a photo in Final Cut, I will make sure I have a larger photo prepped in Photoshop. I set a new sequence in Final Cut for all of my photo moves and immediately export it and reimport the clip to my main sequence. That way the computer processor doesn't have to continually munch on the full-size photo every time it plays back or renders. If I receive a graphic from a client that needs to be bigger, I increase its size in Photoshop and then bring it to Final Cut. Photoshop does a much better job of scaling up.

I also use Photoshop for video tricks, if I have time, I use Photoshop as a rotoscoping program. Beginning in CS3, you could actually edit video in Photoshop, though I prefer to go old school and simply export my video as Image Stills, setting the proper settings in the export box. Then importing these as layers into Photoshop. It is much easier to do this with shorter sequences, I will usually work on only 2 or 3 seconds of footage at a time, so I never have more than 90 layers to deal with.

This technique can be more for just fixing your footage. I also will use this technique to trace outlines of people or scenes, or create an animated line that appears to draw itself into a face or shape. It is a simple "stop-animation" style of filmmaking, where you just trace the outline of the imported stills, growing the line a little more each frame (this is why I will also usually limit my effects to 2 or 3 seconds, it can be a lot of tracing, especially if you are editing at 30 fps). The effect looks unique at its completion, but it was easy to do and took just time and tracing.

I couldn't imagine turning out client work without Photoshop!

8

TRAVELING MATTES, SHAPES, AND ROTOSCOPING

This chapter is a mix of old and new techniques in both Final Cut Pro (FCP) and Photoshop, which editors tell me they enjoy a great deal when I present them in my seminars.

We will look at a special kind of compositing called "traveling mattes." This involves creating new images based on elements from multiple images. This sounds complex, but you've watched these all your life; now learn how to do them.

This chapter starts with a simple traveling matte created entirely in FCP. Then, we'll improve it using some custom-created shapes from Photoshop. Finally, we'll tackle a new feature in Photoshop called Quick Selection and discover the joy – and pain – of rotoscoping.

But, first, let's define some terms.

Getting the Definitions Out of the Way

This chapter uses a number of technical terms, so before we get all wrapped up in the process, let me define a few terms. This won't take long.

Alpha Channel. Special information retained inside some still images and some video formats that indicate what portions of an image, or clip, are transparent. PSD, TIFF, and PNG files are examples of image files that can contain an alpha channel. Only video files using the ProRes 4444 or Animation codecs (or TGA for image sequences), have alpha channels. The easiest way to think about an alpha channel is that it determines the amount of transparency each pixel contains.

Chroma-key. The process of removing a specific color, such as green or blue, from an image so that the rest of the image can be superimposed on another image. While this process generally uses blue or green backgrounds, you can actually use any color, as long as it isn't also in the foreground portion you want to retain. This is also called "green-screen," or "blue-screen," keying.

Composite. Combining two or more images to create a new image. The process of creating a new image is called "compositing." Compositing always involves more than one layer of video.

Keying. An older video term that means to superimpose one image on another. Most often, this refers to text placed upon a background image.

Mask. While often used synonymously with matte, a mask is commonly a drawn shape, often using vector tools, to define the edge of a shape in the image. The key difference between a mask and a matte is that a mask uses a shape, while a matte uses an image.

Matte. While often used synonymously with mask, a matte is an image used to define or control the transparency of another image. In Final Cut, masks have three parts: the portion of the mask that is completely opaque, the portion that is completely transparent, and the portion that is partially transparent. Final Cut indicates transparency with black, opacity with white, and translucency with gray. This will be much easier to understand when you see it in action, I hope. Although not the same as a mask, these two terms are often used interchangeably, generally to confuse the unsuspecting.

Rotoscope. Originally coined in 1917 by Max Fleisher, this is the process of frame-by-frame painting on an image. For instance, to replace a live actor with a cartoon, or remove wires, or replace the background behind an actor. Rotoscoping is most often done by hand for each frame in an image, which means that it can be very time-consuming.

Superimposition. The process of putting one image on top of another image. For example, text is always superimposed on the background image.

Travel Matte. A special kind of composite where one image changes (travels) over time, generally by moving from one position to another in the frame. In Final Cut, this is most commonly created when one video plays in the background, while a second video is inserted into a hole cut by a shape into that background. The effect requires a minimum of three layers to create in FCP.

That gets us oriented. Let's see what happens when we put these terms to work by creating a simple traveling matte.

Creating a Simple Traveling Matte

Traveling mattes are my favorite effects (see Fig. 8.1). They are easy to do; once you learn how to do them. They are always fun to watch, and they are endlessly variable. Although not specific to the latest version of either Adobe or Apple software, this effect often requires the use of both to create.

At a minimum, a traveling matte in FCP requires three layers, though I almost always make them with four. Using Motion, or LiveType, you can make these more easily, but I want to have you understand how these are constructed because it will be relevant as we move into Photoshop later in this chapter.

Figure 8.1 This is the effect we are about to create. Note that we have video on the background with a different video playing inside the letters.

To get started, create a new project in FCP. (This effect can be easily integrated into an existing project, but, as usual, we'll keep things simple by focusing on just this specific effect.) Here are the steps.

1. Put the video you want to use as your background image on V1 (Fig. 8.2). Traveling mattes don't require audio, so in this case, we will create this video-only. For this example, I'm using a background from LiveType called **Space > Solar wind**, which is why it displays a red render bar in the Timeline. (See my LiveType note on the next page.)

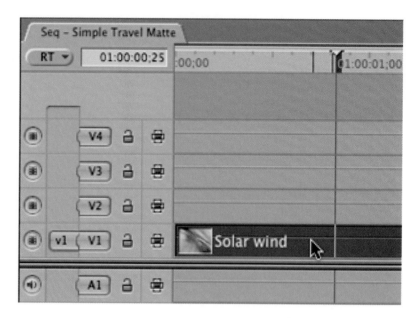

Figure 8.2 The clip you want to use as the background image goes on V1.

A Quick Note on LiveType

I wrote this chapter of the book before Final Cut 7 was released, which is why I used LiveType backgrounds. They are fun and easy to create. When I discovered that LiveType did not make it into the new version, I debated rewriting this chapter. However, whether you use backgrounds from LiveType, Motion, Digital Juice, or video that you shot yourself, the process of creating a travel matte is the same.

Figure 8.3 When you superimpose a text clip using the Canvas overlay menu, it is always trimmed to the length of the clip your playhead is in and is placed on the track immediately above the v1 patch on the left of the Timeline.

2. Put your Timeline playhead anywhere in the middle of the background clip.
3. Create a new full-screen text generator (press **Control + X**).
4. Before making any changes, drag the newly created text clip from the Viewer into the Canvas and drop it on top of the **Superimpose** overlay menu that appears (or press **F12**) as shown in Fig. 8.3.

Note that Final Cut automatically places the text clip on the next track above the background clip and superimposes the text so that you can see both the background and the text. Final Cut determines which track to place the video by the position of the V1 patch. Superimposed images are always placed one track above the track containing the V1 patch.

5. Double-click the text clip to load it back into the Viewer, so you can make changes. (This is a standard pattern for creating text in Final Cut: generate the clip – superimpose the clip – and double-click the clip, to load it into the Viewer.)

6. Go to the **Controls** tab in the Viewer (Fig. 8.4) and change the settings for your text. Always use the Controls tab for text changes – it provides greater flexibility and much higher quality than the Motion tab. Here are the changes I made:

Text: **Desire**
Font: **Impact**
Size: **200** points
Origin: H: **11.25** V: **76**

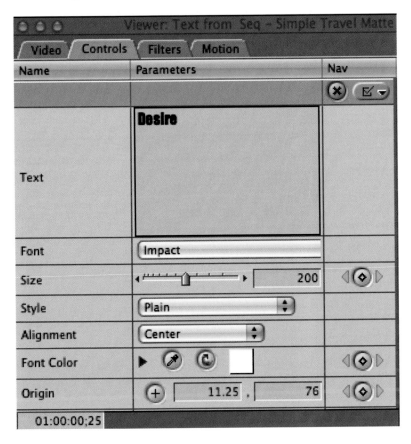

Figure 8.4 In the Controls tab, I changed the text to Desire, so I could make it bigger in the frame, and then changed the font to **Impact** and size to **200** points.

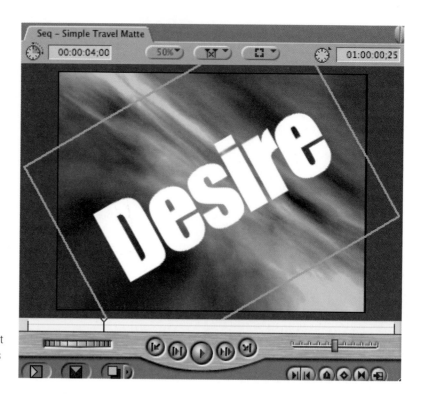

Figure 8.5 Here's what our effect looks like with the first two layers in place.

7. Then, just to show off, I went to the Motion tab and set Rotation for the text to **−30** (Fig. 8.5). This put the text on an interesting angle. You now have white text keyed against the background.

On V3, which is the track above the text, we will put the video that goes inside the white text. This is why we use the term *matte* in describing this effect. The text on V2 used to matte, or cut a hole, in the background so that we can put different video into the hole cut by the text.

8. To create the final effect, add another video clip to V3, directly above these two clips. Again, while you can use any clip for the insert image, it is generally a good idea to look for something that contrasts both in color and texture with the background. Here, I've used another LiveType background: **Space > Alien Fire** (Fig. 8.6).

9. The only problem is that, by default, since video clips in FCP are always full screen and fully opaque, when we add the V3 clip it totally blocks the clips below it. This is where the magic comes in. Select the V3 clip, then . . .

10. Select **Modify > Composite mode > Travel matte – Alpha.**

11. Sha-ZAAM!! Instantly cool effect (Fig. 8.8).

The Case for Title 3D

One of the advantages for using Title 3D for text is that you can rotate the text while retaining its vector shape, which is something that can't be done in Final Cut.

The problem with our text is that, because of the low resolution of video, text is hard to read. We need to separate it from the background, and that means we need to add a drop shadow. But where do we add a drop shadow? We can't add it to V1, that's the background image and full screen.

We can't add it to the V2 clip because it messes up the effect. We can't add it to the V3 clip because V3 is only contained inside

Figure 8.6 With the three layers now added, your Timeline should look like this.

Creating Motion Backgrounds

Motion ships with hundreds of animated, full-screen backgrounds (see Fig. 8.7). Getting them into Final Cut is easy. In Motion, choose the Library tab, select the Contents category on the left, then Backgrounds on the right. Double-click the icon of the background you want to use to add it to the Motion Timeline. Adjust the length as necessary, then save the Motion project. You don't need to render the movie first, Final Cut will do that automatically. Import the Motion project into Final Cut and continue editing. I find myself frequently referring to the Motion and LiveType libraries whenever I need an animated background.

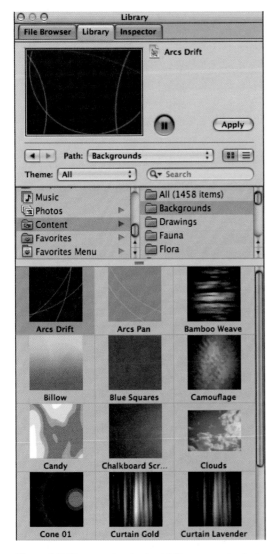

Figure 8.7 There are hundreds of full-screen, animated backgrounds in Motion, which can easily be imported into FCP.

Figure 8.8 Here's our finished effect ... except, it still has a bit of a problem.

Why This Works

This effect works because all text in your Mac has a built-in alpha channel. Final Cut knows where the text is (the part of the text that is white) and where it is not (where there is no text). FCP then says to itself: "Where there is no text, I'll display the background. Where there is text, I'll display white."

Then, when we change the composite mode from Normal to Travel Matte – Alpha, Final Cut continues its conversation with itself by saying: "Hmm ... All text has an alpha channel, so where the text is transparent, I'll display the background and where the text is white, I'll substitute the V3 clip."

(Um, lest you think I'm going completely nuts, I know that Final Cut does not talk to itself. I was just using this as an illustration of the programming involved. Sheesh.)

Larry's Rule of Text

My strong suggestion to all my students is that whenever they superimpose a text over a background, they should always add a drop shadow to improve readability, especially, when the color of the text closely matches the color of the background. Video has very low-resolution images – adding a drop shadow makes all your text a lot easier to read.

the letters, and the drop shadow needs to be outside the letters.

In fact, we need to create a new layer specifically for the drop shadow. This is why I say that while a traveling matte can be created using only three layers, in most cases, you'll actually use four.

Here's what you need to do.

Select the V2 and V3 layers and press **Option + Up Arrow**. This moves both the selected video clips up one track. (This shortcut of Option + Up/Down Arrow is a great technique, but it can only be used with video-only, or audio-only, clips. Linked clips can't be moved this way until you unlink them.)

Hold both **Shift** and **Option**, and drag the V3 clip down to make a copy of it to V2. (Shift-Option is another of my favorite keyboard shortcuts – it duplicates clips.)

Double-click the V2 clip to load it into the Viewer.

In the Motion tab, check the box for drop shadow, and then twirl it down and enter my favorite drop shadow settings:

Offset: **1.5** for SD video, 2.5 for HD video
Softness: **30**
Opacity: **90**

With these settings, even if the color of the text is the same as the color of the background, you'll still be able to clearly read the text (Fig. 8.9).

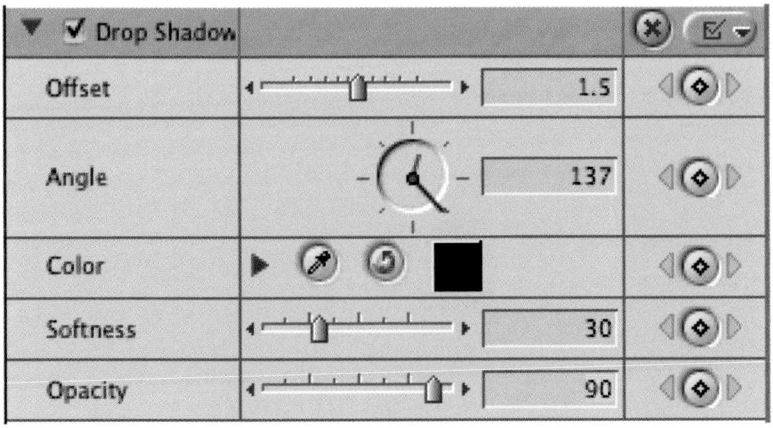

Figure 8.9 Here are my favorite drop shadow settings for SD video. I always add them to any text that I wish to superimpose in FCP. For HD video, I change the Offset to 2.5.

Another Way to Create a Drop Shadow

Another way to create the drop shadow is to nest the V2 and V3 clips, and then apply the drop shadow to the nest.

The benefit to this approach is that you can animate the nest, and the shadow moves with it. So many choices . . .

Whew. While that seems like a lot of work, it really isn't – it just takes a while to explain.

What we've created is a four-layer effect: V1 is the background layer, V2 is a text clip with a drop shadow, V3 is the same text clip as V2 without the drop shadow, and V4 is the video that goes inside the text (see Fig. 8.10).

Figure 8.10 Here's the finished, four-layer effect.

The Limitations of Masks in FCP

A traveling matte is a very cool effect and the one that I use frequently with a wide variety of backgrounds and inserted images.

The problem comes when I want to create a mask using something other than text. Here, we run into a significant limitation of Final Cut – we can't draw custom shapes, and our masking tools are limited to squares, rectangles, circles, ovals, and rounded rectangles, not a large geometric selection by any means.

This means we need to consider other tools to create custom shapes. There are many to choose from, but my first tool of choice is Photoshop, and that is what we cover next.

To Prevent White Pixels Showing around Your Text

A trick you can use to prevent the white text from V2 from leaking around the edges of the V3 clip is to load the V2 clip into the Viewer, select the **Controls** tab, click the Eyedropper tool next to Color, and then click the Eyedropper on one of the letters in the Canvas (Fig. 8.11). This converts the color of the V2 clip to match the color of the final effect. In almost all cases, this will make your overall effect look better.

Figure 8.11

Creating Custom Shapes in Photoshop

In the last example, we used text generated in Final Cut to cut the hole in the background, which we then filled with a video. Let's stay with this concept of video playing inside another video, but let's replace the text with a custom shape.

While FCP has a very limited selection of custom shapes – specifically, a circle, diamond, rectangle, and rounded-rectangle – it does support any text shape that can be generated from a symbol or dingbat font. However, for this example, none of these is a roly-poly running man, which we will use as the source for this example.

That's where the custom shape tool in Photoshop comes in. We can create any number of shapes, which have their own alpha channels, which we can use inside FCP.

Creating the Image in Photoshop

Let me illustrate.

1. Create a new Photoshop document; in this example, I named it "Running Man." While this technique works for any video format, to keep our screen shots small for this book, I'll create this for an NTSC DV 4:3 project. Note that I set the background to Transparent, assigned the **SDTV NTSC** color profile, and used the image dimensions from Chapter 6 (Fig. 8.12). As we discussed in chapter 6, we can use the SDTV NTSC or SDTV PAL color profiles as well as sRGB. All three profiles provide the correct gamma setting for SD video.

Note: Image Sizes Still Matter

Chapter 6 was devoted to explaining how to create images that size properly for video. In this exercise, we are creating a PSD image in Photoshop for import into Final Cut. Be sure to follow the steps detailed in Chapter 6 to properly size your images, so they import correctly.

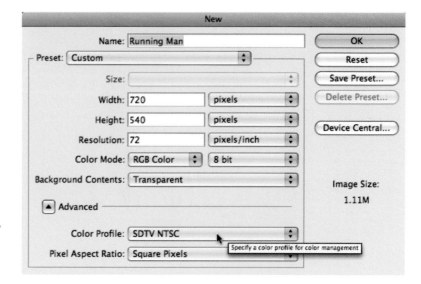

Figure 8.12 Create a new Photoshop document. Here, I'm creating a document for NTSC DV 4:3. Note that I created this with an SDTV NTSC color profile, a transparent background, and sized according to the table in Chapter 6.

2. PSD files retain all their alpha (transparency) channel information when we move them into Final Cut, so all we need to do is create our running man shape and leave the rest of the image transparent.

3. Normally, as you create elements in Photoshop, you add layers to hold them. However, shapes are always created in a new layer.

4. Buried near the bottom of the Photoshop tool palette is the Line Tool. Inside that menu, select the Custom Shape Tool

Pick the Right Color Space

Whenever you create something in Photoshop for use in FCP, be sure it is set to RGB 8-bit Color Mode. Don't use 16- or 32-bit. You can set this in the New Image screen or change it later using **Image > Mode > RGB Color** (see Fig. 8.13). Color spaces other than RGB, such as CMYK or LAB, are designed for print and will not display properly if you try to use them in Final Cut. RGB images are required for display on the web and video.

Figure 8.13

Layer Transparency

If you don't set the background to transparent when you create a new image, then, by default, the background layer is opaque. To allow the background layer to display transparency, double-click it in the Layers tab to unlock it. The name changes from Background to Layer 0. At this point, you can delete the contents of the layer to make it transparent.

To create a new layer, click the New Layer icon at the bottom of the Layers palette (Fig. 8.14). Any layer added above the background retains its transparency when imported into Final Cut.

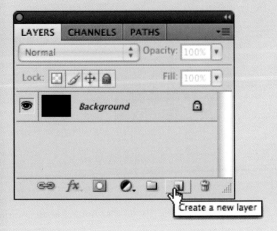

Figure 8.14

(Fig. 8.15). While there are a number of other shape tools, the Custom Shape Tool is the most fun.

5. At the top, in the toolbar, are two additional controls that make this tool even more useful to work with. Click the blue bar next to the word Shape and dozens of shapes are displayed for you to pick from (see Fig. 8.16).

6. If your screen doesn't match mine, click the small fly-out menu in the top-right corner (it's a tiny arrow) and select **All** (Fig. 8.17). This menu gives you a variety of ways to view the available custom shapes, as well as sort them into different categories.

7. For this example, we will select the small, solid black, roly-poly running man (Fig. 8.18). Photoshop calls this shape Blob 1 – but I know, in his heart, he wants to be the roly-poly running man.

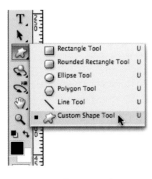

Figure 8.15 Select the Custom Shape Tool from the tool palette.

Any of these shapes can be used in a traveling matte. Video keys into the portion of the shape that is black. You'll see the background video through that part of the shape that is white, or transparent.

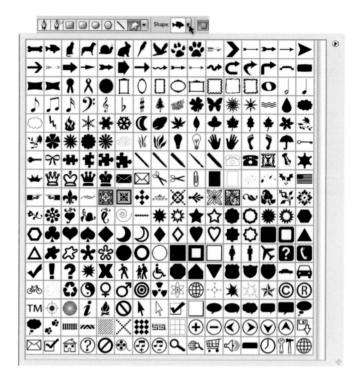

Figure 8.16 There are dozens of vector-based custom shapes. Vectors can scale to any size flawlessly and the wide variety of shapes offers plenty of choice.

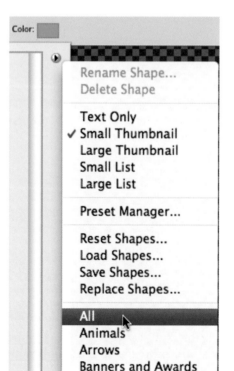

Figure 8.17 If you don't see all the shapes I do, click the small, right-pointing arrow, which is a fly-out menu in the top-right corner and select **All**. This menu gives you a variety of ways to view the available custom shapes.

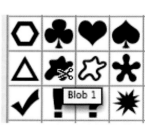

Figure 8.18 Select the shape you want to use by clicking it; in this case, we'll select Blob 1.

8. The shape now appears in the small box next to the word "Shape" in the toolbar. To the left of that is a dialog that allows you to customize the size, aspect ratio, and other parameters of this custom shape (Fig. 8.19). Although the defaults are fine for this example, you should know that they are there.

9. Because we want the shape to be used to create a custom matte inside Final Cut, we need the shape itself to be solid white. The color of the shape is selected from the Color chip in the toolbar at the top of the main window (Fig. 8.20).

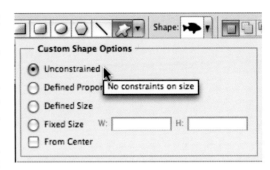

Figure 8.19 This dialog, to the left of the Shape window, allows you to constrain the custom shape you just selected.

Figure 8.20 The color of the shape is determined by this Color chip. Click it to set the color; in this case, we want it to be white.

10. Now the fun begins. Draw a shape as you want it to appear in Final Cut (Fig. 8.21). Once you import it into Final Cut, you have limited options for changing it.

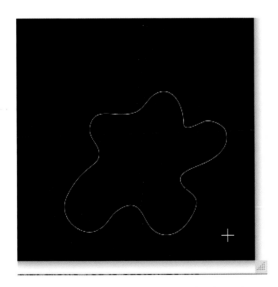

Figure 8.21 Draw your custom shape to the size and at the location you want it to appear in your Final Cut project. As you draw, the shape will be displayed as an outline. When you let go of the mouse, the shape will fill with the white color you selected.

Shortcut Keys Can Help

As you are drawing your shape, press the **Shift** key to constrain the aspect ratio of the shape. Or, after you start drawing, press the **Option** key to draw from the center of the object. Finally, once you start drawing, press both **Shift** and **Option** to constrain the aspect ratio and to draw from the center. Drag the object to reposition it.

11. To move the shape, press **V** to select the Arrow (Vector) tool and drag the shape where you want it. In this case, I'll move it to the lower right corner.

12. By default, a new shape layer is named "Shape," followed by a number. In this case, it is called **Shape 1**. Double-click the layer name in the Layers palette and rename it to something more useful. In this case, I named the layer **Running Man** (Fig. 8.22).

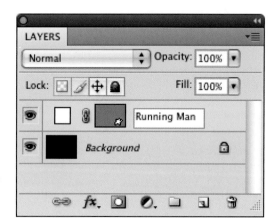

Figure 8.22 You can rename any layer by double-clicking the name. You can change the stacking order by dragging the layer up or down in the Layer palette.

13. Save the file as a Photoshop document (Fig. 8.23). The Save dialog defaults to the name you entered when creating the image. Be sure both Layers and Embed Color Profile are checked. If a second dialog appears asking whether you want to maximize compatibility, say Yes.

14. Finally, squish the image, so the aspect ratios match by saving a second version of the file. To do this, go to **Image > Image size** and change the size according to the PSD sizing table in Chapter 6. In this case, we resize the image to 720 × 480. Then, save the file using a different name.

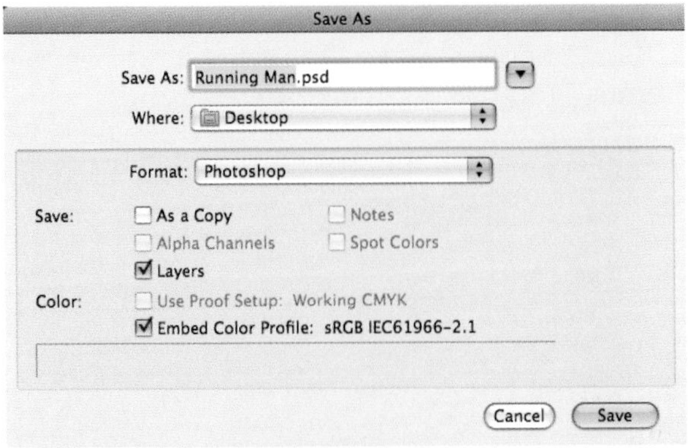

Figure 8.23 Save the file. Be sure to retain the layers and save it as a Photoshop document (PSD).

Adding the Image to the Effect in FCP

Switch back to Final Cut and import the squished image. Remember to set Easy Setup to match your sequence settings prior to import, or your imported image will not look correct.

As we discussed in Chapter 6, PSD images come in as sequences, with each layer converted to a separate clip on its own track in FCP.

Now, we need to create a traveling matte using the blob as the shape we will fill with video.

Double-click the PSD file in the browser to open it in the Timeline; remember it's a sequence, so it opens in the Timeline automatically (Fig. 8.24).

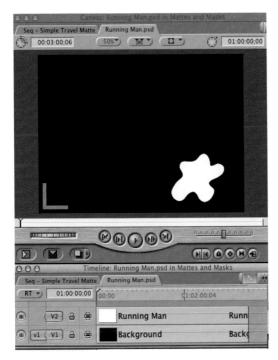

Figure 8.24 The Photoshop image imports into Final Cut, with each layer as a separate clip.

Select the Running Man clip on V2 and choose **Edit > Copy**.

If you still have the sequence you created earlier for the simple traveling matte, remove the two text clips from V2 and V3, and paste the Running Man into the V3 track (see Fig. 8.25). Because of the composite mode you applied to the V4 track, the V4 video will instantly fill into the V3 Running Man matte.

Figure 8.25 From the traveling matte we created earlier, remove the two text clips from V2 and V3, and paste the Running Man clip into the sequence on V3.

Note

If you paste the Running Man clip into V2, the effect won't work. The foreground video and the image that cuts the hole must be next to each other.

As a way of refreshing your memory, duplicate the Running Man clip by **Shift-Option**-dragging it from V3 to V2. Then, apply a drop shadow to the V2 clip in the same way we did earlier in this chapter (Fig. 8.26).

While we used a running man to introduce the Custom Shape Tool, this technique of creating a traveling matte using shapes or text created in Photoshop, or FCP, applies to any shape or text that is stored to its own layer in a PSD file and imported into Final Cut.

There are two types of travel mattes: Alpha and Luma. An Alpha matte uses the transparency data in the PSD file to determine what is foreground (opaque) and what is background (transparent).

A second way to create a travel matte is the Luma matte. Using an older technology than an Alpha matte, it uses luminance to determine opacity. In this case, white is replaced by the foreground (white), black is replaced by the background (black), and gray is the translucent boundary (feathering) between them.

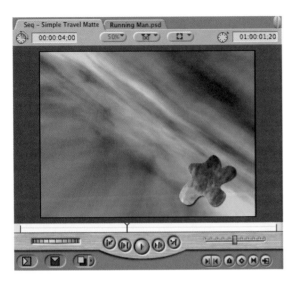

Figure 8.26 Here is the finished effect, complete with drop shadow. While we used a running man, this technique can be used with any shape or text created in Photoshop and saved to its own layer.

Extra Credit

For extra credit, and the ability to pat yourself on the back, create a shape in Photoshop that has soft edges. The softness represents translucency. When imported into Final Cut, the soft edges will translate into a soft blurring of your travel matte (see Fig. 8.27).

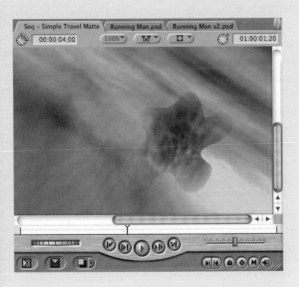

Figure 8.27

To apply this effect, select the top clip, V4 in our example, which is the image that fills the matte, then choose **Modify > Composite mode > Travel matte - Luma**.

The Next Step: Creating a Mask Using Rotoscoping

So far, we've created effects where the alpha channel was built-in, first with text inside Final Cut, and then with shapes created inside Photoshop. But what can we do when we have an image that does not have an alpha channel? Worse, what if we didn't realize it needed to be composited until after we shot it? Figure 8.28 illustrates the problem – we didn't create the image using a blue- or green-screen background.

(a)   (b)

Figure 8.28 (a) Our starting image is on the left – a polar bear standing on a rock in front of a cement wall. (b) Our ending image is on the right – a polar bear standing on a rock on the edge of eternity.

How about Rotoscoping in After Effects or Motion?

Both Adobe After Effects and Apple Motion support rotoscoping. However, neither of them have the wealth of selection tools that Photoshop provides. (Sadly, none of the three allows us the ability to animate the rotoscoping process.) After Effects only allows rotoscoping using Bezier curves, while Motion provides both B-spline and Bezier curve control. But Photoshop has even more options, I tend to prefer Photoshop.

(Well, that's not true. I strongly prefer not rotoscoping at all . . . but when it is necessary, I turn to Photoshop first.) However, at some point, the process of rotoscoping becomes so cumbersome that using a more advanced tool becomes the best choice. A good tool is Studio Artist by Synthetik (www.synthetik.com).

Well, all is not lost, but the process – called "rotoscoping" – is time-consuming, and it requires a combination of Photoshop and FCP. Rotoscoping isn't hard, really, it's just painstaking, persnickety, and time-consuming.

The Process of Rotoscoping

In this example, we want to create a closing image for a video about the impact of global warming on the arctic. I have some video of a polar bear taken at the Toronto Zoo. I need to remove the background and key the bear into something more dramatic.

In the process, I'll showcase a couple of new tools that Photoshop CS4 makes available.

Here we go.

Open the image that contains the background you want to remove into Photoshop. In this case, it's the Polar Bear video (Fig. 8.29).

Figure 8.29 Here's the video we want to clean up, loaded into Photoshop. Note the image looks "stretched." This is OK, we are working with video here, and the aspect ratio should not be changed.

Note that when the video is opened, the image looks stretched. That's the issue of square vs. rectangular pixels we discussed in Chapter 6. In this case, it is critical that you *not* resize the video because you are bringing it back to Final Cut when you are done in Photoshop. Also, if it is interlaced, do not deinterlace it.

To easily move between frames in the video, select **Window > Animation** to display the Animation Timeline. Make sure the CTI (playhead) is at the start of the clip.

What about Interlacing?

All SD, and some HD, video are interlaced. Interlacing is indicated by thin horizontal lines radiating off moving elements in the picture. Interlaced footage makes rotoscoping much harder in Photoshop because Photoshop does not know how to select between fields. Don't deinterlace the footage you plan to continue using as video – this only reduces the resolution and makes all your images soft. If you are working with interlaced video, and you don't like the results you are getting in Photoshop, you'll need to use software specifically designed for the task, such as Studio Artist by Synthetik (www.synthetik.com).

Figure 8.30 The Quick Selection tool makes fast the work of removing a background when all the colors to be removed are similar.

What we want to do is remove the gray background behind the bear. Fortunately, Photoshop CS4 has a great tool that makes this easy – the **Quick Selection** tool. It's the fourth tool down in the tool palette (see Fig. 8.30).

1. Adjust the brush size in the Brush menu at the top, so it isn't too big or too small for the area you want to select. Personal preference is probably a good judge. In this case, I selected a 30-pixel brush size and left the other settings at their defaults (Fig. 8.31).

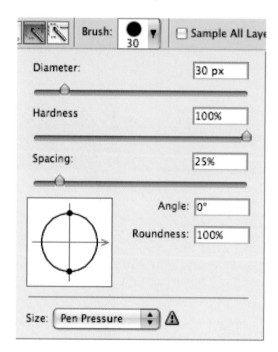

Figure 8.31 From the Brush menu at the top, select a brush size that isn't too big. For SD video, a brush size between 30–50 works fine.

2. Starting from the background you want to remove, drag the tool a short distance. Photoshop will select all the contiguous pixels that match the area you dragged across. Press the **Delete** key to make them disappear. Do this again for every region of the background you want

Benefit to the Quick Selection Tool

One of the things I like about the Quick Selection tool is that it does a better job of selecting around soft edges, like the fur of the bear, than other tools. While this tool is new, it has become one of my favorites. I tend to use this first; only when it doesn't work, I will try other tools.

Figure 8.32 Drag the tool in short sections to select portions of the background to remove. Press Delete to remove them.

to remove. In the case of the polar bear, it took me two swipes to eliminate the background (Fig. 8.32). Working in sections is faster and easier than trying to select everything at once.

3. The good news is that removing the background was fast and easy using this technique. The bad news is that we need to repeat this process for every frame in our video – this explains why I am not a fan of rotoscoping. So, click the right-pointing arrow in the Animation window, and repeat this process for every frame in your video from which you want to remove the background.

Don't worry. I'll wait.

4. In my case, because I want to show you the process, and not create a complete video, I'm only going to do the first 15 frames. (I always knew there was a benefit to writing about video in a book . . .)

In this example, it took me about 6 seconds per frame to remove the background. Exercises like these remind me of just how many images are in 30 frames per second.

Don't Deselect between Frames

You could press **Command + D** to deselect the background region as you move between frames. But, if the foreground doesn't move between frames, a better option may be to leave everything selected and use Quick Select because it retains its shape from one frame to the next.

You can easily add to the selection by pressing the Shift key and dragging the tool across the new portion of video. Or remove portions of the selection by pressing Option while dragging.

Exporting the Video

What we've done, in removing the background, is that we have created a region of transparency in the clip. The next step is to export this clip so that the transparency is retained and able to be imported into FCP.

When you are done rotoscoping, it's time to save your work. Remember, we *save* images, but we *export* clips. Here's how:

1. Select **File > Export > Render Video**.
2. The Render Video dialog determines what kind of video we want to create. At the top, give the file a name and a location. (I added the word "roto" to remind me this is the roto-scoped version of the video (see Fig. 8.33).)

Figure 8.33 Give the file a name. I used the word "roto" to remind me this is the rotoscoped version.

3. Because I want to do additional effects work once this gets back into Final Cut, click **Settings** next to QuickTime Export. **Sound** will be grayed out because Photoshop doesn't export audio, and **Prepare for Internet Streaming** should be unchecked. Click **Video > Settings** in the Movie Settings window (Fig. 8.34) to open the Standard Video Compression Settings window.

Figure 8.34 Click **QuickTime > Settings** and then **Video > Settings** to configure the export for FCP.

4. Because I want to retain the alpha channel information with the clip, set the Compression Type to **Apple ProRes 4444** (Fig. 8.35). This is both the highest quality you can export from Photoshop and one of only two codecs that support alpha channels. (Older systems should use the **Animation** codec.) Also, be sure **Compressor > Depth** is set to **Millions of Colors+**.
5. Click **OK** to accept these compression settings.

Remember, when exporting to go back to FCP, never apply output filters, don't change the image size, don't check Sound, don't check Prepare for Internet Streaming, and don't deinterlace. Click **OK** to return to the Render Video window.

6. Range allows you to specify which frames you want to export. Normally, you would export all of them. In my case,

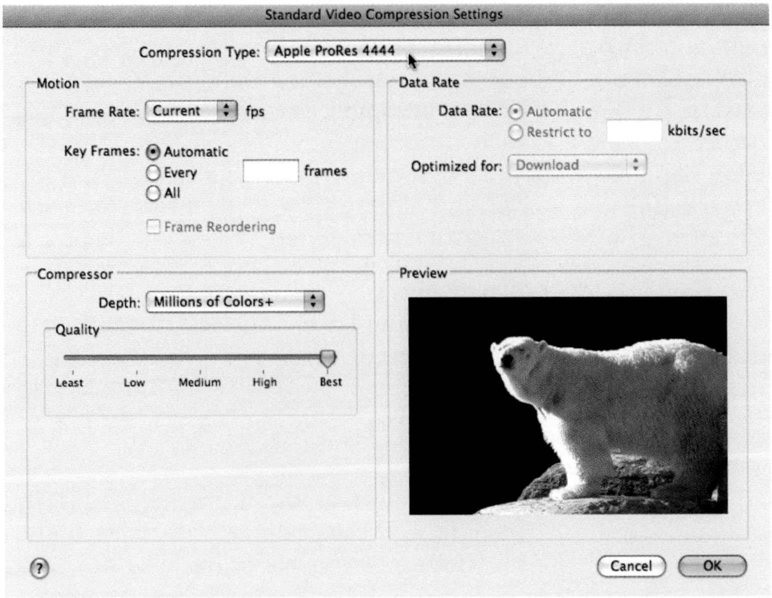

Figure 8.35 When you want to retain transparency information in the clip, be sure to set the Compression Type to ProRes 4444, or Animation for older systems, and set Depth to Millions of Colors+.

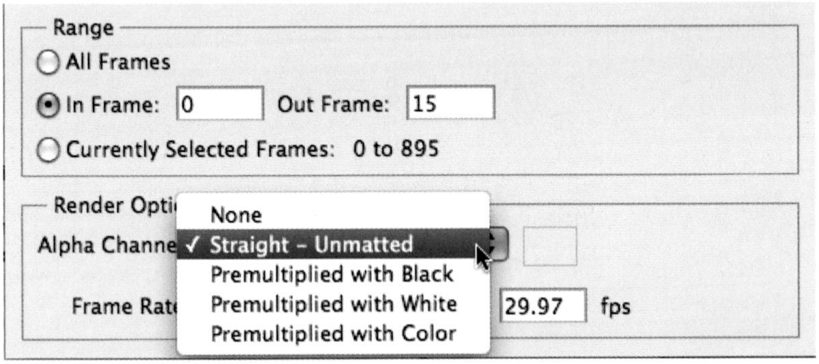

Figure 8.36 Normally, set the Range to **All Frames**. In this instance, however, I only want to export the first 15 frames. Next, set the Alpha Channel to blend the edges based on the luminance level of the background.

however, as I only rotoscoped the first fifteen frames, I only want to export the first fifteen frames.

7. Premultiplying the alpha channel, see Fig. 8.36, confuses a lot of people. Premultiplying determines the blending of the edges between the foreground and the background. Here's how to know what to pick:
   - NEVER select **None** when you want to include the alpha channel in a clip.
   - When in doubt, select **Straight – Unmatted**.
   - When compositing the foreground against a darker background, you may get better results by selecting: **Premultiplied with Black**.
   - When compositing the foreground against a lighter background, you may get better results by selecting: **Premultiplied with White**.
   - NEVER use **Premultiplied with Color**, as Final Cut does not support it.

Adjusting Final Cut

Whatever choice you make here, you need to match the setting in Final Cut – I'll show you how when we get there.

In this case, because the background we are using has both light and dark elements in it, I'll leave this set to **Straight**. This is also the default alpha channel setting for Final Cut.

Click the **Render** button, and after a period of time, your new clip is exported and ready for Final Cut. The amount of time this takes depends upon the length of the clip, the speed of your processors, and the complexity of your effect. However, you generally always have time to get a cup of coffee.

Finishing the Composite in FCP

Now that we've created the alpha channel and exported the clip, its time to see the results of our work:

1. Import the clip into Final Cut's Browser.
2. Edit the clip you want to use as the background to V1 of the Timeline.
3. Edit the rotoscoped, polar bear clip immediately above it to V2 of the Timeline, and select the V2 clip. Note that as soon as you do, you'll see your effect because the background of the polar bear retained its transparency.

Remember, the alpha channel settings we set as part of the Photoshop export? Well, now we need to match them in Final Cut. To do so, select the V2 clip, go to **Modify > Alpha type**, and set it to **Straight** (Fig. 8.37). By default, when Final Cut senses an alpha channel, it defaults to **Straight**.

However, the edges of the bear have a heavy black line. This is a good example of trying different alpha channel settings to get the best results. Select the bear clip and change the alpha channel to **match the setting you used in Photoshop** and, as Fig. 8.38 shows, the edge cleans up a lot.

5. To see the results of your hard work immediately, press **Option + P** – this plays an effect without first rendering it. (It goes slower than real-time, but it sure beats waiting for a render.)

This is a truly cool effect, and not that hard to create, once you know how.

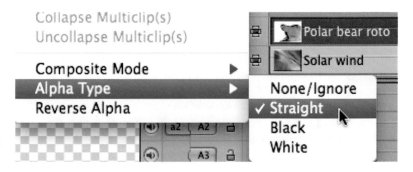

Figure 8.37 To match the alpha channel settings you used in Photoshop, go to **Modify > Alpha type** and set it to **Straight**.

 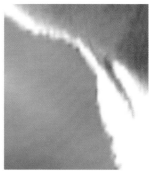

Figure 8.38 Here's a really good example of the benefit of adjusting the alpha type. The heavy black edge along the bear's fur on the left disappears when you match the Alpha Type setting in Final Cut with the one you used in Photoshop.

Summary

I really like this chapter because it takes effects that we've seen for years and gives us lots of new ways to create them to keep our projects looking fresh.

My Story: Using Photoshop to Match Your Text to Your Sequence

George Mauro
Apple Certified Trainer and Editor
www.geocities.com/geomauro/

I've edited for over 30 years, and I'm all about thinking ahead. In the old days – excuse me while I get my walker out – we used to have to roll many tape decks at one time to create an effect like dissolving a picture inside another picture with text overlaid on top.

All these items had to go through a switcher and keyed on top of one another. It was like orchestrating a symphony. Now it's as easy as drag, drop, plop, fizz, it's done.

I'm going to explain how to save some time and to organize files to make life a little easier when it comes to multiple layers of text and images.

Photoshop and FCP are perfect for this. I'll show you how to take a Photoshop document with multiple layers of text and images, and import it into FCP. You'll set markers on the Timeline, and then nest one sequence into another. You'll see how planning ahead will save you lots of time later on.

Figure 8.39 George Mauro.

I do a lot of "how to" videos. Whether it's for a cooking show or a medical procedure, it doesn't matter. What matters is timing, how to time your fade up and fade down of text, or footage according to the narration.

I always cut to sound. You know that speaking about a procedure takes less time than seeing the procedure. Try this. Tell someone to make pancakes.

Read out loud:

- Two cups of whole-wheat flour
- Two eggs
- Tablespoon of baking powder
- Teaspoon of salt
- Half cup of fat-free milk
- Half cup of applesauce
- A touch of cinnamon
- Mix well and cook

If you were to say this, it'll only take about 15 seconds. However, this same narration would take almost a minute to show the viewer how to do this. Right?

Okay. Here's what we do.

In your first sequence, let's call it The Primer, we'll create the audio track and adjust it for timing. Take your narration and place it in your sequence. You are going to space out the description according to your editor's internal clock. You set the tempo of a scene by slicing your narration and by moving the pieces apart to allow for the video to show what you've just said.

Use the blade tool [press **B**], look at the waveform in the Timeline [type **Command + Option + W**] and use the Flying V? The what? Press **Control + V** while the playhead is moving down the Timeline and watching the waveform, you can cut on the fly . . .

Move your pieces apart by using any one of these processes: Drag – Numeric – Brackets. You can either click-and-drag these pieces downstream or highlight them, and use either the numeric keypad to dial in a distance to move them or the brackets to nudge them down. Personally, I grab the suckers and yank them down by dragging, and then fine-tune with the left and right brackets to set them where they should go.

Once you have your V1 footage and narration done, you're ready to add the text over this video. All of which come from the Photoshop document.

Let's keep using the pancake example to keep it all simple.

In The Primer, we have video on layer one and audio sliced and spread out.

Now, make your Photoshop.psd and import it into FCP. Make a separate layer for each ingredient for the pancakes, and add an image for each one as well; that's just extra credit if you want. Save it as a Photoshop document (PSD), and import it into FCP.

If you double-click this doc, it'll open as a sequence. The length of each layer is 10 seconds if you leave your user preferences in the default settings. Let's stretch these layers out to make sure that we have more than we need. If you've ever placed a sequence inside a sequence, called nesting, and then edited the eggs in the nest after the fact, you'll see the nest updates in the final sequence, and usually not in a good way.

Now, go back to The Primer and place your nest on the next video layer and over your narration.

Highlight your photoshop.doc nest and get ready to start marking your spots. Once the playhead is moving, you can hit **M** on the fly to mark where you want each of your layers to fade in or out. Because the nest is highlighted, the markers will go into this clip. Now, double-click the nest to see the eggs. Note the markers you made in the clip are now markers in the nest's timecode ruler.

The rest is simple. Move each layer into positions under each marker – make sure snapping is turned on to make it easier – add your **Command + T** transitions to fade up/down each layer. Go back to The Primer and you're done! All timed perfectly.

9

CREATING BLU-RAY DISCS

If ever an exciting new technology had a star-crossed life, it has to be Blu-ray Discs.

From its initial death scrum with Toshiba's HD DVD format to its current challenge from digital downloads, Blu-ray has battled obstacles both from the marketplace and of its own making. These include multiple hardware specifications, exorbitant licensing fees, limited replication facilities, and a lack of market perception and penetration.

Given all those drawbacks, why should anyone still be interested in this format? The answer is simple. It provides massive, high-speed, high-quality video in a package optimized for retail distribution.

In this chapter, we'll take a look at the Blu-ray format and present four different workflows we can use to create Blu-ray Discs on the Mac. In doing this, I'll show you how to use tools in Final Cut Studio, Roxio Toast, and Adobe Production Premium.

A Quick Lookback

Apple joined the Board of Directors of the Blu-ray Disc Association on March 10, 2005. Naturally, that led many of us to assume that Apple would immediately begin supporting Blu-ray Discs in forth-coming Macintoshes.

But that isn't the way it's turned out.

Currently, Blu-ray Discs cannot be played on any Macintosh computer. When asked why, in October, 2008, Apple CEO Steve Jobs replied: "Blu-ray is just a bag of hurt. It's great to watch the movies, but the licensing of the tech is so complex, we're waiting till things settle down and Blu-ray takes off in the marketplace."

This inability to play Blu-ray Discs means that program authors need a more circuitous workflow to create and test their discs. While the latest release of Final Cut Studio makes some steps in the direction of Blu-ray, current software provides far from full support.

When Blu-ray was first announced, the Blu-ray Association also announced fees that we had not encountered when authoring standard DVDs: license fees for mandatory copy protection (AACS) and using the Blu-ray logo. In addition to normal manufacturing costs, these fees were significantly higher than a standard DVD. Initially, these license fees were in the thousands of dollars per title, making this new technology out of reach for all but the most well-heeled production companies.

Thanks to the tireless negotiating efforts of Bruce Nazarian and the International Digital Media Alliance (http://www.idmadvda. org), these license fees have been significantly reduced in recent months.

There are two ways a Blu-ray Disc can be created: replication and duplication. Replication is a manufacturing process that stamps out large numbers of discs like a cookie cutter. Replication makes sense when you are creating a thousand or more copies of the same disc.

The second option is duplication. When you duplicate a disc, you use standard optical-disc-burning technology to make the copy. The reason for this distinction is that license fees apply only to replicated discs, not duplicated discs.

So, if you only need a few dozen copies of your project, you don't need to worry about license fees at all.

Limited market share is more worrisome, in that no one wants to invest in a format that only addresses a limited audience. As this book is being written, the reported market share for Blu-ray Discs is less than 10% of all DVD players in the market. Sales appear to be growing, but slowly. In fact, Toshiba – long the foe of Blu-ray – recently announced support for Blu-ray Discs with its own Blu-ray players.

Another significant threat facing Blu-ray is the impact of digital downloads. In today's world of "I've got to have it NOW!" the instant gratification of immediately downloading the file you need is hard to resist. Apple, too, seems to agree, with its continued support and marketing for the iTunes and App Stores. Apple's interest in downloads is not matched by their Blu-ray efforts.

So Why Bother with Blu-Ray?

There are several key benefits to the format that can't be met by either digital downloads or standard DVDs, which make it impossible to simply dismiss the format.

These include massive data storage, extremely high quality, a product format ideally suited for retail distribution, and a higher perceived price point for the same content.

Both the Web and Blu-ray use the same data codec: H.264. However, because the storage of Blu-ray is so much greater, the

Downloading Movies Is Not Trivial

A high-quality 1080p Blu-ray movie requires approximately 30 GB for storage. Given a 2 Mbps Web download speed, it would take more than 33 h to download a video of comparable quality to Blu-ray.

Clearly, waiting a day and a half to watch your download makes Blu-ray a much more attractive delivery option.

The key question then becomes: what's the balance between the image quality of Blu-ray, vs. the instant fulfillment of downloads vs. the difference in costs?

optical media format allows much higher data rates, providing far better image and audio quality, than anything you could reasonably download from the Web.

A Blu-ray Disc can currently hold up to 50 GB of data (there are technology previews showing storage capacities of more than 100 GB per disc), which makes Blu-ray attractive for both media and simple data storage.

Because of this huge storage capacity, Blu-ray provides much higher image quality due to its ability to support much higher data rates than the Web. This makes the format especially attractive to those subjects which put a premium on image quality.

Blu-ray also simplifies the ability to deliver surround sound along with image quality.

There is a lot of impassioned debate on the Web currently as to whether retail distribution will soon be supplanted by Web-based businesses.

However, as someone who sells both online and through traditional retail distribution, it is interesting to me that there is a higher perception of quality, and a correspondingly higher price point, for the same content sold on an object you can hold in your hand compared to a download.

Download distribution is cheap, but it doesn't command one-tenth the price of a physical object. For producers who need to provide finished goods with a high-perceived value (i.e., wedding videos), the value of Blu-ray far exceeds downloads.

Which format will ultimately win the distribution battle has yet to be determined. However, for now, producers should definitely keep Blu-ray in their arsenal of potential product offerings.

Get the Right Hardware

Given the speed with which technology changes, it would be a waste of paper to spend much time discussing specific brands and model numbers in a book that will last far longer than any piece of technology currently on the market.

However, here are some general guidelines.

Macintosh computers do not currently record or play Blu-ray Discs using their built-in SuperDrives. (There is a work-around to this – called an AVCHD disc – which is described shortly.) This means you need to get an external Blu-ray burner and a way to play your finished discs

Complicating the hardware choice further – and nothing in our industry seems to be getting simpler – there are three different Blu-ray specifications, which means there are three different types of Blu-ray players. These are called by the catchy names of: Profile 1.0, Profile 1.1, and Profile 2.0. (While all Blu-ray players support all three formats, these differences become important when you are authoring, or creating, the Blu-ray Disc.)

Profile 1.0 was the first version of Blu-ray released to the market. While machines following this spec can play videos, many of the higher-level features we take for granted are missing here. These machines are characterized by their lower price.

Profile 1.1, also called "Bonus View," added the ability to display picture-in-picture.

Profile 2.0, also called "BD-Live!," added Internet connectivity and improved interactivity. Many Hollywood titles are designed to this spec.

There are solid Blu-ray burners from Sony, Panasonic, and other companies that range in price from $200–$400.

If you are just looking for a full-featured Blu-ray player, the current favorite is the Sony Playstation 3. There are lots of them in the market, they work great, and if you love games, you get two goodies for the price of one. Be sure, by the way, to purchase the remote control if you plan to use this for Blu-ray playback.

Get the Right Media

I should mention that you also need good media for recording your projects. There are three types of media that can be used for Blu-ray: a standard DVD, for short Blu-ray projects; write-once, called BD-R; and write-many, called BD-RE. All work well; however, the BD media holds far more data. Of the two BD media, BD-R costs less.

There are wide variations of media quality in the market. Don't buy solely on price. Generally, if a manufacturer makes good DVD media, they will also make good Blu-ray media.

Four Workflows to Blu-Ray Production

You would think that Apple's DVD Studio Pro would be the tool of choice to create Blu-ray Discs… you'd think so, but you'd be wrong. Even in the latest release of Final Cut Studio, DVD Studio Pro only creates SD and HD DVD, DVDs.

But wait a minute, I hear you say, what about this HD DVD format the manual talks about? Sadly, the HD DVD format died a couple of years ago. There is no relationship between HD DVD and Blu-ray Disc.

So, this means that we need to use other tools to create Blu-ray Discs. With the release of latest version of Final Cut Studio, Apple now provides two different options for the creation of Blu-ray Discs. Final Cut Pro 7, using the new Share function,

---

A Note on the Word "External"

Throughout this chapter, I refer to using an external Blu-ray burner. As this book goes to press, Blu-ray burners that connect inside your Mac are starting to appear. So, for this chapter, I define "external" as a DVD burner that is separate from the DVD burner that shipped with your system, that is purchased from someone other than Apple, and that can be placed either inside or outside your Mac.

provides a very simple method to export and burn one movie to a Blu-ray Disc. Compressor 3.5, also, provides the ability to create Blu-ray Discs, through its new Job Actions. However, both FCP and Compressor only provide simple menu templates, and not complete authoring.

Because of the challenges in creating Blu-ray Discs, there are four different workflows we can use:

- Share in FCP 7 to create a simple one-movie "screener."
- Roxio Toast to create a Blu-ray Disc containing multiple movies burned to a standard DVD with 30–60 min of total content.
- Roxio Toast to create a Blu-ray Disc containing multiple movies burned to an external Blu-ray burner with up to 2 hours of total content.
- Adobe Encore to create a complex, customized Blu-ray Disc burned to an external Blu-ray burner for movies up to 4 hours in length.

These four workflows range from creating simple projects (Final Cut) to very complex ones (Adobe Encore). Let's take a brief look at each of these to get a better sense of when to use them.

Workflow #1: Using Share in FCP 7

One of the new features in FCP 7 is the ability to create a Blu-ray Disc directly from FCP. There are two ways Blu-ray can be burned to a disc by Final Cut: using a standard DVD (creating an AVCHD disc) and an external Blu-ray Disc burner. If you plan to burn Blu-ray Discs, you need to purchase an external Blu-ray burner.

The advantage to this workflow is that it is easy and built into Final Cut. The disadvantage is that it only supports putting one sequence (containing as many clips as you want) on the disc. You can't use this to author complex, or even moderately sophisticated, titles. This is designed to make it easy to put one HD movie on a Blu-ray-compatible disc, such as a review copy or screener.

Here's the executive summary: edit your HD sequence as you would normally. When you are done and it is ready to export, use the **File > Share > Blu-ray** setting to create a Blu-ray compatible file and burn it to a disc.

Let's see how this works in real-life.

1. Select the sequence, clip, bin, or range of Browser clips to burn to disc.
2. Choose **File > Share** (Fig. 9.1).
3. From the Output Type pop-up menu, select **Blu-ray** (Fig. 9.2).

What's a Movie?

 In the latest version of Final Cut, we can export a single clip, range of clips, bin containing clips, or sequence to Blu-ray Disc. However, all selected clips are turned into a single movie, with the option to place chapter markers at the start of each piece. Neither Compressor nor Final Cut allows putting more than one HD movie on a Blu-ray Disc.

Apple Introduces a New Term

 With the release of FCP 7, Apple has introduced a new term: AVCHD Disc. This refers to Blu-ray media burned to a standard DVD burner in your Mac using the AVCHD codec. Apple says this format can be played on most Blu-ray players. However, this format is not the same as a Blu-ray Disc. The data is in a similar format, but the discs themselves are different.

According to Apple, these AVCHD discs can be created by either Final Cut or Compressor.

Macintosh Can't Play Blu-Ray Discs

 Just as a reminder, current Macintosh hardware can't burn or play Blu-ray Discs. Even if you have a Blu-ray burner, you still can't play a Blu-ray Disc on your Mac.

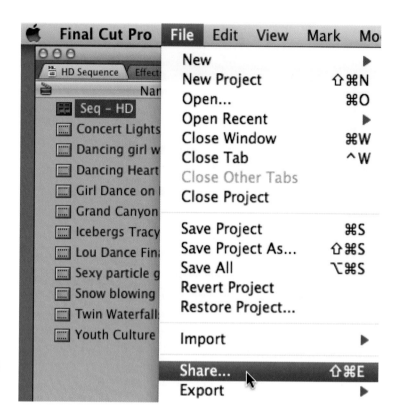

Figure 9.1 Select your sequence in the Browser first, then choose **File > Share**.

Figure 9.2 Select **Blu-ray** from the Output Type pop-up.

4. Final Cut provides a default file name. You can change this by selecting the contents of this text box and adding your own file name.

5. To see what is about to happen, click the small Show Info "i" to the right of the file name (Fig. 9.3).

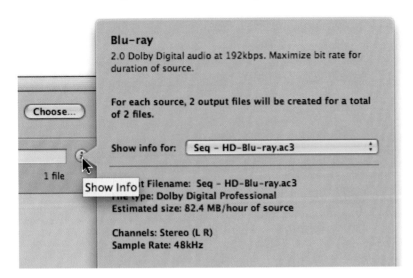

Figure 9.3 This window displays information about what you are about to do.

6. If you want FCP to actually burn a Blu-ray Disc, and prompt you to insert a blank disc for burning at the appropriate time, check the **Create Blu-ray Disc** checkbox. If this is left unchecked, FCP only outputs the compressed media files to the hard disk destination you specify, which allows you to copy the files yourself to a disc at a later time.

7. If Create Blu-ray Disc is checked, the Action Drawer appears. You can customize these settings as necessary (Fig. 9.4).

8. Settings in the Action Drawer include the following:

Output Device. This is used to tell FCP where to burn your media.

Disc Template. This is used to select from a variety of included menu templates for your Blu-ray Disc (Fig. 9.5).

Title. This is the name that appears for your disc.

When Disc Loads. Similar to "First Play" in DVD Studio Pro, this determines what happens when you put the completed disc into a Blu-ray player. Your choices are to either display a menu or immediately start playing the movie.

Figure 9.4 This Action Drawer appears when Create Blu-ray Disc is checked. You can customize this as necessary.

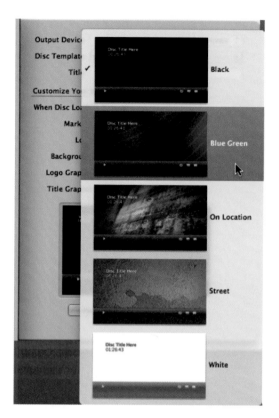

Figure 9.5 Choose your menu from a variety of prebuilt Blu-ray templates.

Background, Logo, and Title. These graphic buttons allow you to customize the template with your own background, logo, and title images.

Main Menu and Chapter Menu. These buttons allow you to preview the look of the template and placement of buttons prior to burning the disc.

9. Once your settings are complete, you have two output options: **Send to Compressor** and **Export**.

Send to Compressor. This sends the file, with all the settings you just applied, into a batch in Compressor. This allows you to take advantage of the additional customization capability in Compressor.

Export. This compresses the file and, if you request it, burns it to a Blu-ray Disc (Fig. 9.6).

10. When compression is complete, another dialog appears asking you to insert a blank disc into your Blu-ray burner (Fig. 9.7).

That's it. Very simple. The limitation of the technique is that it provides only one movie on a disc. Think of this more as a fast way to easily provide screeners and review discs rather than as an authoring tool.

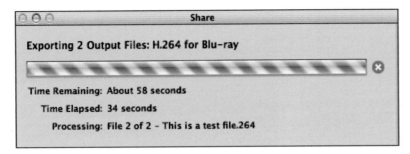

Figure 9.6 After you click the Export button, FCP compresses the file and displays a progress bar showing how much time is left in the process.

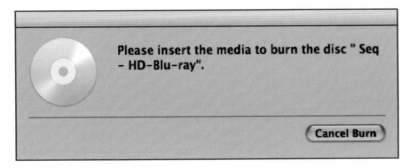

Figure 9.7 When compression is complete, and if you haven't yet inserted a blank disc into your Blu-ray burner, this window will remind you.

If you want to author a disc with more than one movie on it, we'll need to look at one of the next workflows.

A Word about Exporting Video from FCP

If you have a version of Final Cut earlier than 7, or if you want to create a master file of your project to retain for a while, Share is not an option. In this case, to get video out of Final Cut for a DVD, we need to export it. Here's the best way to do this.

1. Edit and finish your sequence, as normal, in Final Cut.
2. Export your sequence using **File > Export > QuickTime Movie**. To maintain the highest quality while still outputting as fast as possible, leave the setting pop-up at **Current Settings**.
3. Give the file a name and storage location, and click **Save**. On my system, I created a folder called **Exported Files** where I store all my exports. This is not required, but it does make them a lot easier to find (Fig. 9.8).

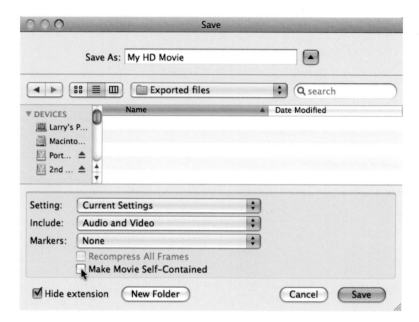

Figure 9.8 Give your exported file a name and location. For fastest speed, don't check Recompress All Frames, or Make Movie Self-Contained.

Time for a Bar Fight

There is a lot of debate on what's the best way to set Export settings for Final Cut Pro. Based on my research and readings, I recommend using **File > Export > QuickTime Movie** with Output set to **Current Settings**. This outputs your sequence in the same format you edited it. Since this is, generally, the same format you shot, you can't get higher image quality than your original image. So, it doesn't make sense to export at higher quality. The net result of changing output settings is that you are transcoding (converting) your media, running it through an extra compression step, and not gaining anything.

It's like pouring a small amount of water into a bigger bucket. The storage space may be bigger, but the amount of water hasn't changed.

There has been discussion that you get higher quality exporting using the Animation codec. My research disagrees. There is a display setting in QuickTime that when it plays a DV or HDV movie, it does so at only ¼ quality. This means that if you judge the quality of your movie by looking at it in QuickTime, the quality is quite poor. However, either changing these display settings or compressing the movie yields results equal to what can be achieved by transcoding into the Animation codec in a fraction of time and file size. Although I have not extensively tested exporting using the latest versions of ProRes, I would expect the results to be similar.

Recompress All Frames should only be checked when you want to force re-rendering every frame of your project. Leave this unchecked.

There is no difference in quality between checking or unchecking **Make Movie Self-contained**. A self-contained movie duplicates all your media and stores it in one gigantic media file. A reference movie simply points to the original source media.

So, if you are going to immediately compress your media on the same system you edited it, you will save time and disk space by *not* checking Make Movie Self-contained.

Workflow #2: Putting Blu-Ray Video on a Standard DVD

One of the more intriguing new ideas is to create a Blu-ray Disc using standard DVD media and burning it on the DVD burner in your Mac. The reason this works is that Blu-ray players can play Blu-ray-formatted media stored on both standard DVDs (burned with a red laser) and Blu-ray Discs (burned with a blue laser). By the way, the fact that Blu-ray is created using a blue-violet laser is how the format got its name.

There are two limitations to using this AVCHD technique:

1. Since a standard DVD doesn't hold as much data as a Blu-ray Disc, we can't put as much media on this disc as we can on a Blu-ray Disc. As a general rule, expect to fit 30–60 minutes of material on a standard DVD, depending on your choice of codec and the compression settings you use.
2. Because a red-laser DVD doesn't transfer data as fast as the blue laser in Blu-ray, our image quality is generally not as high.

Still, for many projects, this can be a very helpful work-around.

We've already established that DVD Studio Pro can't create any form of Blu-ray Disc. This means we need to use other software. In this case, a simple tool of choice is Roxio Toast. You can use either Toast 9.02 with the Blu-ray plug-in or any version of Toast 10. (The screen shots in this book are from Toast 10 Titanium Pro.)

Start by opening Toast and click the Video clapper slate at the top to switch to the video section of the application (Fig. 9.10).

Big Note

 After upgrading to Toast 10, in preparation for writing this book, I went to create a Blu-ray title – only to discover that the Blu-ray options were not available! To enable Blu-ray, you need to go to **Toast > Preferences > General** and turn on **Show Blu-ray video projects** (Fig. 9.9). At which point Blu-ray now appears in the menus. (This small point was omitted from the Toast manual and I won't tell you how long it took me to discover it. Sheesh..!)

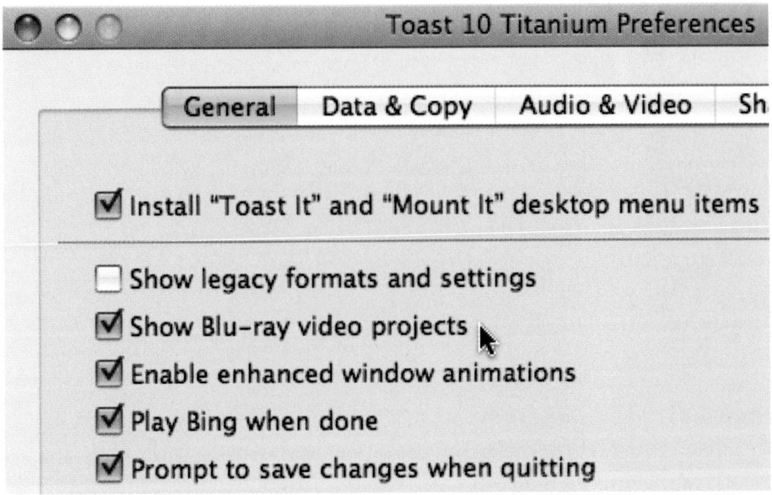

Figure 9.9 To create a Blu-ray Disc you need to turn this option on in Toast > General preferences.

Figure 9.10 Whether you are burning to a DVD or Blu-ray Disc, be sure to select Blu-ray Video.

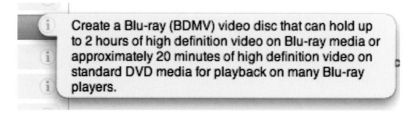

Create a Blu-ray (BDMV) video disc that can hold up to 2 hours of high definition video on Blu-ray media or approximately 20 minutes of high definition video on standard DVD media for playback on many Blu-ray players.

Figure 9.11 Click the Get Info "i" to learn more about the burning option you've selected.

Figure 9.12 Click the name of your burner to display a list of devices to choose from to burn your disc.

Figure 9.13 Drag the movie(s) you want to add to your disc by dragging them into the large window on the right.

From the list on the left, click the **Blu-ray Video** option. Click the Get Info "i" to learn more (Fig. 9.11).

At the bottom of the Toast window is a list of DVD, or Blu-ray, burners attached to your system. Select the one you want to use to burn this disc (Fig. 9.12). (If you only have one burner attached to your system, clicking the burner name causes Toast to scan your system for additional devices, but not display a list.)

Drag your HD movie into the large area on the right (Fig. 9.13). It now appears as a small thumbnail with a title at the top of the window. (You can drag in as many movies as will fit onto a disc.)

You can change the name of your disc by clicking the default My Movie name at the top of the window disc (Fig. 9.14).

Figure 9.14 Change the name of your disc by clicking My Movie and entering a new name.

Figure 9.15 Editing your movie allows you to change text or video settings prior to compression.

Toast Recognizes FCP Chapter Markers

If you added chapter markers in FCP, and exported your movie to include these chapter markers, Toast uses these chapter markers as it builds the DVD.

Toast v9, and early versions of Toast 10, reportedly have problems with chapter marker placement. The markers are offset by approximately 7 seconds in the video! If you plan to use chapter markers in your projects, be sure to use the latest Toast update.

Click the **Edit** button to the right of the file name to edit either the text information associated with your movie or the video (Fig. 9.15). For instance, in the Video tab, you can add an In or Out marker to include just a portion of the video on your disc, add chapter markers to the disc, or change the poster frame of your movie.

One of the hidden benefits to using Toast is that you have an easy way to add menus to your titles. Click the Options button (Fig. 9.16) in the lower left to show a new set of menus allowing you to pick a menu style, and adjust encoding settings.

Clicking the Menu Style pop-up displays dozens of template options to choose from (Fig. 9.17). Click the small icon to the right of the pop-up menu to display settings for your **Disc**, **Menus**, and **Encoding**. (You can also click the **More** button at the bottom of the Options window to get to the same screen.)

Figure 9.16 Toast provides a great deal of control over your DVD by clicking the Options up-arrow in the top right corner.

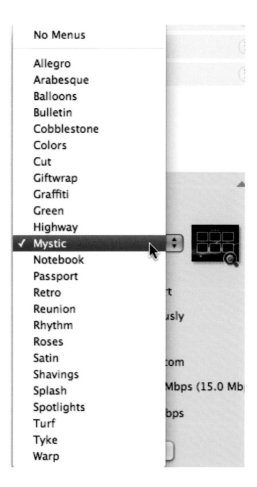

Figure 9.17 Click the Menu Style pop-up to display dozens of menu choices. Click the small menu icon to display the menu settings window.

At the bottom of the Options window are the controls for encoding your files. You can keep things simple by leaving this set to **Automatic**, or if you like to tweak, set this to **Custom**.

However, while you can switch the encoding options here, you need to adjust them in another window. So let's go there now.

Click the **More** button at the bottom of the screen to open the settings window. There are three tabs: Disc, Menus, and Encoding.

The **Disc** tab (Fig. 9.18) allows you to rename your disc, set it to automatically play when inserted into a player, and add your own customized slide shows.

The **Menus** tab (Fig. 9.19) allows you to change the template, rename the menu title, control how many buttons are displayed on the screen, add buttons for scene menus and slideshows, and tweak the overall look. While you can't design your own template, this still provides a significant amount of control over the template itself.

While you can't change the position of the buttons and their poster frames within the menu, you can change the background image by dragging a new image on top of the menu icon. (For best results, size the menu image to the same size as your video file.) Click the magnifying glass to see an enlarged view of your selected menu template.

The Encoding tab has two options: **Automatic** and **Custom**.

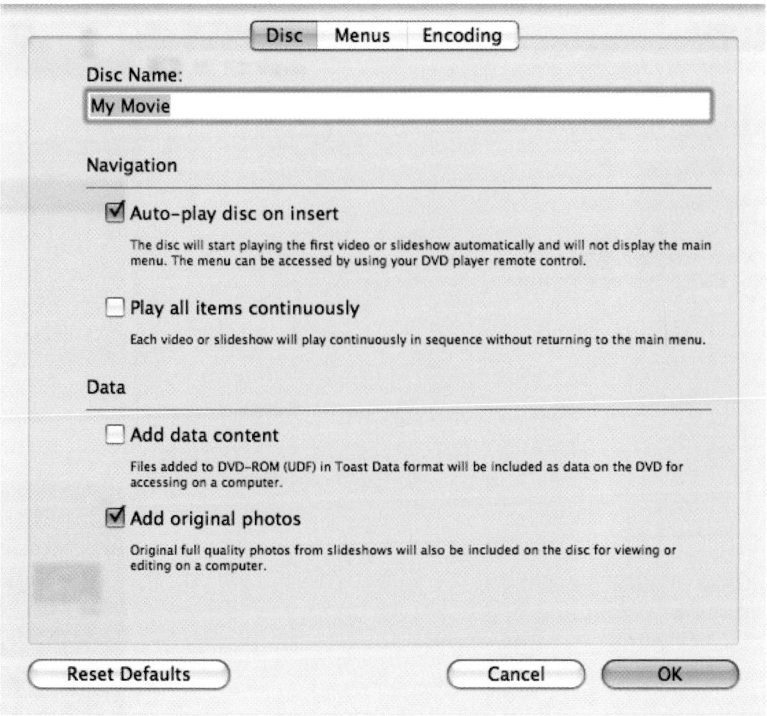

Figure 9.18 The Disc tab determines the name of your disc, whether it autoplays your movie, and other settings.

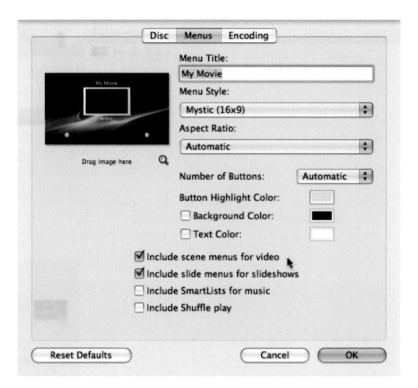

Figure 9.19 The Menus tab allows you to change menu templates, background images, and control the overall look of the template.

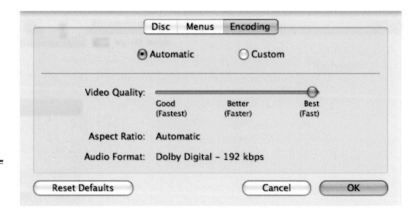

Figure 9.20 Clicking Automatic in the Encoding tab provides a simple way to select between faster encoding or higher quality. Audio defaults to Dolby Digital.

Important Compression Note

The codec you choose in Custom remains the selected codec when you return to Automatic, which means it really isn't automatic at all. To be safe, always check your compression settings using Custom. Be very careful using Automatic.

If you select Automatic encoding (Fig. 9.20), the only thing you can adjust is the quality slider. This allows you to set the balance between encode speed and quality. In this setting, audio is Dolby Digital (192 kbps) and can't be changed. Because of these, and other, limitations, I strongly encourage you not to use the Automatic settings.

If you click the **Custom** button (Fig. 9.21), the Encoding tab displays a lot more options. Figure 9.19 illustrates the settings I recommend for encoding HD to a standard DVD.

Set the Video Format to **MPEG-4 AVC** (this is another name for H.264). This codec offers the smallest file size with the highest quality. However, it takes longer to encode than MPEG-2. It is important to set the codec first, before adjusting compression settings.

A variety of settings – similar to what we find in Compressor – appear. These provide a great deal of control over image quality and file size. For detailed descriptions of what these controls do, consult the Toast documentation.

Now that you have added your movies, configured the disc, menus, and set the encoding levels, it's time to create your disc. Before you do, though, check the estimated size of your media in the lower right corner (see Fig. 9.23), just to make sure everything will fit on your disc.

Now comes the fun part – push the big red button (Fig. 9.23)!

There's one last window. Here, you can change the drive that burns your media, change the write speed, and indicate how many copies you want it to make (Fig. 9.24).

Load fresh media into your drive and press **Record**.

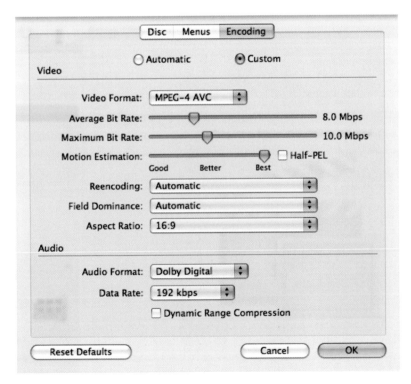

Figure 9.21 Clicking Custom allows you much more control over the encoding process. These are the settings I recommend for encoding HD to a standard DVD.

Be Sure You Have Enough Space

Prior to burning your disc, Toast needs to create a variety of very large temporary files during compression and final compilation of the disc. It is a good idea to have at least 30 GB of free space. To set Toast's scratch disc to a volume with plenty of room, go to **Toast > Preferences > Storage**.

On my second drive, which I use as a scratch disk, I created a folder called **Roxio Converted Items**. I then point the Converted Items menu to that folder by clicking the **Change** button at the top of the screen.

Then, at the bottom of this window, I pointed the **Temporary Storage** to the second drive as well (Fig. 9.22).

Important Caution

The quality of any encode is not only dependent on the encoder, but on the content being encoded. Therefore, the data rate numbers I recommend in this chapter are only a guideline, and not a guarantee of an acceptable encode.

As the amount of movement in your video increases (think of a talking head compared to a football game), your data rates will need to increase.

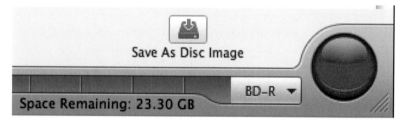

Figure 9.22 Go to **Toast > Preferences > Storage** to set your scratch disks to a drive with plenty of room.

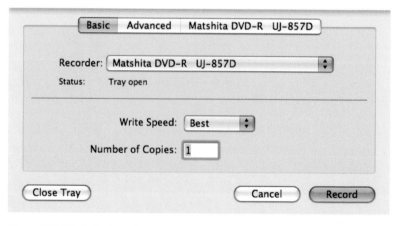

Figure 9.23 Be sure to check the size estimator next to the big, red button to make sure your media will fit on the disc. Then, to burn your disc, push the big red button. If it helps, imagine giant klaxons going off in the background.

What Speed Should You Burn?

In the past, I opposed the idea of burning optical media as fast as possible. The faster you burn, the more errors creep into your discs. So, for this reason, I recommended burning CDs no faster than 16x and DVDs between 2x and 4x. Using these speeds, I've never had a burn failure. Blu-ray is still new technology, and burning speed wisdom is scarce. For now, I recommend leaving the Write Speed setting at Best, but keep track of any burn failures. If they start to appear, slow your burn speed down.

Figure 9.24 This is the last window before burning. Use it to make sure you've selected the right burner, burn speed, and copies.

At this point, things take a while. Use this opportunity to rediscover your family, your pets, or sleep.

In the background, Toast is compressing your media according to your settings, combining audio and video (a process called "muxing") with the menus into the finished Blu-ray BDMV folder, and then, finally, burning that folder to the disc. If you are making multiple copies, it only does the encoding and muxing once, which means all following discs burn faster than the first one.

During this time, Toast displays a variety of status screens, so you know that it hasn't forgotten you. Still, this process can take a long time.

When the disc is finished, pop it into your Blu-ray player – remember, you can't view Blu-ray Discs on your Mac even if you have an external burner connected because the OS doesn't support it – and admire your work.

Workflow #3: Creating Actual Blu-Ray Discs Using Roxio Toast

The cool part about creating actual Blu-ray Discs is that the process is virtually identical to what we just went through in putting Blu-ray media on a standard DVD.

In other words, you already know how to do this, even though you haven't done it yet!

Since the only changes are in the encoding settings and the burner we use to create this disc, you can now squeeze up to 4 hours of media on a dual-layer disc, and with the faster data rates Blu-ray allows, your Encoding settings can be faster, providing higher quality.

My suggested encode settings are illustrated in Fig. 9.25. (While every video is different, often necessitating slightly different encoding settings, these will get you close.)

Workflow #4: Sophisticated Blu-Ray Production Using Adobe Encore

Final Cut allows us to create a simple, one-movie Blu-ray Disc. Toast allows us to work with templates to create titles containing multiple movies. But what if you want more complete control over a much more sophisticated title? That requires Adobe Encore.

Similar in capability to DVD Studio Pro, but far exceeding it with HD media, Adobe Encore provides a number of advantages over anything we've seen so far. These include the ability to

- Create fully customized menus.
- Create motion menus.
- Create pop-up menus.
- Create dual-layer discs supporting up to 50 GB of media.

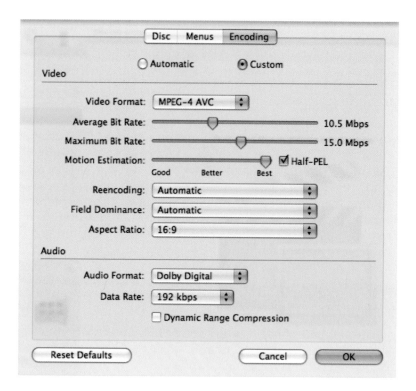

Figure 9.25 To get you started, these are the encode settings I recommend for media encoded for a Blu-ray Disc.

- Compress our video in Compressor, then import that into Encore.
- Export a DVD or Blu-ray project to the Web as a Flash movie with navigation. (I'll discuss that in the next chapter.)
- Tight integration with other Adobe applications, similar to how DVD Studio Pro integrates with other Final Cut Studio applications.
- Display your Blu-ray Disc layout as a Flowchart (similar to DVD Studio Pro's Graphical View).

While a complete discussion of all Encore's features is impossible in this book – there just aren't enough pages available – I do want to spend some time showing how to create a Blu-ray Disc using Encore.

Here's the basic workflow:

- Create and export your video in FCP.
- Compress your video using either Apple's Compressor or Adobe's Media Encoder. In this chapter, I'll show you how to use Compressor; in the next chapter, I'll show you how to use the Adobe Media Encoder.
- Create your Blu-ray Disc using Encore.

We've already seen how to export our media from Final Cut, so let's start by looking at how to compress it using Compressor.

Compressing Blu-Ray in Compressor

The advantage of using Compressor to encode your media is that you are using an application you may already know, that works seamlessly with FCP, and creates files that are fully compatible with Adobe Encore.

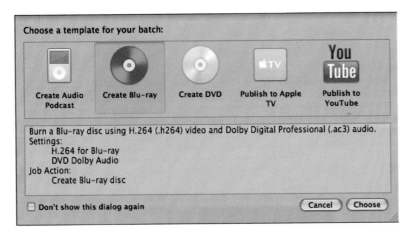

Choose a template for your batch:

Create Audio Podcast   Create Blu-ray   Create DVD   Publish to Apple TV   Publish to YouTube

Burn a Blu-ray disc using H.264 (.h264) video and Dolby Digital Professional (.ac3) audio.
Settings:
    H.264 for Blu-ray
    DVD Dolby Audio
Job Action:
    Create Blu-ray disc

☐ Don't show this dialog again   Cancel   Choose

Figure 9.26 When Compressor starts, it offers this job template. However, selecting Blu-ray Disc only creates an AVCHD disc, instead of the Blu-ray stream we need for Encore. Click **Cancel**.

When Compressor first starts, it displays a job template (see Fig. 9.26), where Blu-ray is one of the choices. However, this option only creates AVCHD-formatted files that are only appropriate for burning to a standard DVD.

You can also use Compressor to burn a file to a Blu-ray Disc; however, again, this is only a Blu-ray-compatible file burned to a standard DVD, unless you have a Blu-ray burner connected to your Mac. The SuperDrive in your system will not burn Blu-ray Discs.

Instead, we want to compress Blu-ray files that we can import into Encore for final authoring.

To compress a video in Compressor, we need to click **Cancel** for the job templates and create our own compression settings.

1. Drag the video you want to compress into the Task Window in the top-left corner of Compressor. You can add as many files as you want, the process is the same.
2. In the Settings window, click the **Plus** (+) button in the top-right corner (see Fig. 9.27) and select **H.264 for Blu-ray**. A new setting, named **Untitled H.264 for Blu-ray**, appears in the Settings window and in the Inspector.
3. In the Inspector, give this setting a name and description, so you can find this again in the future. (This is one of the big benefits of using settings in Compressor. Once you create a setting that you know works, you can use it over and over again.) Figure 9.28 illustrates my suggested settings.
4. Make sure Stream Usage is set to Blu-ray. AVCHD stream files only work on SD discs.

Definition: Authoring

Authoring is the process of creating a DVD or Blu-ray Disc. Authoring is what happens after your video, audio, and image elements are created. It includes file compression, disc design and layout, adding and linking elements, scripting, testing, and creating of the final master disc.

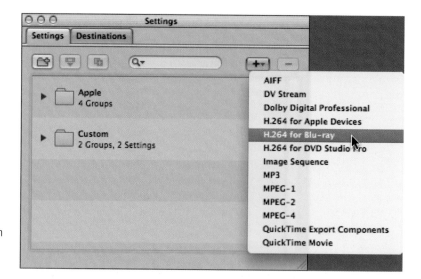

Figure 9.27 Click the Plus button to create a new setting. Be sure to pick **H.264 for Blu-ray**.

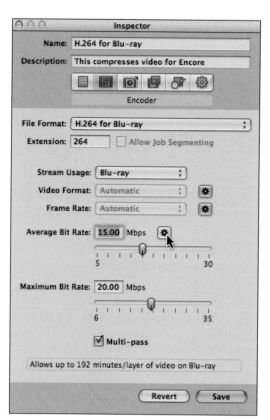

Figure 9.28 The Encode tab determines how your video is compressed. Here are my suggested settings. Click the small gear next to a setting to take it off automatic mode.

5. The new version of Compressor has a series of automatic "sensors" that determine Video Format, Frame Rate, and Bit Rates. Click the gear to turn off the autosensor and switch it to manual mode.

6. Multi-pass is off by default. Similar to 2-pass compression for MPEG-2, you will get better quality by turning this on. However, encoding will take longer.

7. When you are done, click **Save** to save your changes to this setting.

8. Other tabs in Compressor are similar to what we used in earlier versions or other compression settings. Since there is nothing specific to Blu-ray in them, refer to Compressor's documentation for instructions on how to use them.

9. Drag your new setting from the Settings pane onto the Task pane of the video you want to compress.

10. Either drag a destination for your compressed file from the Destination tab or Control-click the Destination setting for the file (see Fig. 9.29), and select where you want the compressed file to be stored.

11. Make sure the file name is correct, and then click **Submit** to start the compression process; this button includes all the files in the Task window. Click **Submit** in the second window, and Compressor moves your files into the background and starts compressing.

Other Settings

 As a general rule, I don't add any filters to video being compressed for either standard DVD or Blu-ray Disc. Also, the settings in the Geometry tab don't need changing unless you are changing the image size of your video. Most of the time you can leave both Filters and Geometry set to their defaults.

Make Sure Your Destination Is Online

 If you select a destination that isn't online, say a hard disk that isn't connected to your system, Compressor compresses your file but never stores it anywhere. This can be somewhat frustrating.

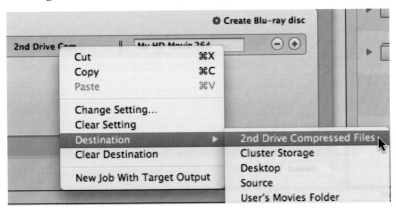

Figure 9.29 Control-click the Destination column in the Task window to select where you want the compressed file to be stored.

12. When compression is complete, Compressor displays a window asking to insert a Blu-ray Disc (see Fig. 9.30). In this case, we don't want to burn the disc yet, so click **Cancel**.

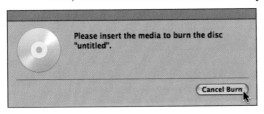

Figure 9.30 When compression is complete, Compressor offers to burn a Blu-ray Disc. Since we want to build the finished disc in Encore, be sure to click Cancel.

Now, it's time to move these compressed files in Adobe Encore.

Building a Blu-Ray Disc in Adobe Encore

Because the process of building a Blu-ray Disc in Encore is similar to building a standard DVD, we'll just look at the differences caused by working with Blu-ray media.

Like DVD Studio Pro, Encore takes a while to start up. When it does, click **New Project** to get started (see Fig. 9.31).

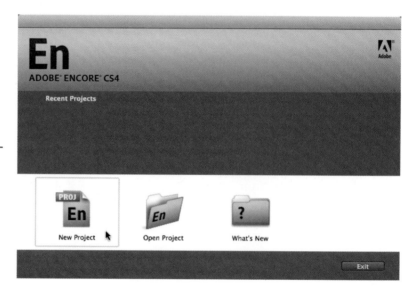

Figure 9.31 Click New Project to start a new project.

Next, Encore asks you to configure the settings for your project. In the Basic tab, give the project a name and location. (As usual, I stored it to my second drive in a folder named "Encore projects." see Fig. 9.32)

Encore creates a series of subfolders in this location, which it needs for its own purposes. So, I don't store my assets here, instead I have a separate folder for storing assets such as compressed files, audio clips, or images for menus.

Click the **Blu-ray** radio button and configure the other settings to match your video. The NTSC vs. PAL pop-up is confusing if you are working with HD. If you shot 25 or 50 fps, select **PAL**. If you shot any other frame rate, select **NTSC**. Set the other pop-ups to match your video.

To keep things simple, we will work with an existing template to create our Blu-ray Disc. So, in the **Library** menu, click the far left icon in the row of the small icons near the top (see Fig. 9.33). This displays some of the template choices. HD menus are indicated by the letters **HD** following the template name. An icon with a folded corner indicates a template containing a motion menu.

At the top of the Library tab, click the **Set** pop-up and select **Entertainment**. From the list, double-click **Studio Menu HD** to load it into the template.

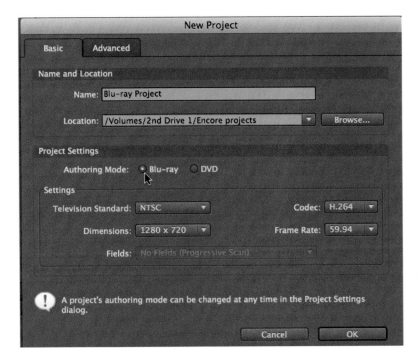

Figure 9.32 Give your project a name and location. Be sure to click **Blu-ray** and set the overall parameters of your project. These can be changed later if necessary.

Figure 9.33 Click the small icon at the left of the row of icons to display the list of templates. Load the template you want to use by double-clicking its name.

Resetting Your Workspace

If you can't find the tabs I mention, it is probably due to the two of us using different workspaces or screen layouts. To reset yours, select **Window > Workspace > Default**.

Blu-Ray Movies May Not Play Smoothly

Because the Mac does not play Blu-ray natively, when you play a Blu-ray movie in Encore, it may not play smoothly. Not to worry, it will play fine when it finally gets burned to a Blu-ray Disc.

Before we can create links between our menu and movies, we need to import and place each movie in a Timeline. DVDs (both SD and HD) are collections of linked objects that contain stuff. ("Stuff" is one of my favorite technical terms.) So, we can't link a button to a movie. Instead, we place the button in a container called a menu, and the movie in a container called a Timeline, then link the two objects.

While you can import the movie as an Asset, then add it into a Timeline, a much faster way to do this is to import the movie and instantly turn it into a Timeline (see Fig. 9.34). To do this, either go to **File > Import As > Timeline**, or **Control-click** in the Project tab. Either way, select your movie in the resulting window.

Each video now appears in its own new Timeline. Even better, though we can't play the compressed movie directly on our Mac, we can play the movie inside Encore. This is a great way to make sure that all our compression settings are correct. (As with Final Cut, you play, or stop, a Timeline movie by pressing the Spacebar.)

Next, we need to tell Encore where to start playing when the DVD is inserted into a player. Because we want the main menu to play before anything else, Control-click the name of the main menu in the Project tab and select **Set First Play** (see Fig. 9.35). If, for example, we want something else to play first, we would assign the first play option to that.

Figure 9.34 Use **File > Import As > Timeline** or Control-click in the Project tab to select the assets you want to import and place them into a Timeline.

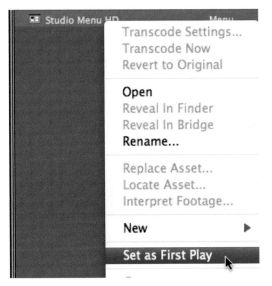

Figure 9.35 Control-click a menu or Timeline in the Projects tab to tell Encore what object you want to play first.

Designing text for buttons in Encore is very flexible because it seamlessly links the menu to Photoshop. In addition, to get us started, the template already has buttons designed.

To select a button, click it. To change a button, select it and go to **Properties > Basic** tab (see Fig. 9.36). Like the Inspector in DVD Studio Pro, you change the name, formatting, and operation of the selected button here.

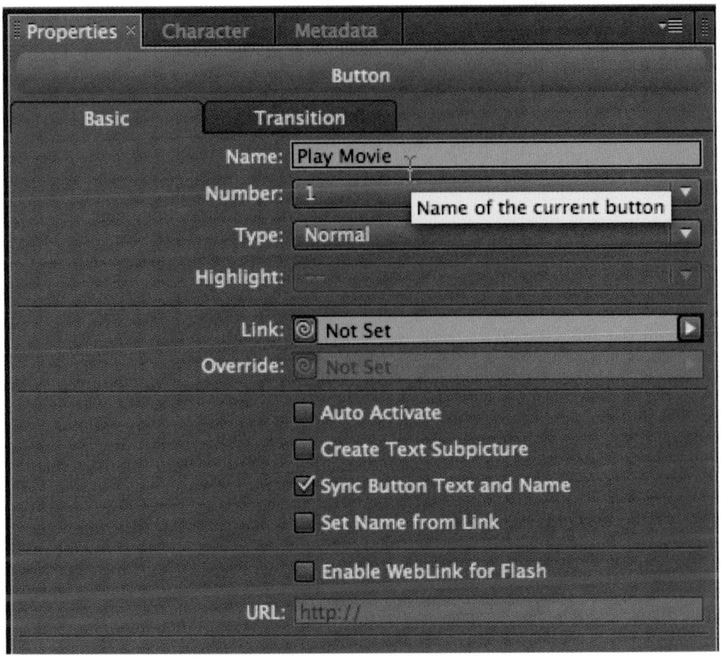

Figure 9.36 Select a button by clicking it, then change its properties in the **Properties > Basic** tab.

To link a button to a Timeline, select the button in the menu, go to the Properties tab, and grab the curled **Pick Whip** icon (see Fig. 9.37). Drag it over to the Project tab and drop it on top of the Timeline object you want to link to it. If you attempt to link to the wrong object, the whip will disconnect without linking.

To see how your project is doing, click the **Flowchart** tab in the top center of the interface (see Fig. 9.38).

Objects that are not yet linked are displayed at the bottom of the Flowchart window. To link objects in this window, drag a line connecting one to the other.

Just as you need to connect a button to a Timeline, you also need to tell the Timeline where to go when it is done playing. In DVD Studio Pro, we call this an End Jump. In Encore, it's called an End Action.

The fastest way to set the End Action is in the Flowchart by dragging from the Timeline object to the menu to which you want it to return (see Fig. 9.39).

When your project is complete and ready to build, click the **Build** tab, next to the Project tab (see Fig. 9.40). Set:

- Format to **Blu-ray**
- Output to **Blu-ray Disc**
- Select your burner in **Destination > Recorder**

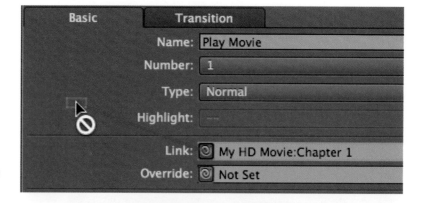

Figure 9.37 Drag the Pick Whip icon from the Properties tab of the select button to connect with a Timeline in the Project tab.

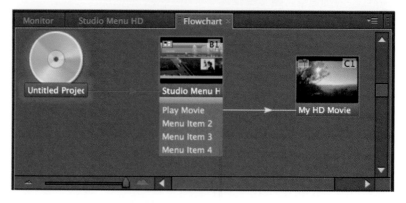

Figure 9.38 The Flowchart tab shows graphically the layout of your project. It also shows objects at the bottom of the window that are not yet linked.

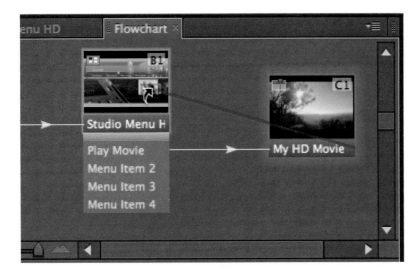

Figure 9.39 Create an end action by dragging from a Timeline object to the menu to which you want it to return.

Figure 9.40 Click the Build tab to make sure all settings are to Blu-ray prior to burning. When everything is set, click the Build button.

After making sure your settings are correct, click the **Check Project** button. On the screen that follows, click **Start** to test your entire project. This will look for any lost links or other missing pieces. It displays a report listing anything that needs to be fixed (see Fig. 9.41).

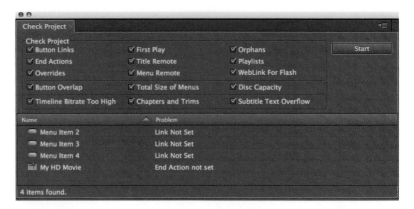

Figure 9.41 Just before burning, check your entire project for missing links by clicking **Check Project**, then **Start**, and reviewing the report. If anything is wrong, this will let you know.

When all links are correct, it's time to create the final Blu-ray Disc. This is called "building" your project. Click the **Build** button in the Build tab to start the process.

That's it. The process of creating a Blu-ray Disc is similar to creating a SD DVD. Yes, there's some new software to learn, but if you are comfortable with DVD Studio Pro, the process of learning Adobe Encore is a matter of a few hours.

The capability to create, output, and sell your HD masterpieces makes the effort fully worthwhile.

Summary

For massive storage, combined with high quality, Blu-ray is a contender. Now, with the latest releases from Apple, Roxio, and Adobe, you have a variety of tools you can use to create your own Blu-ray Discs – including burning them to standard DVD media to save time and additional hardware purchases.

My Story: Creating Blu-Ray Discs

Mike Chapman
Senior Editor/Associate Producer
DigiNovations, Inc.
www.diginovations.com

As good as Apple's DVD Studio Pro is, the integration between Adobe Encore, Photoshop, and After Effects makes the production of dynamic Blu-ray DVDs a snap. Here's how I do it in my shop:

First, I export my finished sequence to QuickTime. We usually work in XDCAM, so I export a finished QT as a reference file by unchecking the "Make Movie Self-Contained" box in the export dialog.

Next, I launch Encore and select **Create a New Blu-ray Project**. I import my QT reference movie as an asset and place it into a new Timeline.

Next, I import a still frame from the show. I had exported it from FCP using **Export > Using QuickTime Conversion**. I import the still as an asset, then create a new blank menu, being sure to check the 16 × 9 radio button in the Properties tab. I drag the still into the menu, then right-click to select **Edit Menu in Photoshop**. I can then add effects, correct the color or position of the still, add elements such as logos, all within Photoshop. When I'm finished, I simply save it and click back into Encore. Adobe's dynamic link updates the menu, and I can then add buttons (which I could also have edited in Photoshop) and specify links.

Figure 9.42 Mike Chapman.

Now, the part that makes our DVDs shine: from the "Menu" menu, I select **Create After Effects Composition . . .** AE opens with a new Comp comprised of the layers of our new menu. From there, I can be as creative with the individual elements, buttons, etc. as time or budget allows. In this case, I make two simple Comps: one that flies the buttons into place and the other that flies them out and dissolves the background to black. These will play before and after my static menu.

The beauty of dynamic linking is that I don't have to render out a separate movie, all I have to do is drag the Comps from the AE project window into Encore's project window. I drag the first Comp into a new Timeline, which I call Preroll. I'll select this Timeline as First Play and specify the static menu as the End Action. I'll then create a new Playlist, and use the Pick Whip to specify my second Comp (which I've dragged to a Timeline) and my main movie as the elements, linking the Playlist to the "Play Video" button.

Now, when I preview the DVD, the menu will fade in from black while the buttons fly into place, before "cutting" to the menu. When I select my "Play Video" button and activate it, the buttons fly off again as the background dissolves to black, followed by the program itself – very smooth and classy, nothing popping on and off the screen. (Some older Blu-ray players will occasionally glitch between the end of the Playlist and the menu. Check with the manufacturer to see if a firmware update is available.)

If I want to go back and change any of the elements, either in Photoshop or After Effects, my Encore menu is updated immediately. This is important and time-saving for fixing those inevitable goofs (like misspellings!) that occasionally slip through.

FCP and Motion are still the quickest and most reliable ways to edit and do quick graphics, but for sheer horsepower and integration, the Adobe Creative Suite is as essential as electricity!

10

CREATING VIDEO FOR THE WEB

Blu-ray not withstanding, the Web is an essential element in any distribution strategy for the projects we create. However, the combination of Final Cut and Compressor has been able to create videos for the Web for many years, why should we be interested in using the applications in Adobe Production Premium?

The answer is simple: Flash.

QuickTime runs on lots and lots of different systems, but it can't begin to touch the ubiquity of Flash. Any morning now I'm expecting to read a news bulletin that Bic just released a Flash-enable gel pen. (Well, maybe not, but 10 years ago, who would have bet that we could watch videos on our phones?)

So, this chapter looks at the process of creating Web videos.

There are four ways we can create video for the Web:

- Final Cut Pro
- Compressor
- Adobe Media Encoder (AME)
- Adobe Encore

The latest version of Final Cut Pro adds new export options to simplify this whole process: **Share** and **Send to Compressor**. Even if you are working with an earlier version of Final Cut, the export option provides a variety of high-quality options to get our video ready for the Web.

The latest version of Compressor builds on its impressive compression capability by adding Job Actions, which combine both compressing and publishing a file – whether to a Blu-ray Disc, YouTube, or a local Web site.

The problem with both Final Cut and Compressor is that, unless you purchase third-party plug-ins, both of them only create QuickTime files. We can't use either of them to create Flash movies.

To directly create Flash movies, we need to turn to two applications in Adobe Production Premium: Adobe Media Encoder and Adobe Encore.

We discussed Adobe Media Encoder earlier in this book. In this chapter, we'll take a closer look at its automation and batch processing capabilities.

Not Strictly True

Although it's true that you can't create Flash movies directly from either Final Cut or Compressor, there is still the trick of exporting an H.264 QuickTime video, then changing the file extension to .f4v to make Flash think it's a Flash video.

Then, we'll wrap up by returning to Adobe Encore. But this time, to look at its ability to create a project, and then by changing only a few simple settings, create a standard DVD, a Blu-ray Disc, or an interactive Flash Web site. Adobe calls it: "Author Once, Write Many." In this chapter, I'll show you how to create a Flash project to post to the Web.

Final Cut Pro 7

With the release of Final Cut Pro 7, Apple added two new options for getting files to the Web: Share and Send. (For those that have an earlier version of Final Cut, all is not lost. We discussed how to create high-quality exports from Final Cut in Chapter 8.)

In talking with editors around the world, one request that I hear over and over is that compressing video is a technically complex process. Anything that can be done to simplify the process without damaging quality would be great. Apple seems to have heard this as well because that's what these two new features do.

Share is a one-stop approach to prepping files for the Web. This allows you to select an Apple preset, export and compress your file, then automatically send it to the location of your choice. It also offers a one-button easy approach for exporting files in a batch. Both Share and Send to Compressor run in the background, allowing you to export a sequence then quickly get back to editing!

Send to Compressor is the new replacement for File > Export > Using Compressor. While they can both do the same thing, the key advantage of Send is that it runs in the background.

When to Use What

Use **Share** when you are satisfied with the existing Apple presets or when you have created and saved customized presets in Compressor. This is very fast, simple, and it runs in the background.

Use **Send to Compressor** when existing presets are not appropriate, and you need to create a customized setting. This is very fast and also runs in the background.

Use **Export > QuickTime Movie** when you want to create a high-quality master file that can be stored, sent to someone else, or compressed at a future date. For files that you intend to store, be sure to select **Make Movie Self-Contained** in the export options. This is fast and provides the highest image quality because it doesn't compress at all. Also, this requires a separate compression step to compress a file for the Web. Think of this as an archiving option.

Use **Export > Using QuickTime Conversion** for freeze frames, or to support third-party plug-ins that don't use Compressor. (Telestream's Flip4Mac comes immediately to mind.)

Sharing Your Files

Share is designed for simplicity. As Apple's manual states: "From the Share window in Final Cut Pro, you can quickly create and deliver output media files in iPod, iPhone, Apple TV, MobileMe, DVD, Blu-ray Disc, and YouTube formats without having to open any additional applications. Just choose Share from the File menu, select the intended playback device or platform, and click Export."

Share has presets for the following formats:

- Apple TV
- Blu-ray
- DVD
- iPhone
- iPod
- MobileMe
- YouTube
- Apple ProRes 422
- Apple ProRes with Alpha
- QuickTime H.264

But Share does more than just compress the file, it also publishes it, which means that Share takes the finished file and stores it in the folder, or Web site, you specify.

You can export a single clip directly from the Timeline or the Browser, or select a variety of clips, bins, or sequences in the Browser and process them all as a group. This is a very fast way to deliver multiple files at once.

Let's take a look at two scenarios for using Share:

- Creating a single video for the iPhone
- Transcoding a group of files from HDV into Apple ProRes 422

Creating an iPhone File

Here's an example of Share at it simplest (Fig. 10.1) Load the sequence you want to export in the Timeline and make sure the Timeline is selected. Then, go to **File > Share** to display the Share window.

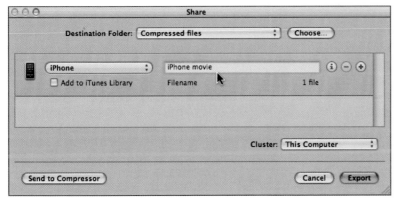

Share Does More

Share isn't just limited to its presets. You can select Other in the Share screen and pick from any Compressor preset, including custom presets that you create and save. Because Share is just a front end to Compressor, it can also be used with a render cluster to speed compression.

Sharing Is Not What You Think

Contrary to what you might at first think, the Share window does not allow multiple people to share the same file, instead it makes it easy for you to share your file with others.

Figure 10.1 In the Share window, pick the output type, destination, and file name for your file.

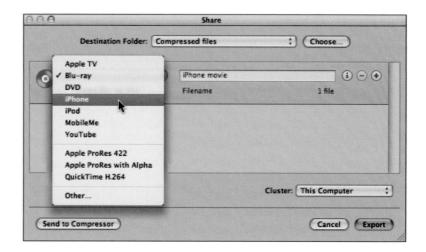

Figure 10.2 You can select to create multiple output types for the same file, or batch of files. All the compression settings are preset by Apple.

An Interesting Note about Filenames

 Share defaults to a filename template, which automates naming files when you export a batch of files (Fig. 10.4). The template uses the name of the sequence, or clip, you are exporting, followed by its compression setting. You can enter your own file names by selecting the contents of this text box and replacing it with your own file name, or integrate your file names with these templates. This template allows you to establish a naming convention for all your clips prior to compression.

The Share window defaults to one destination setting and one output-type setting (Fig. 10.2). At the bottom, it allows you to send the file to Compressor (which I'll talk about in the next section), determine where the file will be compressed (**This Computer** is always the safest option), and start the exporting process.

Although there is no limit to the number of output types you can create for each file, you are limited to one destination per Share window.

From the output type pop-up, select **iPhone**. This applies Apple's recommended compression settings for iPhone videos to your export. You can add more output types, for example, to create one version for an iPod and another version for a YouTube to this same video, by clicking the **plus** button to the right side of the window. (To remove an output type, select it, and click the **minus** button.)

Make sure the file name is what you want. If you are using the filename template, position your mouse over the Filename text box. The yellow tooltip shows you the actual file name.

You can see the specific settings for the file by clicking the small **Show Info** button (Fig. 10.3). When everything is set to your satisfaction, click **Export**.

Share exports the file in the background, so you can quickly get back to work in Final Cut. The simplicity of the Share window, combined with background exporting, makes this feature a huge time-saver.

Transcoding Several Files into ProRes 422

While the simplicity of the Share window is cool, the power of Share appears with batch processing. For instance, imagine that you've just captured a flock of HDV clips via FireWire. However, to simplify your editing and speed up

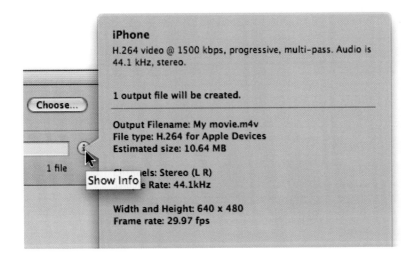

Figure 10.3 Click the small Show Info icon to see the settings you are applying to your file.

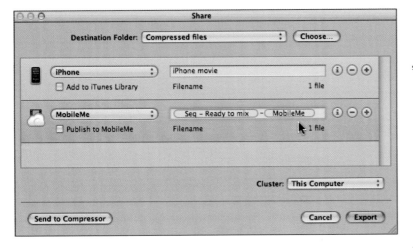

Figure 10.4 While the Filename text box defaults to a template, you can override this by entering your own file name.

Customization Means Compressor

If you want to create customized compression settings, this requires Compressor. However, as long as you save your customized settings, you can still use Share to create your export.

your render times, you've decided to transcode (or convert) them all to ProRes 422 before starting the editing process. (For HDV, ProRes 422 is more than sufficient. You don't need to use ProRes HQ or ProRes 4444.)

In the past, you'd use Batch Export in Final Cut Pro or Compressor. However, Share means you can do it all in Final Cut, and run it in the background.

In the Browser, select the clips you want to transcode. You can select single or multiple clips, bins, or sequences. In this example, I have five HDV clips in a Bin that I want to convert to ProRes. So, I Control-click the Bin and select **Share** (Fig. 10.5).

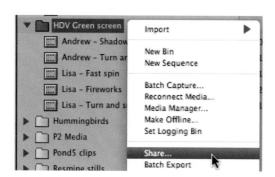

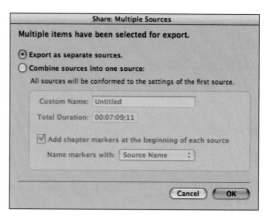

Figure 10.5 To process a batch of clips, select them in the Browser and then go to **File > Share**. In this case, I selected a bin of HDV clips to transcode.

Figure 10.6 This menu, which appears when you select more than one clip for export, allows you to export each clip individually or combine them into a single clip.

When more than one clip is selected, Final Cut asks whether you want to export them as individual clips or combine them into a single clip (Fig. 10.6). If you combine them, Share automatically adds chapter markers at the beginning of each clip. This is a fast way to build a DVD or Blu-ray screener of multiple clips using the DVD capabilities of Share to automatically create a chapter menu based on these chapter markers.

This is a great feature. It means you don't have to compile your edited sequences into a master sequence and manually add chapter markers before exporting. Simply select the sequences, and Share compiles them with chapter markers for QuickTime, DVD, or Blu-ray.

Once you decide how you want your clips exported, click **OK**.

Apply the **Apple ProRes 422** output type as the compression setting. I suggest you create a folder called "Transcoded clips" on your media drive. Click **Choose** in the Share window to change Destinations to this folder.

Click **Export** when you are ready to go. Figure 10.7 illustrates the status report Share provides to track your work.

Figure 10.7 As Share does its work, it displays a status box indicating how much time remains on your job and allowing you to cancel it if you get really impatient.

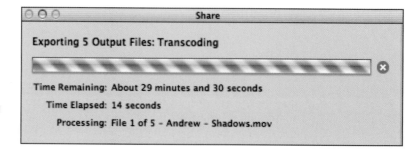

As a note, you can monitor the status of all files in compression, whether originating from Share or Compressor using either **Utilities > Batch Monitor** or the revised History panel in Compressor. More on that in a few pages.

When the export is complete, all your newly transcoded files are stored in the Destination folder.

In summary, Share is the tool of choice when you want to export files quickly and easily, in the background, using presets supplied by Apple, or saved by yourself. However, if you need to send files automatically to remote sites, or want to use the flexibility of Compressor to tweak settings, Share is not the best option. Instead, use Send to Compressor.

Sending Files to Compressor

Compressor is a high-quality video and audio encoder that we can use to create a variety of formats for DVD or Web distribution.

In earlier versions of Final Cut, we could round-trip files (what Adobe calls Dynamic Linking) by sending them between Final Cut and Motion, or between Final Cut and Soundtrack Pro. In Final Cut Pro 7, Apple added a new option: Sending Files to Compressor.

You can send files to compressor from either the Share window or the File menu. The benefit to using Send from the File > Share menu is that you can preset compression settings or destinations. The benefit to using Send from the File > Send menu is that it is fast: select the clips you want to compress in the Browser, or select a sequence in the Timeline, and select **File > Send to Compressor**.

Regardless of the option you select, the huge benefit from Sending Files to Compressor, unlike the Export > Using Compressor option in earlier versions of Final Cut, is that sending happens in the background.

In fact, while you are sending a sequence from the Timeline, you can be editing the exact same sequence! This is a huge time saver.

In this example, I'll send an HD sequence to Compressor, then modify the compression setting and add a job action, so it uploads it directly to my YouTube account.

I've opened an HD sequence in Final Cut, which I shot on a Panasonic P2 camera in 720p/60 mode. The portion I'll be working with here runs about 30 seconds.

With the Timeline selected, go to **File > Share** to open the Share window (Fig. 10.8).

In Share, I applied the **QuickTime H.264** output type, set the Destination to the **Compressed Files** folder on my second drive, and verified the filename template. After the file is prepped, click

New Compressor Feature

The latest version of Compressor has added a new feature called a Web Reference Movie.

The benefit to using the Share window is that you can create batches more easily and apply a compression setting to the clips before sending them to Compressor. This option creates a reference movie that enables a Web browser and a server to automatically select the right movie for any device or connection speed, without requiring the viewer to make a choice.

While we won't be covering this feature here, this has the potential to provide significantly greater quality without adding a lot of time to your workflow. For this reason, I wanted to mention it to you.

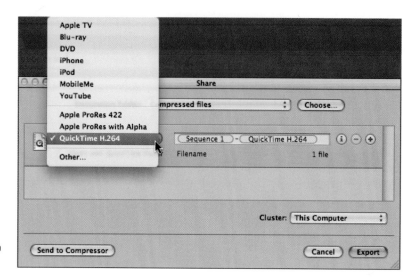

Figure 10.8 By opening the file in the Share window, I can apply basic settings before sending it to Compressor.

Send to Compressor. Final Cut Pro starts Compressor and loads my sequence, including all settings directly into Compressor (Fig. 10.9).

Why Not Use the YouTube Template?

The YouTube template, which appears when Compressor first opens, contains both compression settings and the YouTube Job Action. This is fine if the compression presets meet your needs. But if you need to customize a preset, such as add a watermark, the template won't work.

In which case, you need to create your own compression settings to the clip, then apply the YouTube Job Action, which is what we are doing here.

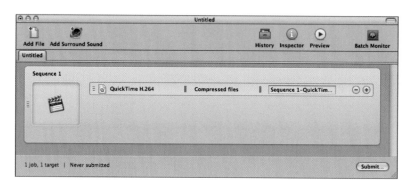

Figure 10.9 When the file comes into Compressor, all the settings from the Share window are retained.

The file loads automatically into the Task window. Note that the poster frame for the movie is the Final Cut Pro icon, unlike a movie imported directly into Compressor that displays the first frame of the movie. Also, the movie is named for the sequence which contained it. You can easily change this by retyping a new name.

At this point, I could assign a compression setting, modify the setting, assign a different setting, add more files to the batch – all different tasks that Compressor supports.

In this case, I want to show how to assign a Job Action to send this file to YouTube when compression is complete. A Job Action is what happens after your video is compressed. Think of Job Actions as automated ways of publishing a file.

In the Inspector is a new tab, titled Job Action. Click the **Job Action** tab and select **Publish to YouTube** from the pop-up list (Fig. 10.10).

In the YouTube pane, enter your account information (Fig. 10.11). (If you don't have an account, you'll need to get one for this option to work.) Note that I left the private video box checked. I tend to always do this. That way, I can make sure the compression and posting process was successful before releasing a video to the world.

Once you apply a Job Action, a gear menu appears in the upper right corner of the task window indicating a Job Action was applied (Fig. 10.12).

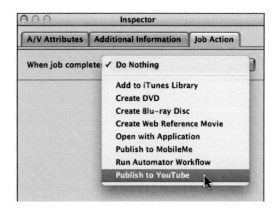

Figure 10.10 A Job Action is what happens to a file after compression is complete.

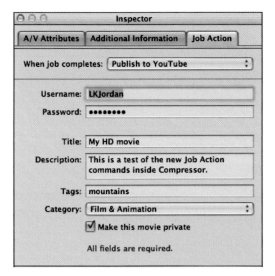

Figure 10.11 Prior to sending your first file to YouTube, you need to obtain a YouTube account, and then complete all the fields in this form.

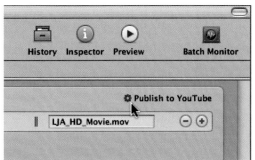

Figure 10.12 Once a Job Action is assigned to a file, the small gear menu indicates what it is.

Finally, because I want to brand my video, I'll add a watermark in the lower right corner during compression (Fig. 10.13). Here's how:

1. Click the compressor setting **(QuickTime H.264)** in the Task window.
2. Click the **Filters** tab in the Inspector (fourth button from the left).
3. Scroll down to find, then check, the **Watermark** filter.
4. Click **Choose** to select a PSD file containing the watermark you want to use.

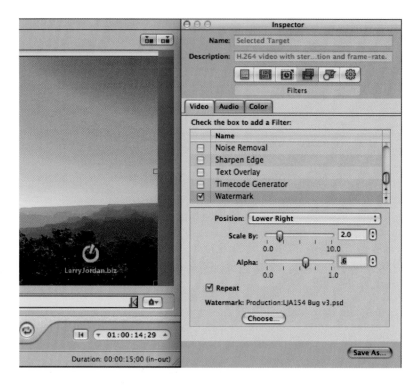

Figure 10.13 Here's what my finished watermark looks like. (Thanks to Pond 5 for the image.)

5. When creating the Photoshop file, I place the watermark in the position I want it to appear. I tend to put watermarks either in the lower right or upper left corner. (Chapter 6 discusses how to size watermark files.)

6. Adjust **Scaling** and **Alpha** until it has the right size and opacity.

When all settings are complete, click **Submit** to begin the compression process.

The YouTube copyright warning appears (Fig. 10.14). Just as you don't want people stealing your work without your permission, be sure to treat the work of others with the same respect. If you don't have the legal right to post your material, please don't. Assuming everything is OK to post, click **OK**.

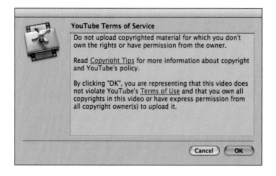

Figure 10.14 Make sure you aren't uploading materials you don't have the rights to post. Then, click OK.

In the final dialog, which asks what computer you want to use to compress the video, most of the time just accept the defaults and click **Submit**.

Depending upon how your Compressor preferences are set, the Batch Monitor appears, allowing you to track the status of your files (Fig. 10.15). Or you can use the display in the History tab. To get more details on how long this will take, click the small Show Info "i" at the right side of the status bar to display the compression log.

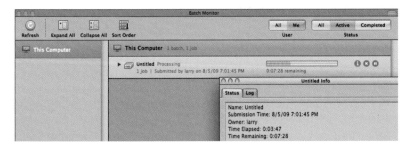

Figure 10.15 Turn on Batch Monitor in **Compressor > Preferences**, then Batch Monitor automatically appears showing the status of your file.

Applying a Job Action before starting compression means that Compressor automatically posts your file to YouTube as soon as the compression is done, and here is the finished movie (Fig. 10.16).

This is very cool!

So, in summary so far, if you want a fast and easy way to compress and post videos to the Web, use **File > Share** inside Final Cut

Finding Batch Monitor

 You can automatically display Batch Monitor by turning it on in **Compressor > Preferences**. Or, run it after compression has started by going to **Applications folder > Utilities folder > Batch Monitor**. This is just a monitoring program, you don't need to run it if you don't want to.

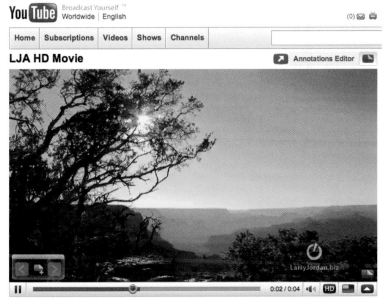

Figure 10.16 Here's our finished file, posted on YouTube. I make a point to test all my videos before releasing them to be sure the quality is OK.

Pro. If you want to use the power and flexibility of Compressor while still exporting your videos in the background without wasting time, use **File > Send to Compressor**.

But, neither of these options allows us to create Flash. That's when we need to turn to Adobe, and we'll start with the Adobe Media Encoder.

Adobe Media Encoder

The Adobe Media Encoder (AME) can create QuickTime files, but its real strength is in creating Flash movies. It can create Flash movies one at a time, or in a batch. It can create video using the latest Flash codec, or support multiple versions of Flash. Plus, it can add all the metadata we've talked about earlier in this book so that your videos can be searched on the Web – provided your media player supports metadata searching.

Let's take a look at how this works.

First, we need to export our video from Final Cut. We've discussed how to do this in detail in Chapter 9 elsewhere, so here's the summary:

1. In Final Cut's browser, select the clip or sequence you want to expor Or, open your sequence in the Timeline and make sure the Timeline is selected.
2. Go to **File > Export > QuickTime movie**. Give the file a name and location. Set Settings to **Current Settings**. If you are compressing the file on the same system you used to edit it, don't check **Make Movie Self-Contained**. If you are going to compress it on a different system, check **Make Movie Self-Contained** (Fig. 10.17). Click **Save**.
3. Open Adobe Media Encoder.
4. There are several ways you can add files into Adobe Media Encoder for compression:

   - Clicking the **Add** button in the top-right corner.
   - Using **File > Add**.

Figure 10.17 These are the settings I use when exporting from Final Cut to get the fastest export with the highest quality. I almost always store exported files to my second drive for its size and speed.

- Select them in the Finder and drag them in.
- Processing a Watch folder.

Watch folders are something that Compressor doesn't do. A Watch folder is a location where you drop files, or, in our case, a folder where we export all the files that need to be converted into Flash movies. This works best when a number of editors are contributing files into a network based server. Periodically, someone runs Adobe Media Encoder and starts the Watch Folder queue. All the files in the folder are compressed based on settings assigned to that Watch folder. When the compression is done, Adobe Media Encoder outputs the compressed files to an Output folder located inside that Watch folder.

While not as automated as Watch folders on other systems, this provides a one-click preset to process a batch of files.

Creating a Watch Folder

In this exercise, I want to create a Watch folder to compress movies that are stored in it. Since Watch folders can have only one compression setting for each folder, I'll set this folder to compress files into a 720p HD Flash movie. (You can also use this technique to compress individual files, without using a Watch folder.)

There is no limit to the number of Watch folders you can create, and there's also no limit to the number of movies you can drop into a Watch folder.

To create a Watch folder, do the following:

1. Open Adobe Media Encoder and select **File > Create Watch folder**.
2. Choose the folder you want to use as a Watch folder and click **Choose**. I always create Watch folders with a very specific name. For example, "Drop HD Files Here for Flash 720p." Like I said, I make the name very specific (Fig. 10.18).
3. Adobe Media Encoder moves that folder to the top of its encoding queue. When processing starts, files in a Watch folder have priority over all other files.
4. Next, we assign a compression setting to apply to all the files that are dropped into this folder. Go to the **Format**

When Is a Watch Folder Not a Watch Folder

Traditionally, when a file is dropped into a Watch folder, it actives an automated process so that the file is processed by whatever application is watching the folder. The key word is "automatically."

In the case of Adobe Media Encoder, however, nothing happens until you start the application. In this case, Adobe Media Encoder handles watch folders more like a batch process, where files are all gathered into one place, then processed when the application starts. The application does not do so automatically.

Figure 10.18 Create a folder you want to use as a Watch folder and give it a name that you'll recognize later. Obvious is good.

column, click the small down-pointing arrow, and pick the format you want to compress your videos into. You are selecting the finished format for your video (Fig. 10.19).

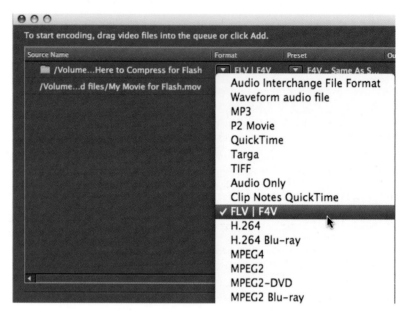

Figure 10.19 From the Format column header, pick the video format you want your compressed files to become. FLV/F4V creates the most recent versions of Flash.

5. Click the down-pointing arrow under Preset to set the compression settings (Fig. 10.20). If you aren't worried about supporting older versions of Flash, set this to version 9 or later. Then, determine the size of your compressed file. The larger the image size, the bigger the file size and the

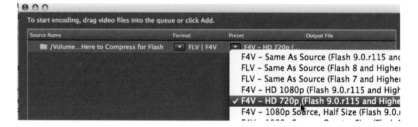

Figure 10.20 There are lots of presets to choose from. The smaller the image size, the smaller the file and the faster the download. Pick the preset that works the best for you.

longer the download. I always want the fastest download possible, so I select the preset that keeps file sizes as small as possible, but still with high quality.

6. At this point, Adobe Media Encoder processes all the files in this folder when you click **Start Queue** (Fig. 10.21). (It's in the middle right side of the Adobe Media Encoder window.)

7. Whenever Start Queue is pressed, Adobe Media Encoder starts compressing all the folders in the Watch folder. (Again, think of this as a batch-processing system.) It also creates two folders inside the Watch folder: Output folder and

Figure 10.21 Click the **Start Queue** button on the right side of the window to tell Adobe Media Encoder to start watching the Watch folder.

Source folder. All your compressed files are stored in the Output folder, while all source files are moved to the Source folder once compression is complete. Unfortunately, you can't change the location of these folders. They are always inside the Watch folder.

And that's it.

The Next Step

Once your Flash files are compressed, you'll find them inside the Output folder inside the Watch folder. At this point, you can view them in QuickTime Player or your favorite Flash player to make sure they look OK. Once you've checked them, post them to the Web for the world to see.

The benefit of using Adobe Media Encoder is that you can create files supporting a variety of Flash versions.

But there's one more very cool thing we can do with Adobe software that Final Cut Studio doesn't support. We can create an Encore project, and, with only a few clicks of the mouse, output that same project as a standard DVD, a Blu-ray Disc, or a Flash-based Web site, all from the same Encore project file. Author once, write many.

That, as they say, is next.

Adobe Encore: Author Once – Write Multiple Times

In the last chapter, we saw how we can take HD video, compress it in Compressor to the Blu-ray spec, then transfer it to Adobe Encore to build into a Blu-ray Disc.

But, Adobe takes this one very large step farther with their concept of "Author Once – Write Many." Specifically, we can create a single project inside Encore, then output that project as a standard DVD, Blu-ray Disc, or interactive Flash Web site.

In the last chapter, we used Compressor to compress our media files into Blu-ray format before importing them into Encore. Although this procedure works well, it only works as long as Blu-ray is the only output format we need from Encore.

However, in this new example, we want to output to potentially multiple formats, which means we need to import source media into Encore. We use source files because Encore it needs to compress the media into different formats for each project – MPEG-2 for DVD, H.264 with high data rates for Blu-ray, and H.264 with low data rates for the Flash.

To illustrate how we can take advantage of this multiple-output workflow, I modified the project we worked on in the last

Watch Folders Don't Support Custom Presets

Although you can create custom compression presets for Adobe Media Encoder, you can't use those custom settings in a Watch folder. That's the bad news. The good news is that the existing presets for Flash do a good job in most situations.

Note: How Long Does Compression Take?

The time it takes to compress a file depends upon the speed of your CPU, the size of the file, the video format of the source file, and the compression setting you selected.

Be Careful of Automatic Posting

I am very leery of automatically posting compressed files to a public Web site without first viewing them. It is very easy to correct an embarrassing mistake, provided you are the only one who sees it. I watch everything before I post it. It takes time, and I don't have a lot of spare time. But the risk of posting something that's wrong is just too great.

chapter for Blu-ray. First, I need to substitute the compressed video with uncompressed source footage, and, to make this project a bit more challenging, I decided to use a variety of different media, especially, HDV 1080i/60, DVCPROHD (P2) 720p/60, and XDCAM HD 1080i/24.

Using source media means that Encore needs to compress the footage based on the specs for each project. To make sure the media is ready to be compressed, widen the Project tab in Encore (Fig. 10.22). This displays the columns that are relevant to how we want our video to look: the Transcode Settings.

Name	Type	Duration	DVD Transcode Status	DVD Transcode Settings	Blu-ray Transcode Status	Blu-ray Transcode Settings
Lisa – HDV.mov	Video file	00;00;30;00	Untranscoded	NTSC Pr... 7Mb VBR 2 Pass	Untranscoded	Automatic
LAPD – XDCAM.mov	Video file	00;00;30;01	Untranscoded	NTSC Pr... 7Mb VBR 2 Pass	Untranscoded	Automatic
Horses – P2.mov	Video file	00;00;30;00	Untranscoded	Automatic	Untranscoded	Automatic
Studio Menu HD	Menu	--	--	N/A	--	N/A
Lisa – HDV	Timeline	00;00;30;00	--	N/A	--	N/A
LAPD – XDCAM	Timeline	00;00;30;01	--	N/A	--	N/A
Horses – P2	Timeline	00;00;30;00	--	N/A	--	N/A

Figure 10.22 Expanding the Project tab allows you to see the detailed Transcode Settings for both DVD and Blu-ray Disc.

When we imported the compressed video into the earlier Blu-ray project, Encore realized that the files were already compressed, so it set the Blu-ray Transcode Setting to **Don't Transcode**, meaning it won't recompress the files (Fig. 10.23).

Figure 10.23 When importing compressed media, for either DVD or Blu-ray Disc, be sure the Transcode Status is set to **Don't Transcode**.

DVD Transcode Status	DVD Transcode Settings	Blu-ray Transcode Status	Blu-ray Transcode Settings
Untranscoded	Automatic	Don't Transcode	Don't Transcode
--	N/A	--	N/A
--	N/A	--	N/A

Now in the current example, I imported uncompressed source footage into Encore using **File > Import > As Timeline**. Because this is uncompressed media, the Transcode Status is set to **Automatic** by default. However, you can change the specific compression settings by Control-clicking Transcode Status to open the Transcode window (Fig. 10.24).

Since we first created the Blu-ray project in the last chapter, I modified it to add a new title and buttons to the menu.

Unlike DVD Studio Pro, Encore expects you to do all your menu work in Photoshop, even if you are using one of the included templates. To send a menu to Photoshop, Control-click anywhere in the menu and select **Edit in Photoshop** (Fig. 10.25).

Encore is tightly linked to Photoshop and uses it for both menu and button design. (Look in Photoshop Layer's palette to see how button highlights are created.) In this case, I added a title, and renamed and repositioned the buttons (Fig. 10.26).

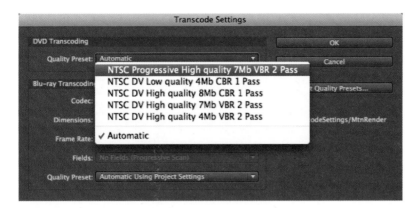

Figure 10.24 By default, compression settings are set to Automatic, you can manually adjust them using the Transcode pop-up menu.

Figure 10.25 To revise a menu, right-click the menu image and select **Edit in Photoshop**.

Figure 10.26 Here's the revised menu displayed in Encore's Menu Viewer, reflecting the changes I made to the Encore template in Photoshop.

Next, I made sure all the video was placed into Timelines and properly linked with the menu. If we look at the revised project from the Flow Chart view (press **Control + Shift + 4**), you can see the current layout (Fig. 10.27).

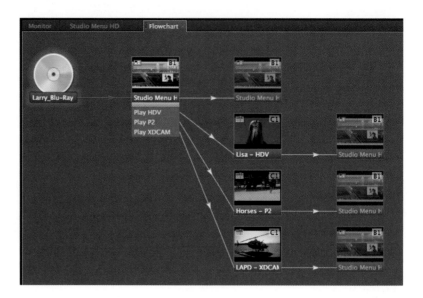

Figure 10.27 Look in the Flow Chart window to see the layout for our new project.

Next, click the **Build** tab and make sure all links are correct by clicking the **Check Project** button (Fig. 10.28). Use this to locate any problems that need fixing before output. (By the way, Encore can create far more complex discs than this illustration. However, I don't need to build a complex disc to illustrate this idea of "Author Once – Write Many.")

Figure 10.28 After a few tests and corrections, the Check Project window showed that all my links were correct and nothing was missing.

You can keep an eye on how much storage you need for your DVD by watching the Disc Info thermometer at the bottom of the Build tab (Fig. 10.29). However, these size settings disappear when you switch to Flash output because they are no longer relevant – the Web has no size limitations.

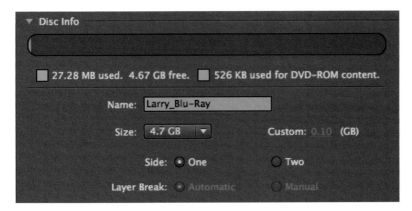

Figure 10.29 Encore tracks storage requirements dynamically. Check in the Build tab to see how much space your DVD or Blu-ray project requires. (This display is not available for Flash output because it is not necessary.)

You can preview your project at any time by Control-clicking any disc, menu, track, slideshow, or other element, and selecting **Preview from Here**. For example, in the Flow Chart tab, if you right-click the disc icon, you'll preview from the beginning of your project. Or, as Fig. 10.30 illustrates, if you click a menu, you'll preview from the element of the project that you clicked on.

Now that the project is complete, previewed, and tested, the fun starts.

Click the **Build** tab, in the top-left corner of the workspace. Inside it is this amazing **Format** pop-up. Click it and, with one mouse click, you can switch the output format between standard DVD, Blu-ray Disc, and a Flash-based Web site (Fig. 10.31), all without having to rebuild anything!

Because we are looking at creating projects for the Web in this chapter, select the **Flash** option. The Build tab reconfigures itself with Flash settings. We'll look at these from the top down in this menu.

Figure 10.30 Control-click any disc, menu, or track to preview from that portion of your project.

Figure 10.31 This is where the magic starts. Click the Format options to switch between creating DVD, Blu-ray Disc, and Flash output – all from the same project!

Unlike a DVD, or Blu-ray Disc, when creating Flash output, there's only one output option: an SWF file (Fig. 10.32).

The Source setting allows you to select the project you want to use. This, too, defaults to **Current Project**.

When creating and testing a Flash site, I find it helpful to use a local hard disk to store files before uploading them to the Web. For this purpose, I created a Destination folder on my second drive titled **Flash project**. Then, I clicked **Browse**, next to Destination, to point to that folder (Fig. 10.33). Once my testing is complete, I'll upload all these files to the Web.

Farther down the Settings section, you can give your project a name (I called mine **Larry_HD_Movies** – feel free to use your own name . . .)

Next, if you want the site to support only the latest versions of Flash, leave the format set to F4V. Otherwise, to support earlier versions, change this to FLV. The F4V files will be smaller with equal or greater quality compared to FLV.

Figure 10.32 The Output pop-up menu configures automatically to Flash output. Unlike a DVD, or Blu-ray Disc, there's only one output format for Flash – an SWF file.

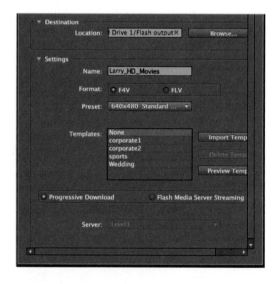

Figure 10.33 The Settings section of the Build tab allows you to configure image size, templates, and whether the data will be downloaded or streamed.

The Preset pop-up menu allows you to set the aspect ratio (4:3 or 16:9, which Encore calls "widescreen"), image quality, and image size.

In this case, since I want to retain the HD image size, I selected 1280 × 720 (Fig. 10.34). My file size will be significantly larger than normal, but since this project is just for a limited audience, I don't need to worry about excess bandwidth costs. If I were creating a project that was going to be seen by thousands or hundreds of thousands of viewers, I'd make the image size smaller to avoid paying for excess bandwidth.

Since you have already created a DVD menu, there's no reason to use a template – so leave this set to **None**.

Finally, unless you have access to a Flash server, leave **Progressive** as the default setting. Otherwise, select **Flash Media Server** and add the server connection settings in the Server pop-up.

When all your settings are complete, click **Build** in the top-right corner of the tab. A **Build Progress** thermometer pops up (Fig. 10.35), showing the progress of compressing your video and creating the Flash version of your DVD.

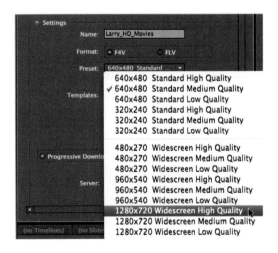

Figure 10.34 Select the image size, aspect ratio, and quality that you want to use for compressing your project.

Compression takes a while, even with a fast computer. I tend to let my longer, or more complex, projects compress overnight. In this case, not only was it compressing my files but it was also resizing two of them from 1920 × 1080 down to 1280 × 720.

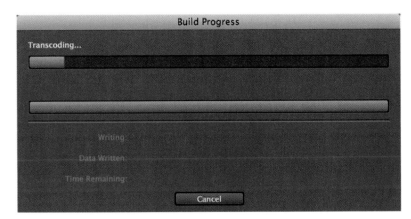

Figure 10.35 This window displays the progress of compressing and creating your final Flash output.

When the project is complete, click **OK** at the bottom of the Build Progress screen. This acts as a reminder that your project is complete – just in case you forgot.

You can view the finished Flash project using your Web browser by opening the folder you created to contain the Flash files and by double-clicking the **index.html** file (Fig. 10.36). Not only did all the files translate perfectly from the DVD format to interactive Flash, with NO coding from me, but the image resizing worked perfectly, too! Buttons and movies all play perfectly.

Figure 10.36 Here's the finished Flash site running in my Web browser. All the buttons work the same as if I were running the title from a DVD or Blu-ray Disc.

A Note of Comparison

 While your results will be different, my three HD source files – HDV, P2, and XDCAM – totaled 309 MB in size. After compression into the HD Flash format, my total file size was less than 40 MB, including all menus and links. I could make the files much smaller still, by sizing them to a much more Web-reasonable size of 480 × 270.

This ability to send the same files to DVD, Blu-ray Disc, or Web via Flash from the same project is just flat-out too cool!

Summary

This chapter has focused on moving our projects to the Web. Whether it is a single movie that needs to be compressed, or a complex creation, the combination of Final Cut Pro with Adobe Media Encoder or Adobe Encore gives you a wealth of opportunities to choose from.

My Story: Why Encore CS4?

Jeff Evenson
President
Motion Post, Inc.
www.motionpost.tv

First, I'll start off with some project details.

This was a doctor educational project for a major pharmaceutical company. Our goal was to educate anesthesiologists on new anesthetic techniques using the companies' anesthetic agents. The budget was not huge by any stretch of the imagination, and we had several hurdles to clear: the Medical Legal department, content experts in three states, and doctors on two coasts. The final deliverable would be a DVD that sales people would use to sell doctors on the use of these agents.

We cut the sequences in Final Cut Pro – 17 different modules in various lengths from 6 to 15 min. Graphics were created with Illustrator, After Effects, Motion, and Photoshop.

After receiving initial approval from the content experts, we started to author the DVD. Since this was an SD project, I really could have done the authoring using DVD Studio Pro, but several factors steered me to Encore CS4: disclaimers, checking the project, and getting reviews and approvals.

Legal disclaimer information is required for this type of sales tool, and it must be precise. We went through a number of rounds of changes as the client and their legal department tweaked the language and composition in these sections. Encore CS4's round-trip integration with Photoshop made this a breeze. They also had us create several other slide shows with prescribing information and references.

This is a great feature of Encore CS4. I was able to catch missing end jumps and broken links before I sent it onto the client for approval.

Figure 10.37 Jeff Evenson

Encore's ability to create a flash site from the DVD project made the review and approval process a breeze. Of course, this project had a tight deadline, and we needed to get approval for the navigation and layout of the menus quickly.

All I had to do was set the pull-down to "flash" and set up the compression. Within 30 min, Encore had compressed all the movies and menus to complete the flash site. I was able to shave days off the process this way. We made multiple rounds of changes in one day, avoiding the delay and overhead of FedEx'ing a check disc to each of the content experts and Medical Legal teams.

11

THE NEW FRONTIER: MOBILE DEVICES

Our industry today is confronting two divergent, driving technologies: the burgeoning growth of high-definition, large-screen video and the explosion in small, portable devices that play video.

We've looked at the high-end of this scale. In this chapter, we look at the other end – creating video for mobile phones.

We'll start with a look at what Apple has released in its latest version of Final Cut Studio, then wrap up our look at Adobe Production Premium with a tour of Device Central – a program that has no peer within the Apple suite.

What's a Mobile Device?

For the purposes of this chapter, I'll define a mobile device as something small enough to fit in your pocket that can play videos, either downloaded to the device or streamed from the Internet.

These devices have a wide variety of screen shapes and sizes. And, while it may be convenient to think of all them as iPhones, the truth of the matter is that the iPhone has a very small portion of the market. What this means is that there is no single video solution that plays perfectly on all devices. As we have come to expect, the situation is more complex than that.

However, unlike wrestling with the many flavors of HD video, creating videos for mobile devices comes down to two choices: video for Apple devices and video for everything else.

For Apple devices, the options are easily met with the new Share feature in Final Cut Pro and recent versions of Compressor. For non-Apple devices, Adobe has come to the rescue with Adobe Media Encoder (AME) and Device Central.

Let's first take a look at the design challenges of creating a video for very small screens, then look at each of these two delivery options, starting with Apple.

Design Considerations for Mobile Video

Entire books are written on design considerations when creating images for video, or the Web, for that matter. And there are always exceptions to every rule.

The key thing to keep in mind is that mobile screens are small, often viewed under poor lighting conditions, and are best suited for viewing short segments rather than long features. This means that the image you are editing will be significantly reduced – squeezed many times smaller – so what you easily see while you are editing is much less visible in the final product.

While screen sizes vary, no mobile device even comes close to providing the resolution of an SD image. Most are far smaller. So, if your goal is to create movies for mobile devices, there's no real call to shoot HD video – since no mobile device's screen size exceeds SD video image sizes.

HD is the preferred format for projects that need to be viewed on larger screens, but there is no reason to shoot a 1920×1080 image, when the final output may be 27 times smaller at 320×180. My preferred image size for projects that need to go to mobile devices, the Web, and HD is 720p. The progressive format removes the need to deinterlace, while the image size provides lots of image detail for HD distribution, while still compressing well for the Web and phone use.

That being said, here are some of my thoughts on how to improve the look of your mobile videos. (By the way, before the shouting starts, this list is not exhaustive, and all are welcome to their own opinions. These are mine.)

Camera

- The key thought here is to frame your shots tight. The playback screen is so small that anything with lots of detail, or very small size, will be lost.
- Shoot your actors using a variety of close-ups. Emotions reside principally in the face, shooting close-ups makes those emotions easier to see.
- Keep the background simple and avoid lots of detail, especially moving detail; like leaves fluttering.
- Avoid hand-held, shaky shots. These are hard to compress well.
- Avoid wide, panning shots that have lots of fine detail, but no central subject.
- In fact, just avoid wide shots with lots of fine detail. Medium shots and close-ups are always better.

Lighting

- The key thought here is that most mobile devices are watched in adverse lighting conditions, with reflections and sunlight washing out the screen.
- Make the important subject in the frame bright. Putting key subjects in shadows makes them hard to see.
- Light for high contrast; the more washed out your image, the harder it is to see.
- Use shadows and highlights to add texture to your image.
- Use lots of color, but avoid highly saturated, bright colors.

Audio

- The key thought here is that most phones have poor audio. They are not being listened to in quiet environments.
- Keep audio levels reasonably loud. However, don't raise your audio levels so loud that they distort.
- Avoid extreme dynamic ranges. Shifting from very soft to very loud is hard to understand on small speakers.
- Avoid very soft audio. This will be inaudible when listening in a moving car or an outdoor environment.
- Most bass sounds will be lost on small speakers. Assume for the purpose of mixing that your mobile device has a frequency range of 350–7000 Hz.

Text, Graphics, and Transitions

- The key thought here is that text that looks good on a big screen will disappear as the screen size shrinks.
- Always scale and place fonts using the Controls tab in Final Cut Pro, not the Motion tab. The Controls tab scales the text itself, whereas the Motion tab scales the frame containing the text. The Controls tab provides much higher quality results.
- Slightly thick fonts without serifs look best. Consider fonts such as Gill Sans, Optima, Futura Medium, Hobo, Lucida Grande Bold, Impact, Stone Sans, and others like them.
- Avoid fonts with "Light" in their names or with very thin lines, like Century Gothic.
- Avoid fonts with very thin bars or serifs at the end of characters, such as Didot, Caslon, Baskerville, or Times Roman. These serifs often get lost, making text hard to read when the image size is reduced. Or the bar of the letter "e" disappears, making the letter look like a "c."
- If you use curly fonts, like Brush Script, use thicker weights. Avoid very thin, curly fonts, like Edwardian Script.
- Keep point sizes large. I use 30 points or larger for HD, when it's going to be compressed to very small image sizes.

- Always add drop shadows. Drop shadows make text much easier to read. However, given the choice, bigger text is better than smaller text with drop shadows.
- Vertically-aligned text is almost impossible to read quickly, use horizontally-aligned text instead. As a design element, vertical text is fine.
- Avoid horizontal lines thinner than four pixels. Thin lines disappear when the image size is reduced. Six-pixel lines are better when working with HD.
- Avoid lines that are almost horizontal or almost vertical. They will stair-step and look jagged.
- Keep text on screen long enough for you to read it twice. Remember, you are paying attention. Most of the time, the attention of your audience will be distracted.
- Avoid lingering transitions. Cross dissolves are hard to compress because the image changes on every frame.

As producers and editors, the challenge we face is figuring how to make our projects look as good as possible on a very, very small screen. These ideas can help.

Once we finish editing our project, we need to compress it for a mobile device – whether iPhone, iPod, or the cell phone of your choice. Apple provides new compression opportunities with the Share option in Final Cut Pro 7. So, let's take a look at Apple's solutions first, then move to the much larger mobile phone market better served with Adobe's Media Encoder and Device Central.

Creating Videos for Apple Mobile Devices

Apple devices range from current model iPhones to first-generation iPods. Screen sizes also range from 480 × 360 on the iPhone to 172 × 132 for first- and second-generation iPods. Earlier devices provided a 4:3 frame size for their screen, whereas newer devices use 3:2.

In other words, there's no assurance at what screen size your final video will be viewed. (Your image, though, will not be stretched to fill the screen; instead, it will be displayed letterboxed or pillar-boxed, as necessary.)

Because it uses a variety of different screens, Apple selected a compression codec that does a nice job scaling between the various screen sizes: H.264.

Apple recommends creating your videos at a size slightly larger than the image size of the device playing them back. In fact, it recommends 640 × 480. (Before you panic, as long as you use one of the Apple presets in Compressor, it automatically adjusts the compressed image size to properly display 4:3 video at 640 × 480, or 16:9 video at 640 × 360.)

Letter-Boxing and Pillar-Boxing

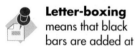 **Letter-boxing** means that black bars are added at the top and bottom of an image – just outside the image area, so your video is not affected – so that a 16:9 movie will properly fill a 4:3 frame.

Pillar-boxing means that black bars are added to the sides of an image – again, outside the image area – so that a 4:3 movie will display properly on a 16:9, or 16:10 frame.

This black framing is done automatically by the device, based on the image size of your video.

The main difference in Apple presets between compressing for an iPhone vs. an iPod is the data rate of the video. iPhones support higher data rates, which means that for the same video, iPhone quality will be higher than iPod quality; meaning the higher setting displays movement more clearly.

Compressing Using Final Cut Pro

There are several ways to create videos for Apple mobile devices within Final Cut Pro. If you have the latest version of Final Cut, select the sequence you want to export in either the Browser or Timeline, then select **File > Share**.

In the Share window, as we discussed in the last chapter on creating videos for the Web, select the compression preset from the pop-up menu. Both the iPhone and iPod have their own presets.

As Fig. 11.1 illustrates, both the iPhone and iPod presets use the H.264 codec with the same audio and video settings, except for data rate. The iPhone compresses data at 1500 kbps, whereas the iPod (Fig. 11.2) at 600 kbps. This means that, for the same video, iPod file sizes are smaller while the image quality of the iPhone version will be higher.

The benefit of using Share is that your videos export in the background, allowing you to continue editing in Final Cut while the export is continuing.

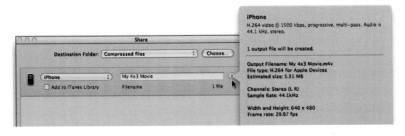

Figure 11.1 Click the **Show Info** box to see the compression settings for iPhone videos. Note that the final image size is 640 × 480. This setting can be used for both 16:9 and 4:3 video, because Compressor sets the correct image size automatically during compression.

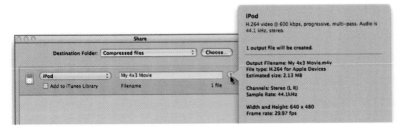

Figure 11.2 Compare the iPod data rate of 600 kbps versus the iPhone data rate of 1500 kbps. Higher data rates generally mean higher quality and better compression of movement.

Earlier versions of Final Cut, which don't have access to the Share window, can use **File > Export > Using QuickTime Conversion** to create a version of their movie for one of these devices. There are three setting windows you need to adjust, which are illustrated below.

1. Open the sequence you want to export into the Timeline.
2. Select **File > Export > Using QuickTime Conversion**.
3. In the **Format** pop-up, you can select presets specifically for the iPod or the iPhone (Fig. 11.3), or you can create a custom setting. Try the presets first. If they work, great. The problem with them is that you can't adjust their settings. If your video doesn't look good enough to you, check out the rest of this procedure, detailed below.

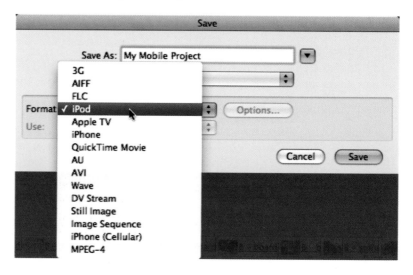

Figure 11.3 File > Export > Using QuickTime Conversion has presets for iPod and iPhone, as well as custom settings.

4. In the next dialog, give the file a name and location, then click the **Option** button.
5. In the Movie Settings window (Fig. 11.4) is a summary of the current compression settings. These are most often

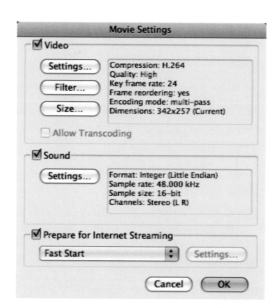

Figure 11.4 The Movie Settings window summarizes your compression settings and allows you to make changes.

incorrect, so here are the settings that match the Apple recommendations.

6. Check **Prepare for Internet streaming**.
7. Click the **Settings** button for audio and set them according to the illustration in Fig. 11.5. If you only have one speaker, for example a video podcast, set the Channels to **Mono** and the Rate to **22.050 kHz**.

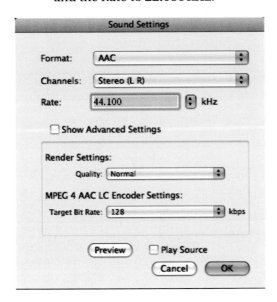

Figure 11.5 Audio settings for a movie containing stereo sound. There are no perceptual differences between 44.1 kHz and 48 kHz audio, but the 44.1 file will be smaller.

8. Click **OK** when you are satisfied with your settings.
9. Click the **Settings** button for video. Figure 11.6 illustrates the video settings to compress a movie for the iPhone. Note that the Compression Type is preset to H.264. If you want to create smaller files for use on iPod, change Data Rate > Restrict to **600 kbps**.

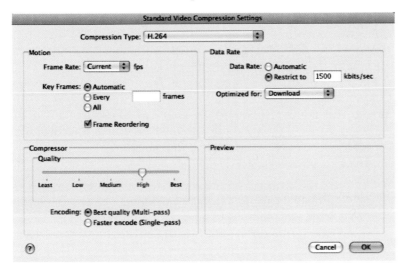

Figure 11.6 Video compression settings for an iPhone. Note that the codec in the top pop-up menu is set to H.264.

10. Click **OK** when you are satisfied with your settings.
11. Click the **Size** button to adjust the size of your image. Figure 11.7 illustrates appropriate settings for a 16:9 video. Deinterlacing video for mobile devices is correct, leave this checked.

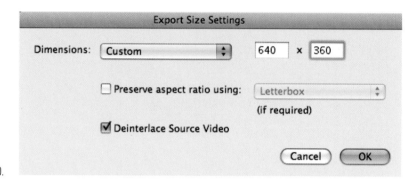

Figure 11.7 Here are the image size settings for a 16:9 video. If you are compressing a 4:3 video change the settings to 640 × 480.

12. Click **OK** when you are satisfied with your settings.

The Movie Settings window now shows a summary of your corrected settings. Click **OK** when everything is ready, and Final Cut will export and compress your video.

Unlike using Share, **Export > Using QuickTime Conversion** takes longer than real time to output your sequence. During the export process, Final Cut is tied up, meaning you won't be able to edit until the export is complete.

Compressing Using Compressor

For me, a much better way to compress files for any device, not just Apple devices, is Apple's Compressor. This is an application that is optimized for compression, with much greater flexibility than Final Cut alone provides.

In the latest version of Final Cut, Apple added a **Send to Compressor** option. This is often the best choice for exporting because it renders and exports the file in the background, allowing you to continue working with Final Cut Pro.

For those with earlier versions of Final Cut, I illustrated in Chapter 9 how to export files using **File > Export > QuickTime Movie**. This is the fastest and the best way to export files for all earlier versions of Final Cut. If you need a detailed review of that process, please refer to the steps in that chapter.

Here's a quick summary:

1. Open the sequence you want to export into the Timeline.
2. Select **File > Export > QuickTime Movie**.
3. Give the file a name and location.
4. Be sure settings is set to **Current Settings**.

5. If you are planning on immediately compressing the file, uncheck **Make Movie Self-Contained**.
6. Click **Save** to start the export process. Figure 11.8 illustrates these settings.

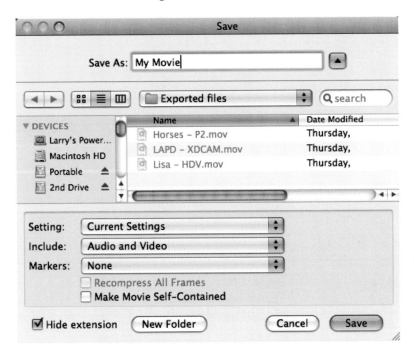

Figure 11.8 Summary of the settings I use when selecting **File > Export > QuickTime Movie**. As the file is going to be immediately compressed, there is no reason to make it self-contained.

Once the master file is created, load it into Compressor for final processing. I wrote earlier about how to use Compressor to compress files. Here, let me point out the specific settings you can use for a variety of Apple devices.

1. When Compressor opens, dismiss the Job Action window by clicking **Cancel**.
2. Import your movie into Compressor by clicking the **Add File** icon in the top-left corner of the Compressor window.
3. In the Settings tab, twirl down the Apple folder, then twirl down the Apple devices folder. As Fig. 11.9 illustrates, there are three choices: **Apple TV**, **H.264 for iPod at 320 × 240**, and **H.264 for iPod at 640 × 480**. For compression to the iPhone, use the **640 × 480 option** (see Fig. 11.9).
4. Once you determine the best compression setting for your video, drag the setting on top of the movie in the Task window and compress it as you would any other file.

The advantage of using Compressor is that it does a much better job of resizing, retiming, and deinterlacing the images than Final Cut, as well as providing the ability to add filters, watermarks, and automation using droplets.

640 × 480 for 16:9 . . . Really??

Yup. Because Compressor is smart enough to tell the difference between 4:3 and 16:9 video. Even when you select the 640 × 480 option, if you send it 16:9 video, the compressed file comes out 640 × 360, perfectly in proportion, automatically. (This adjustment works the same for the 320 × 240 setting as well.)

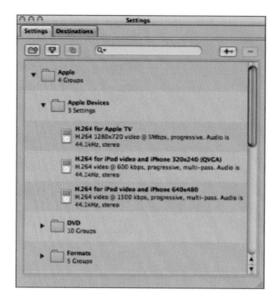

Figure 11.9 The Apple presets for creating mobile video using Compressor.

Chapter 9 showed how to create Flash movies for the Web. Cell phones require different presets, with far smaller files. And, then comes the process of testing your video. Testing is important because, just as we have eight billion different versions of HD, we have 17 kajillion different cell phone formats. (Well, OK, maybe that's a bit of an exaggeration, but not by much.)

This is where Adobe provides some answers.

Putting Video on Mobile Devices

If the Internet seems like a bit of a free-for-all, it is civility itself compared to the rugby scrum of the cell phone industry. All manufacturers are looking for ways to differentiate their phones from the competition. Screen sizes, file formats, features, and functionality vary widely even between phones from the same manufacturer.

Worse, there was no central clearing house for developers to go to that provided information on all the different options.

To solve this situation, in March 2007, Adobe released the first version of Device Central as part of the CS3 software suite. Its primary purpose, as Wikipedia reports, "is to offer both professional and individual creative professionals, Web designers, and mobile developers an easier way to preview and test Flash Lite, bitmap, Web, and video content for mobile devices. It is accessible from all of the Creative Suite editions."

Device Central is software for testing movies on cell phones. By far, the most popular video format is 3GPP. As the iPhone and iPod Touch only support QuickTime, you won't find them in Device Central. But, you will find everything else.

Device Central allows you to preview and test the appearance, performance, and behavior of mobile content on a computer. It simulates the behavior of cell phones, without requiring you to purchase hundreds of different phones for testing.

You can also simulate various display conditions, such as back-light timeout and sunlight reflections. In other words, this allows you to get a much better feel for how your videos look in the real world.

The largest market for Device Central are Flash developers who need to test and debug their mobile-enabled Web sites. So, there are emulation features in the software that video producers don't need to worry about.

But, the ability to see how our videos will look is a great advantage, and once you understand how Device Central works, testing your projects before release isn't hard to do.

Device Central

Adobe's Device Central is a great application that answers three critical questions when preparing video for cell phones:

1. What image size should I use?
2. What codec should I use to compress it?
3. How will it look in real life?

The only way we can learn these answers is using Device Central. And the way we do this takes three steps:

1. Select the devices you want to test and determine what video formats they support.
2. Compress your video to match those specs.
3. Test your video to see how the final results are likely to look in reality.

The first and last steps are handled by Device Central; step 2 is the realm of the Adobe Media Encoder.

New with the CS4 version of Device Central is a dynamically updated library of mobile devices, improved video support and integration, tighter integration with all of Adobe's CS4 software, higher-quality video playback, and the ability to upload files from Device Central to the FTP site of your choice.

Step 1: Selecting the Devices You Want to Use

When you first start Device Central, it displays the Welcome screen (see Fig. 11.10).

In this case, we want to do some browsing to figure out what kind and size of files to create to meet the common characteristics of the phones we want to support. So, click **Browse Devices** to display the main screen. In the center is an empty window, which will soon contain device profiles. On the left are three tabs:

- Device sets
- Local Library
- Online Library

Figure 11.10 Upon starting Device Central, the welcome screen appears. Click **Browse** Devices to get started.

Inside the Local Library is a set titled: **Flash Lite**. Click it to display a series of generic Adobe devices in the main window (see Fig. 11.11).

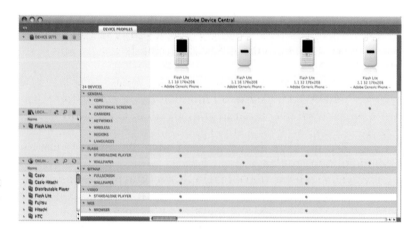

Figure 11.11 This is the main interface for Device Central. Click the Flash Lite folder on the left to display these generic devices.

On the lower left side is a tab titled: **Online Library**. This is a listing of all the different manufacturers and their phones. This is dynamically updated via the Web by Adobe so as new phones are released, they are automatically added to your list.

As an example, scroll down to **Motorola**, click the twirl-down triangle, and click **Motorola RAZR V3m**. Specs on the phone are displayed in the main window.

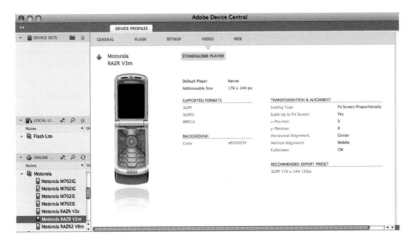

Figure 11.12 Click the name of a phone to display its specs.

Click the **Video** tab along the top, and the video settings for this phone are displayed (see Fig. 11.12).

Each phone has a vast array of technical specifications, but the portion we are concerned with is in the **Video** tab. Specifically, we want to know the following:

- The addressable size of its screen
- The video formats it supports
- What it uses as a video player

In the case of this Motorola phone, Fig. 11.13 shows that it has an addressable screen size of 176 × 144; it supports 3GPP, 3GPP2, and MPEG4 video formats; and it uses a standalone player to display video.

Select different phones from the Online Library and see how the specs differ from phone to phone. If the specific phone you are looking for isn't here (and remember, the iPhone won't be on this list because it doesn't support Flash), click the **Refresh** button (see Fig. 11.14) at the top of the Online Library to check for updated phone profiles.

However, since we aren't developing interactive phone applications using Flash, but, rather, trying to figure out how to compress our videos to work on the greatest number of phones, twirl down the **Flash Lite** collection in the Local Library tab.

This is a listing of generic devices, assembled by Adobe, that represents common settings for phones that implement different versions of Adobe Flash for cell-phone playback.

For example, as Fig. 11.15 illustrates, select three devices: **Flash Lite 1.1 32 176 × 208, Flash Lite 2.0 32 240 × 320**, and **Flash Lite 2.1 32 240 × 320**. (To select more than one device, press the **Command** key while clicking.)

Display Size versus Addressable Screen Size

The Display size, listed next to the phone name in the Online Library, is the total size in pixels of its display. The addressable screen size is the total size, in pixels, that can be used for video. Width is always listed first, and not all phone screens are oriented horizontally. As an example, look at many of the Nokia phones, such as the 3600.

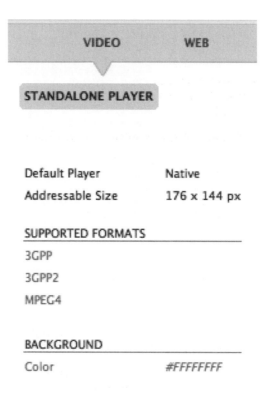

Figure 11.13 The Video tab displays the key settings we need to know to properly compress our videos: screen size, video formats, and player.

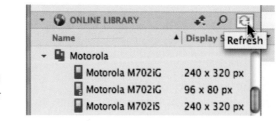

Figure 11.14 Click the Refresh button to update Device Central with any new phone releases or changes.

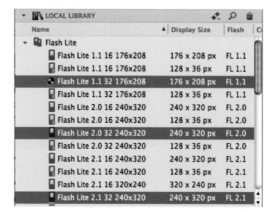

Figure 11.15 Command-click to select multiple phones to compare specs between devices.

The main window displays a comparison between the selected devices. Twirl down **Video > Standalone Player** and make note of the following specs:

- Whether the device supports video
- The addressable size of the screen in pixels
- All supported video formats

For example, Fig. 11.16 shows the specs for one of the phones.

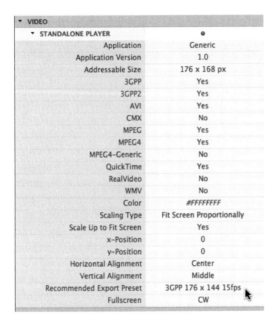

Figure 11.16 While all these specs are important, at the bottom is the **Recommended Export Preset**, which provides a minimum standard.

Compressing for Cell Phones Using Final Cut Pro

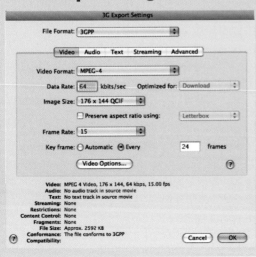

You can also take the Device Central information and use it to create settings for direct export from Final Cut with **File > Export > Using QuickTime Conversion** select the **3G** format and have access to 3GPP or 3GPP2 compression, which pretty much covers every non-iPhone mobile device (see the screen shot below). There are also 3GPP and 3GPP2 presets in Compressor. These can be accessed from the Share module selecting **Other > Apple > Other Workflows > Mobile Devices**.

While using either Final Cut or Compressor to create 3G files works, what I like about using Adobe Media Encoder, however, is how easily it allows me to test my videos using Device Central.

using a standalone player (see Fig. 11.17). Also, there is a common setting supported by all three that we can use to compress our video:

- Format: 3GPP
- Screen: 176 × 144 15 fps
- Codec: H.264 (this is also called MPEG-4)

▼ VIDEO			
▼ STANDALONE PLAYER	●	●	●
Application	Generic	Generic	Generic
Application Version	1.0	1.0	1.0
Addressable Size	176 x 168 px	240 x 280 px	240 x 280 px
3GPP	Yes	Yes	Yes
3GPP2	Yes	Yes	Yes
AVI	Yes	Yes	Yes
CMX	No	No	No
MPEG	Yes	Yes	Yes
MPEG4	Yes	Yes	Yes
MPEG4-Generic	No	No	No
QuickTime	Yes	Yes	Yes
RealVideo	No	No	No
WMV	No	No	No
Color	#FFFFFFF	#FFFFFFF	#FFFFFFF
Scaling Type	Fit Screen Proportionally	Fit Screen Proportionally	Fit Screen Proportionally
Scale Up to Fit Screen	Yes	Yes	Yes
x–Position	0	0	0
y–Position	0	0	0
Horizontal Alignment	Center	Center	Center
Vertical Alignment	Middle	Middle	Middle
Recommended Export Preset	3GPP 176 x 144 15fps	3GPP 320 x 240 15fps	3GPP 320 x 240 15fps
Fullscreen	CW	CW	CW

Figure 11.17 By comparing the Recommended Export Preset for multiple phones, you can quickly determine the minimum specs your video needs to support.

This screen gives us the information we need to go to step 2: com-pressing our video so it fits on these phones.

Step 2: Compressing Video Using Adobe Media Encoder

Cell phones, even more than the Web, demand microscopic files containing very small image sizes. Many people pay per downloaded byte, so they certainly don't want to pay for any more data than absolutely necessary. And, even if your viewers are on an "all-you-can-eat" plan, the bandwidth used by phones is not as fast as a hard-wired Internet connection.

For all these reasons, we need to squeeze our videos down as small as possible. To do this, we will use Adobe Media Encoder to create the files we need.

So, leave Device Central running in the background and launch Adobe Media Encoder. Whether creating videos for the Web or for cell phones, the process is the same, except for the settings.

Here is the summary of this process:

1. Open Adobe Media Encoder.
2. Import the file(s) you want to compress into the Source window.

3. Go to **Settings** and select a **Format** and **Preset** to match the requirements of phones on which you want to view your video.

4. As part of the Settings panel, be sure the **Open in Device Central** checkbox is checked, so the compressed video opens directly into Device Central, allowing you to review it before posting.

With that as an overview, let's go through the specific steps.

Launch Adobe Media Encoder and when it opens, click the **Add** button in the top-right corner to import your video (see Fig. 11.18). In this example, we'll work with an XDCAM HD video shot by Jody Eldred about the helicopters used by the LA Police Department. You can also add videos by dragging them directly into the central window.

The default compression settings are not designed for cell-phone video; we need to change them. To do this, select the video and click **Settings**.

The **Export Settings** window opens (Fig. 11.19). While this allows us to set In and Out points, preview our source footage,

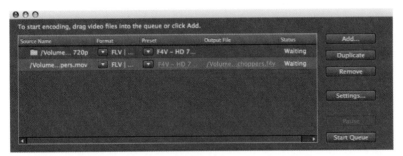

Figure 11.18 Click the **Add** button to import your videos, or just drag them into the central window. Then, click **Settings** to change compression settings.

Figure 11.19 This window allows complete customization of compression settings. However, the area we are most interested in is the top-right corner.

add Flash cue points and all kinds of other cool stuff, we want to focus on compressing our video for cell phones. To do that, we need to refer to the notes we made in Device Central.

1. We learned that the phones all supported MPEG-4. So, change the Format pop-up (Fig. 11.20), from FLV/F4V to **H.264**.

Figure 11.20 The default Format setting should be changed to H.264, which is the video format used by the cell phones we examined earlier in Device Central.

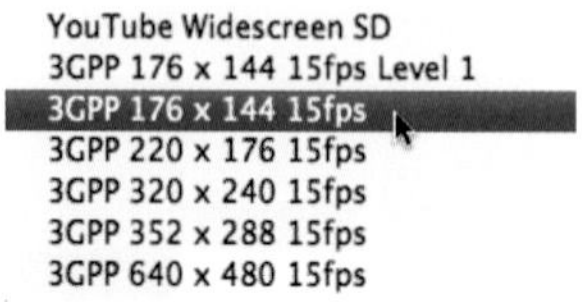

YouTube Widescreen SD
3GPP 176 x 144 15fps Level 1
3GPP 176 x 144 15fps
3GPP 220 x 176 15fps
3GPP 320 x 240 15fps
3GPP 352 x 288 15fps
3GPP 640 x 480 15fps

Figure 11.21 Change the Preset to match the specs we wrote down earlier when looking at the minimum specs for the phones we want to support: 3GPP 176 × 144 15 fps.

2. In the Preset pop-up, change the setting to **3GPP**, which is one of the video formats supported by the phones.
3. But, which 3GPP format? Again, the research we did in Device Central comes to the rescue. Remember the screen sizes of the phones? It determines which version of 3GPP to use. In this case, **176 × 144 15 fps** (Fig. 11.21).

Be sure that **Open in Device Central** is checked. Normally, selecting a cell-phone format automatically checks **Open in Device Central**. It tells Adobe Media Encoder to automatically open the compressed file into Device Central for testing.

4. Click the orange letters in Output Name (Fig. 11.22) and give your file a name and location. I usually save this into my Compressed Files folder, which I created on my second drive.

Click **OK** to apply these settings to the file.
Click **Start Queue** to begin the compression.

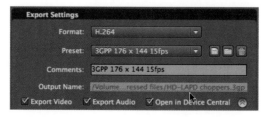

Figure 11.22 Click the orange letters next to Output Name to give your file a name and location.

During the compression, a status bar shows how much time remains, and, depending upon how you set the preferences in Adobe Media Encoder, it also shows images of your video during compression (Fig. 11.23).

Figure 11.23 During compression, Adobe Media Encoder displays a status bar showing time remaining as well as images of your video.

Now, here's the cool part. The instant your video is compressed, Adobe Media Encoder opens the video automatically in Device Central and places it into the last selected phone. And that brings us to the last step in this process.

Step 3: Testing Mobile Phones Using Device Central

Without any help from me, when compression is done, Adobe Media Encoder opens the file in Device Central and starts playback of my video in the last selected phone (Fig. 11.24). Very, very cool.

Figure 11.24 Here is the finished video playing inside a simulated phone in Device Central.

You are viewing your actual compressed video using a simulated device showing how it would look in a cell phone in the real world. This is a great way to check your compression and image quality.

The controls at the bottom of the window (Fig. 11.25) allow us to control playback, rotate the phone, (which does not automatically rotate the video because not all phones support that feature) take snapshots of the screen, and zoom in or out of the phone itself.

The image may not fill the frame because not all pixels are addressable and the screen shape is not optimized for video playback.

Here's another cool feature. Want to see what your video looks like on other phones? Just double-click the name of the phone you want, and it instantly replaces the phone you are currently examining. For instance, try the **Motorola RAZR V3m** (Fig. 11.26).

Figure 11.25 The controls at the bottom of the screen allow us to control playback of our video.

Figure 11.26 Double-click the name of a different phone and it replaces the currently displayed phone. This is a great way to check how your video looks on different phones.

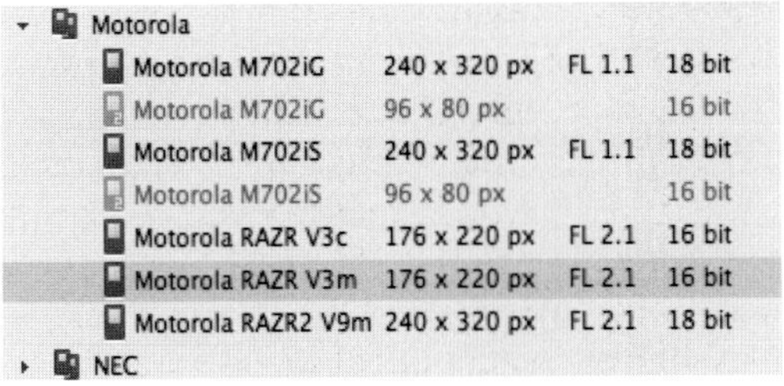

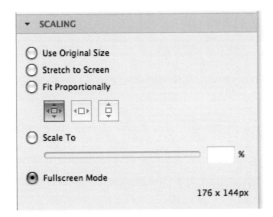

Figure 11.27 Other phones.

Why Are Some Phones Grayed Out?

As you look through the phone lists, some phones have their names grayed out. This is because the screen size of the phone is too small to display the video you have currently loaded into Device Central (Fig. 11.27).

Now that our video is compressed and loaded into the phone of our choice, check out what the simulator can really do.

1. Click the **Rotate Counter-clockwise** arrow in the Controls panel below the phone.
2. In the Scaling tab, click **Fullscreen Mode** (Fig. 11.28). Ta-DAH! Your video is playing as big as the phone will allow. Different phones support different scaling options.

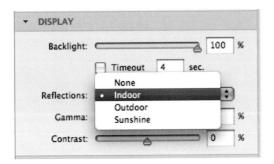

Figure 11.28 Your video is now playing as large as that particular phone supports.

3. Go to the Display tab and change the Reflections setting to **Indoor** (Fig. 11.29). This adds reflections to the screen of the phone similar to lighting in a typical office (Fig. 11.30). (Yes, I know, it's very discouraging. The "Sunshine" display setting is far worse – don't show the results to your lighting designer.)

Figure 11.29 Changing the display setting simulates the effect of different lighting conditions on the screen of your selected phone.

Figure 11.30 These simulated reflections show what your video would look like under normal office lighting.

4. Some phones allow alignment changes. However, in general, just assume your video will play in the middle of the screen.

When you are done testing, quit Device Central. This is testing-and-simulation software, so there's nothing to save. By the way, my original XDCAM HD video was 159 MB, and the 3GPP compressed version was 1.6 MB.

Summary

Mobile devices are becoming increasingly important in getting people to watch the videos we create. So, this means we need to make sure our projects look good on really, really small screens.

This chapter shows that we can edit our videos using Final Cut Pro and export them to the iPhone using Share or Compressor. For all other phones, we now have a very fast way to export from Final Cut, compress in Adobe Media Encoder and make sure they look great using Device Central.

This chapter illustrates the central tenet of this book. Video technology is exploding, and no one application should be expected to meet all our needs. Using the power of Final Cut Pro, we can edit professional grade programs. When you combine the power of Final Cut with the extended reach and capability of

Adobe CS4 Production Premium, we can meet the needs of more clients, in less time, with the quality we expect.

And that translates into money in the bank.

My Story: Creating Flash Videos

Simon Walker
Principal
On a Deadline
www.onadeadline.com

I'm a freelance shooter, editor, and graphic designer. My daily challenge is to create videos to be viewed on clients' Web sites. I'm also an Apple certified trainer (in Final Cut, Motion, and Color), and so as well as running the Apple certified classes, I teach courses on video compression and filming techniques. While having to solve deadline problems late at night (and then having to solve students' problems when they ring even later at night!), I've found a number of practical techniques that help to keep the video quality high.

My clients are increasingly moving from just hiring me to shoot and edit videos, to wanting to edit some of the videos themselves, and to be involved in the production process. So, these days I find myself troubleshooting clients' systems and workflows. They usually buy Final Cut Studio and Adobe Production Premium, and the discipline I use is the concept of only using these two packages when producing the project.

The end video format of choice is, of course, Flash, or rather FLV files. But Final Cut and Compressor don't export FLV files out of the box. I know that you can buy plug-ins to do this (CRAM Compressor, for example, is a great plug-in for Compressor), but once my clients have shelled out for two expensive software packages, they are reluctant to have to buy any more software to complete the job.

The advantage of FLV videos wrapped in an SWF player embedded in a Webpage is that the video starts playing immediately, while still downloading the rest of the content. But this only happens if your broadband speed is higher than the data rate of the FLV file. And if you reduce the data rate of the file, the quality also reduces.

So, lots of movement needs bandwidth, and the more bandwidth you have, the larger the video, and the longer it takes to download. From all the tests I've done, based on the average broadband speed of clients and the people who'll view their Web sites, the thing to do is to encode the videos at between 400 and 700 kbps.

The usual horse-trading that happens when dealing with clients is that they want as much movement on the screen as possible, and I'm trying to make the video look as good as possible. Both of these techniques need bandwidth. Keeping the camera still helps keep the quality up, so I try to include a number of static shots in the video to compensate.

So, the workflow is shoot the video, capture, and edit in Final Cut Pro, and then use Compressor to resize the video to the correct size for the Web site (keeping up the data rate all through the process). The last stage is to transcode to an FLV file. The best way I've found is to then use the Adobe Flash CS3 Video Encoder. It's an easy-to-use interface, and you have the option of typing in exactly which data rate you want to use.

Adobe renamed the software with the release of CS4, to Adobe Media Encoder and this does a better job of encoding, as it uses the H.264 codec.

INDEX

Class:

Accession No:

Type: